The Theory and Measurement of

Business Income

The Theory and Measurement of Business Income

By EDGAR O. EDWARDS

PHILIP W. BELL

University of California Press

BERKELEY AND LOS ANGELES 1961

University of California Press
Berkeley and Los Angeles, California

Cambridge University Press
London, England

Library of Congress Catalog Card Number: 61–7534

Printed in the United States of America

To Our Parents

Preface

This book is an attempt to develop a meaningful theory of business income and to show how it can be applied in terms of accounting records and reports. It attacks directly problems which, because they have fallen in that no man's land between economics and accounting, have seldom been explored systematically. And when such efforts have been made, as in the case of Irving Fisher's *The Nature of Capital and Income,* they have not received the attention they deserve.

The need for development of a rigorous concept of business income, one which rests on sound theoretical underpinnings yet is measurable in practice, is indisputable. Business income is one of the key elements of information upon which the functioning of a private, free enterprise economy depends. A proper measure of such income is essential for sound business management, for the internal evaluation of business decisions taken in the past in order to make better decisions relating to an uncertain future. It is needed by persons or groups outside the firm, such as investors, creditors, and even regulatory agencies to judge the performance of individual firms and make comparisons among different firms or groups of firms, for such outsiders also influence the allocation of resources in the economy. Finally, a sound concept of business income is essential if there is to be equity in matters of taxation.

The problem of income measurement has been an especially perplexing one in part because economists have approached it with essentially subjective concepts derived from expectations concerning future events, while accountants have insisted on objectivity and the measurement of actual, unfortunately often historic, events. The apparent impasse between these two points of view has led many to resign themselves to the impossibility of reconciliation, and thus has tended to widen the gap between the two disciplines. Yet, except for the difference in perspective, the two often deal with related problems and rely on similar data. Because both points of view have proved themselves so useful in regard to their own special problems, a reconciliation is needed which does not at the same time destroy either the subjective approach of the economist or the accountant's emphasis on objective events. Our major theoretical effort is directed to this end.

The central concept of business income which emerges depends upon objective events but differs in many respects from the traditional concept employed by accountants. While many readers may feel inclined to skim over the theoretical half of the book, the developments there are necessary, we feel, to a full understanding of the limitations inherent in the traditional accounting concept and of the modifications necessary to eliminate them. These modifications depend upon an understanding of the theory of the behavior of the firm under conditions of uncertainty, and upon the relating of concepts of value to this behavior. They also depend upon a clear recognition of the distinction between changes in prices of individual asset and liability items and changes in the general price level. In part we are trying in this work to fill the void indicated by Professors Moonitz and Nelson in their 1960 survey of accounting theory:

If accountants and businessmen are so indifferent to the impact of inflation that they ignore it in their financial statements, why should

Congress and the Treasury be ready to recognize it in the income tax return? And if the type of tax "relief" we do get is unpalatable to us as theorists, to what extent does the fault lie in our failure to develop a clear, cogent theory of the relationship among changes in individual prices, in the general price-level, and the conventional standards underlying the preparation of financial statements? [1]

While one principal concept of income, a concept which we term "business profit," stems from the theoretical chapters relating to the theory of the firm, we recognize that business income measurements serve many purposes, from the evaluation of business decisions through reports to owners and tax authorities to the aggregation of data on industries and the economy as a whole. Accounting techniques are needed, therefore, which are sufficiently flexible to provide data for the business profit concept as well as for certain additional profit concepts, shown to be intimately related to business profit, but techniques which at the same time do not burden the firm with the unnecessary cost of multiple daily records. The second half of the book is devoted to the development of such techniques. We attempt to demonstrate the feasibility of accumulating data which can be used in a flexible manner to yield all the necessary measures of profit and their components, but which nevertheless involve only end-of-period adjustments in accounts maintained according to existing practices.

The principal stumbling block to the implementation of such a system, the matter of practicality, is examined in the concluding chapter. We feel that this hurdle, however, may be largely imaginary, a product of viewing current needs against historic resources. In a dynamic economy even criteria of practicality are subject to rapid change.

In works of close joint authorship, such as this, the responsibility for the writing of individual chapters is often hazy even before they are put on paper and tends to become very much blurred during the process of revision and rewriting. The ideas basic to Part One, however, were originally worked out by Mr. Edwards while he was in Sweden in 1954–55 as a John Simon

[1] M. Moonitz and C. L. Nelson, "Recent Developments in Accounting Theory," *Accounting Review* 35 (April, 1960), p. 213.

Guggenheim Memorial Fellow on leave from Princeton University.

It is literally impossible to identify all those who have been kind enough to read parts or all of the manuscript at one stage or another and who have contributed comments. Especially helpful were Professors W. T. Baxter, of the London School of Economics, S. T. Beza, of Princeton University, D. S. Brothers, of Rice University, S. Davidson, of the University of Chicago, L. A. Doyle and M. Moonitz, of the University of California, Berkeley, G. V. Rimlinger, of Rice University, A. W. Sametz, of New York University, and J. Worley, of Vanderbilt University, each of whom read all of an early draft of the manuscript and offered many thoughtful suggestions. We have also been aided by various of our students who have worked through parts of the manuscript or debated some of the ideas contained therein with us.

Mr. Edwards wishes to acknowledge support from the Guggenheim Foundation for help in financing his year in Sweden in 1954–55, and from the Ford Foundation for research funds administered through Princeton University during the summer of 1958. Mr. Bell wishes to acknowledge support from the Social Science Research Council and the Earhart Foundation for help in financing a year of research in London in 1956–57. Both authors are indebted to the Institute of Business and Economic Research of the University of California for financing the typing of the final manuscript. Finally, but only because it is customary, we wish to express appreciation to our wives, who have held their breath, if not their tongues, while grudgingly typing draft after draft.

Edgar O. Edwards
Hargrove Professor of Economics
Rice University

Philip W. Bell
Associate Professor of Economics
Haverford College

Contents

PART ONE: Development of the Theory

Tables

Figures

Statements and Schedules, XYZ Corporation

General Statements

Supplementary Statements

Supporting Schedules

I *The Problem and the Challenge:*

ECONOMIC NEEDS AND ACCOUNTING RESPONSIBILITIES

The suggestion that accounting and economics are related sciences is not a new one. Both are intimately concerned with the activities of the business firm, and in this context both deal with similar variables and their impact on profit. Yet the difference in time perspective which distinguishes the two sciences from each other has served also to keep them further apart than logic would suggest. It is true, of course, that for much of economics the past is dead, whereas for much of accounting it is the future which is nonexistent. Economics deals with the future and the decisions which will determine that future, while accounting is primarily concerned with historical description. It is our contention, however, that this difference in time perspective, far from being a divisive factor, provides the principal relationship between accounting and economics. We intend to establish this relationship in this chapter, to explore the function of accounting data in this light, and to examine briefly the extent to which existing accounting principles and various suggestions for their modification fulfill this function.

Demand for Data in a Dynamic Economy

The economics of the firm is essentially the economics of decision-making: How should the managers of a firm allocate its resources in order to maximize profit? The kind of decisions that must be made can be grouped, in accounting terminology, under three headings: (1) what value of assets to hold at any time (the expansion problem), (2) in what form to hold these assets (the composition problem), and (3) how to finance the holdings of assets (the financial problem). To make these kinds of decisions, for example, whether to replace a machine, to develop a new research laboratory, to build a new plant, to produce a new product, to select a different process of production, management must entertain expectations about future events. If we leave luck aside for a moment, the successful management is one that acts upon expectations that are relatively accurate. And any management that can increase the relative accuracy of its expectations and the ability of the firm to act upon those expectations should increase the profitability of the firm.

Managerial Competition

This pressure to increase what we might call "managerial ability" is a product of a dynamic society. In a stationary state "where tastes, technique, and resources remain constant through time,"[1] such pressures are nonexistent because the future is certain. The existence of certainty about the future follows automatically from the conditions of constant demand for and supply of both factors and products. It is uncertainty that breeds a demand for managerial ability and creates the pressures to increase that ability over time. Tastes, technology, and resources are in

---

[1] The stationary state also implies that savings and investment are zero, that income equals product, that actual prices experienced by entrepreneurs equal prices expected by them, and that the money rate of interest equals the real rate of interest. See J. R. Hicks, *Value and Capital*, pp. 117–119.

fact constantly changing, and the uncertainty that accompanies these changes makes business decisions necessary. As efforts are made to increase the ability of management to collect and communicate data, to develop relationships among variables, to analyze data according to these relationships, and to act upon the resulting information, the profit-making potential of a firm may increase. Whether this potential will be successfully realized or not depends upon the changing complexity of the problems management must analyze. If this complexity increases more rapidly than the managerial ability needed to solve them, profit realized by a firm may well decline. One of the important contributors to problem complexity is undoubtedly the rate of increase of managerial ability in competitive firms. To be successful over time, then, a firm must not only employ top-level management but it must also be geared to increase its managerial ability at a rate at least as great as that in business generally. It is a high relative, not absolute, level of managerial ability that is most likely to result in higher profit.

The hypothesis that managerial ability tends to increase over time accords closely with observable facts. The increasing proportion of managerial personnel to nonmanagerial personnel, the weight given higher education in the recruitment of junior executives, the intensified executive training programs in many business firms, the increasing emphasis on product and market research, experiments in managerial organization, and the development of extensive computation centers are but a few examples of the abundant evidence.

Evaluation of Business Decisions

It is in the evaluating of business decisions, we believe, that the demand for accounting data exists. For unless one holds firmly that all decisions are essentially intuitive in nature, the improvement of managerial ability and related decision-making processes must lean heavily upon an evaluation of past decisions. And of all the alternative courses of action considered in past decisions, the most important one, of course, is the alternative that was in fact adopted. We suggest, therefore, that a principal function of accounting data is to serve as a fundamental tool in the evaluation of past decisions, a function that would clearly not exist in a stationary state.[2]

The mass of accounting data is accumulated voluntarily by the individual firm. It is true, of course, that the demands of certain external parties influence the kind of data gathered by the business firm. The tax authorities, the owners of the firm, security analysts, and the public at large should probably be counted among those who influence the kind of data produced. Nevertheless, the bulk of accounting data is never made available to people outside of the business firm itself. Thus it seems safe to conclude that accounting information must principally serve the functions of management. In this sense accounting data serve as a means of protecting against fraud or theft; but, much more important, the data serve as a means of evaluating business decisions, thereby contributing (1) to the control of current events in the production process, (2) to the formulation of better decisions in the future, and (3) to the modification of the decision-making process itself. It is the development of data to serve the evaluation function that is of primary concern to us in this book.

The overwhelming test of the adequacy of accounting data as developed for any particular period must be their comparability with the expectations originally specified for that period. Where economics deals with a set of expectations and an expected profit which represents a summary of those expectations, accounting attempts to develop a list of actual events and the actual profit which results from them. Properly formulated, a comparison of these two views of the events of a period should reveal errors in expectations, and these errors, properly analyzed, should serve as a basis for altering events where such control is possible or for altering expectations where the events themselves cannot be controlled. For example, if the amount of raw material used in production is higher than expected, an attempt might be made to reduce waste, but if the price at which it is purchased is market-determined and higher than expected, management would probably alter its expectations of that price in the future. The effective isolation of errors in expectations requires, of course, that

[2] For an excellent discussion of this hypothesis, see H. V. Finston, "Managerial Development: Challenge to Accountants," pp. 32–35. (For full citation of references, see Selected Bibliography.)

the accounting data developed be directly comparable with the set of expectations originally specified. This means clearly that, insofar as possible, accounting data must measure the actual events of a particular period, no more and no less. Events of earlier periods must not be confused with events of the current period; nor must any events of the current period be omitted. We shall find this criterion useful in evaluating the existing set of accounting principles.

While accounting data must serve internal functions first, it does not follow that the kind of data developed will be useless if made available to outsiders. That outside users of accounting data such as stockholders, stock analysts, labor union officials, government statisticians and policy makers, and economists are mostly by-product beneficiaries is undeniable. Certain data are made available to tax authorities and regulatory agencies as a matter of law, but other external users cannot insist on data of any kind; rather they must be satisfied with what is offered them. Nevertheless, both a growing sense of social responsibility and an awareness of what may be considerable self-interest at stake are leading businessmen to be more and more concerned about the external users of accounting data. Further, many outside uses of accounting data may be of help to the businessman himself. Economists' research on business growth, efficiency, and relative profitability, for example, may contribute directly to the improvement of business decisions; business managers are coming to depend upon national income data, input-output tables, flow-of-funds reports, and the like in making plans for the future. Published accounting data should serve other social functions as well: promoting a more efficient allocation of capital, calling attention to monopoly profits, and providing relative profitability figures to potential entrants into an industry, for example. Whether the kind of data developed for the internal purposes of the business firm will serve these external functions equally well is a matter we shall want to investigate. But just as management uses such data primarily for purposes of evaluation, most external uses involve similar evaluations. It should not be surprising then if the same set of accounting principles can be used to develop data suitable to external as well as to internal users.

It has been pointed out that if the demand for data is predicated largely upon the existence of change and uncertainty in the economy, accounting data, to be most useful, should be designed to report changes as they occur. Unfortunately, the kind of accounting data currently being developed for both internal and external users falls far short of this ideal. To highlight this deficiency, we shall take as our first task the demonstration that traditional accounting procedures are predicated implicitly on the utter absence of change.

Supply of Data and the Stationary State

Over a great many years, going back before the famous treatise by Pacioli on double-entry bookkeeping, accounting has slowly been developed into a systematic body of knowledge through gradual acceptance of certain ad hoc conventions and principles which can be applied to specific problems.[3] When this complex of practices is peeled away and the basic framework laid bare, it is clear that present-day accounting would yield accurate and truthful results only under very special circumstances. A critical analysis of the premises underlying accounting practices and of the conventions and principles which accountants follow in order to bypass these obviously unreal assumptions will help to indicate the nature of the gap between the demand for and supply of accounting data.

The Necessary Assumptions for Validity: The Stationary State

The basic purposes of accounting are to measure for a business unit[4] its efforts (costs), its accomplishments (revenues), its suc-

[3] For some interesting early history of some of these developments, see W. T. Baxter, *Studies in Accounting* and A. C. Littleton and B. S. Yamey, *Studies in the History of Accounting,* as well as Littleton's older *Accounting Evolution to 1900.* The best treatment of the development of specific principles and conventions is Littleton's *Structure of Accounting Theory.*

[4] The business unit itself in accounting is conceived of as an entity which is a continuing concern in quest of profit. The accounting unit need not, of course, coincide with the legal unit, and the boundaries may not be unambiguous, especially where there are interests in affiliated companies involved. Furthermore, some firms clearly do not contemplate more than a temporary existence, an arrangement to sell Christmas trees, for example. Nevertheless, the entity assumption, the going-concern assumption, and the objective-of-profit assumption underlie all of business accounting. With these assumptions we have no fundamental

cess (the difference) over time, and its position (what it owns and owes) at any moment of time. These purposes are represented among a firm's published reports by the profit and loss statement and the balance sheet. The functional assumptions of accounting outlined below are a description of a set of conditions under which these statements, as presently compiled, would be complete, truthful, and unambiguous.

1. *Money unit of account assumption.*—It must be assumed that all activities and properties relevant to the firm can be measured in terms of money and that the purchasing power of money is stable so that its uses as a unit of account and as a standard of value are complete, truthful, and unambiguous.

2. *Cost-market value identity assumption.*—It must be assumed that the cost of anything purchased or produced is equal to its market value. In its raw form this means that the present market value of plant and equipment and the values of its services can be derived from its original cost. It also implies that the costs of all factors of production attach to the product produced and that this accumulated cost is equal to the market value of the product. Keeping records in terms of cost is therefore a legitimate practice.

3. *Certainty assumption.*—It must be assumed that the future is known to the firm for certain. Only then can the allocation of costs and revenues among past, present, and future periods be certain. This is necessary if the operations of a continuing firm are to be measured accurately for fiscal periods.

The accountant might hesitate to accept these assumptions as his own, but they are necessary to ensure the accuracy of the data he collects. He does (1) keep records in money terms, (2) measure values in terms of costs, and (3) make reports for fiscal periods. If data collected and reported in this fashion are to yield complete, truthful, and unambiguous results, (1) all raw data must be measurable in money units and prices must be constant, (2) cost and market value must be identical, and (3) knowledge of pertinent future events must be certain. Only then would the techniques the accountant applies be safe from criticism.

---

argument. For an excellent discussion of these and other assumptions of accounting, see W. A. Paton and A. C. Littleton, *An Introduction to Corporate Accounting Standards,* pp. 7–23.

It is perhaps paradoxical that the practical science or art of accounting can be related, even remotely, to such unreal assumptions. Yet all elements of a firm's operation and position must be measurable in money terms if statements are to reflect the full relevance to the firm of its activities. The relevant elements must be identifiable, and appropriate values must be assignable. The unit in which these values are measured must be stable if ambiguity is to be avoided; the difficulty of comparing money profits over time when the price level has been changing is an abvious example of possible ambiguity. Few would deny the necessity of the first assumption if current accounting techniques are to yield the desired results.

The identity of cost and value is a harsh assumption. Yet record-keeping on the basis of cost can be fully vindicated only if the condition holds. The "current position" of a firm suggests a description in terms of market values. To develop such a description in the records would necessitate the recognition of profit as market values change rather than at the point of sale (goods in process, for example, could not otherwise be recorded at market value). Thus, in order to describe completely and truthfully with present accounting techniques the current position of a firm and its profit as it accrues, recorded costs must be equal to market values.[5]

The certainty assumption is necessary if the arbitrary allocations of cost among different periods is to be unambiguous. Because many firms have a long life span the development of interim statements and the use of the fiscal period device are mandatory. But the accurate measurement of the operations of a firm for short periods requires, in addition, that the firm be in possession of complete and certain knowledge of future events. The cost of a plant whose use extends over several fiscal periods cannot

[5] Some accountants argue that asset data on the balance sheet should represent a firm's current position in terms of *unallocated costs*, that portion of historic cost that has yet to be designated an expense on the profit and loss statement. It can be argued that this is a rationalization of what in fact is done. Nevertheless, both purposes, unallocated costs and current position at market values, could be served by present techniques only if cost and value were identical. The question of whether unallocated *historic* cost is the appropriate cost to be deducted in determining profit is as yet unresolved. See S. J. Broad, "Cost: Is It a Binding Principle or Just a Means to an End?", and this book, Chapters II, III, and IV.

be allocated correctly among periods without this full advance knowledge of the extent and value of its use in future periods. Without certainty, errors in judgment would often be discovered after cost allocations had been made, and some errors might never be fully determined.

To summarize, present accounting practices would be fully valid only if prices, quantities, and qualities of both factors and products were unchanging over time, i.e., if there were a stable general price level (the first assumption), stable individual prices (the second assumption), and perfect certainty about the future (the third assumption). But this is a situation clearly akin to the stationary state. The certainty it implies bars by definition the very existence of profit as a return for bearing uncertainty. The implicit assumptions of accounting eliminate that which it has set out to measure! [6]

Substitution of Three Accounting Conventions

Accountants are fully aware that the heroic assumptions we have imputed to accounting are not typical of the real world in which they keep records. In applying accounting techniques, which might be fully valid in a stationary state, to the actual problems of the business firm, accountants claim much less for their data than the foregoing presentation might suggest. Rather than adopt assumptions that are clearly unrealistic, accountants have adopted conventions which purposely restrict and circumscribe the scope and validity of accounting data as they are currently developed.

1. *The money convention.*—Instead of assuming that all relevant variables can be measured in money whose purchasing power is stable, accountants claim to measure only those variables that can be measured in money; those that cannot must be judged by nonaccounting means. They adopt as a goal the measurement of money magnitudes (revenues, costs, and profits) so that adjustments for changes in the value of money itself are not presumed to be a bookkeeping function. Accountants, of course, assist in the interpretation of data and are now more and more

[6] F. S. Bray has noted the close relationship between the economic concept of the stationary state and accounting assumptions. See his *The Measurement of Profit,* p. 16.

accepting as "part of the job" the special interpretation necessary because of the changing value of the dollar. But there has as yet been no general acceptance within the profession of a means for incorporating these adjustments in the basic records of the firm.

2. *The realization convention.*—Instead of assuming the identity of cost and value, accountants have adopted the convention of recognizing profit only upon sale; no pretense is made of measuring profit as it accrues either in production or as a result of simply holding assets as their prices rise. Reporting assets at historic cost represents a consistent application of this convention; a record at market value would involve a recognition of gain prior to sale. Those who use accounting data are fairly warned by this convention that the interpretation of a firm's position or operation on the basis of market value is not the responsibility of the accountant as record-keeper. The accountant shares the interpretative responsibility with other members of management, however.

3. *The fiscal-period convention.*—Instead of assuming certainty the accountant recognizes the arbitrary character of interim reports and attempts to designate by appropriate terminology those estimates that are most tenuous, such as depreciation and bad debts.

These conventions represent an honest recognition and warning of many accounting limitations involved in the design of accounts. They are not very helpful to the users who must interpret accounting data. Strong arguments can be advanced for maintaining a dichotomy between the design and interpretation of accounts, but it is important to recognize the limitations which the conventions impose. They can be summarized in the following way:

1. Within the framework of present accounting practices, no capital gains or losses are recorded as they arise, i.e., as individual prices change; this limitation in turn has three main implications:

a) The capital gains (losses) for any one period are incomplete; i.e., they are not recognized until the assets are sold or used in the production of goods which are sold, and profit is therefore *under*stated (*over*stated);

b) Some capital gains (losses) of former periods are recognized as capital gains (losses) of this period when assets which have risen in price over an extended period of time are sold in this period, thus *over*stating (*under*stating) profit;

c) Balance sheet values are badly distorted.

2. Capital gains and losses which are realized through use of an asset whose price has changed and the subsequent sale of the product for which the asset was used are included as part of normal operating profit although the profit results from holding activities rather than using activities per se; this difficulty stems from keeping records at original purchase cost with the result, for example, that one of the expense deductions from operating revenue is depreciation based on the historic cost value of the fixed asset.

3. There is no recognition of changes in the general price level and thus no separation of *real* and *fictional* elements in reported profit figures as well as no true statement of real net worth on the balance sheet.

All of these limitations, which are based on one or more of the three basic conventions listed above, will become clearer as we move ahead, specifically in Chapters III and IV. Exposing their nature and significance, establishing firmly the characteristics of the gap between needed data and supplied data, is one of our major purposes.

The Gap and the Degree of Error

In considering the present-day supply of accounting data, there remains one central question: How far from reality can it be? For this we have no authoritative answer; the errors involved have never, to our knowledge, been subjected to systematic analysis. Our own review of existing accounting principles suggests that those events of a particular period which represent quantity data are being adequately recorded. The fundamental shortcomings of accounting data can be traced to the treatment of price data which, when applied to the quantity data, yield the values that lift accounting above mere counting.

The price events of any particular period can be divided into two kinds, movements in the general price level and movements in individual prices. The most thorough studies of accounting limitations have dwelt on those shortcomings that result from movements in the general price level. It is our thesis, however, that while this is a kind of error that should be corrected, the really significant limitation of accounting data lies in the failure to account for changes in individual prices. Attempts to indicate the magnitude of this kind of limitation are spotty indeed; in fact, comprehensive statistical estimates of the accounting error involved in neglecting individual price movements are urgently needed. Those who have dealt with this problem at all have generally limited their attempts to the error involved in the existing treatment of fixed asset prices. Nevertheless, the evidence is sufficient in our view to warrant the conclusion that the neglect of price dispersion causes a deviation of supplied data from desired data of the first magnitude, a deviation that exists, of course, even when the price level is stable.[7]

Price Level Error

But the magnitude of the price level error, the deviation of accounting data from reality because of the "money convention," has itself been great in recent years. The pioneering study was that of Ralph C. Jones, who surveyed nine steel companies in the United States, representing 80 per cent of the industry's ingot capacity, for the period 1941–1947. In adjusting the reports of these firms for price level changes over this period, he found the following discrepancies between the reported data and the adjusted data:[8]

Reported Data	*Adjusted Data*
Dividends earned by a substantial margin every year.	Dividends not earned in any year since 1941.
Income retained to provide additional capital, $543 million.	Dividends, interest, and income taxes *paid out of capital,* $409 million.
Working capital increased 51% during seven-year period.	Working capital increased 2% during seven-year period.
Fixed assets decreased 6% during seven-year period.	Fixed assets decreased 19% during seven-year period.

[7] We shall buttress this conclusion in Chapters V, VI, and VII, drawing on empirical evidence beyond that used in the studies completed thus far and reported on below.

[8] R. C. Jones, "The Effect of Inflation on Capital and Profits: The Record of Nine Steel Companies," p. 13.

In a more recent study prepared for the American Accounting Association, Professor Jones has investigated the price level error in four companies of different types over an extended period of time. His summary of the error in the Reece Corporation for the period 1940–1951 is typical of the other three firms investigated.

> Assuming that the same price, financial, and dividend policies had been followed, statements expressed in uniform dollars would have shown that the increase in annual gross income from 1940 to 1951 was 55 per cent instead of 187 per cent; that net income was 6 per cent instead of 10 per cent of the gross income; that the average income tax was 67 per cent instead of 57 per cent; and that the rate of return on the common stockholders' equity was 4.9 per cent instead of over 8 per cent. Such statements also would have shown depreciation charges to have been 22 per cent higher, and they would have made clear that dividends exceeded net income.[9]

No one would deny that these discrepancies are serious. Whether management was sophisticated enough to recognize the deficiencies of the reported data in actually making decisions is a moot question, but it is doubtful that the managements involved in these studies would knowingly have dispersed real capital as they apparently did. The possibility that outsiders, investors, labor unions, and others have recognized fully the consequences of price level changes is even more remote.

Lest it be thought that the errors specified in these studies result primarily from historic fixed asset valuations alone, let us look at another study in which depreciation was a minor element. Applying techniques similar to those of Jones to a department store, Donald Corbin was able to show that the price level error was substantial; moreover, the error fluctuated considerably from year to year, suggesting that an estimate of it by non-computational means would be extremely hazardous.[10] His figures were as follows:

---

[9] R. C. Jones, *Price Level Changes and Financial Statements: Case Studies of Four Companies,* pp. 128–129. The other three companies treated and the periods covered in the study are the New York Telephone Company (1940, 1946–1952), Armstrong Cork Company (1941–1951), and Sargent and Company (1929–1952).

[10] D. A. Corbin, "The Impact of Changing Prices on a Department Store."

Percentage Excess of Reported Earnings over Real Earnings

1946	1947	1948	1949	1950	1951	1952	1953
0	16	41	7	−14	28	58	12

Large as this price level type of error is, we shall argue below that its magnitude tends to exaggerate its importance and has garnered for it more attention than it probably deserves.

Price Dispersion Error

As already noted, studies of the magnitude of the errors introduced into the accounts by the neglect of changes in particular prices are incomplete and have usually been limited to a revision of depreciation estimates. Some idea of the magnitude of the error for the individual firm, however, can be gained by examining two studies related largely to the depreciation error.[11] In a study of the Armstrong Cork Company, A. L. Bell showed that during the years 1948, 1949, and 1950 profits were overstated by approximately 19 per cent because of underdepreciation alone. Historic cost depreciation charges in money represented only about 50 per cent of depreciation computed on a current cost basis. Some of his substantiating data can be summarized as shown below.[12]

Year ending	Historic cost depreciation (millions of dollars)	Current cost depreciation (millions of dollars)	Excess of current cost over historic cost depreciation (millions of dollars)	Excess as per cent of historic cost depreciation
6/30/48	2.2	4.3	2.1	95
6/30/49	2.6	4.7	2.1	81
6/30/50	3.2	5.8	2.6	83

In a study of an unidentified farm equipment company, Myron Gordon has shown that the adjustment of expense items to a current cost basis converted after-tax operating profits of $16,400

[11] The aggregate error for the economy as a whole in the case of inventory and depreciation costing is treated at the beginning of Chapter VII.

[12] A. L. Bell, "Fixed Assets and Current Costs."

and $27,100 for 1947 and 1948 to profits of $2,000 and $17,800, respectively. If, however, capital gains on assets whose prices rose while they were held by the company were counted (an adjustment that Bell did not consider), this reduction would be more than offset because these amounted to $23,800 and $15,900 in the respective years.[13] The propriety of (1) counting holding gains from changes in prices of individual asset and liability items at all and of (2) combining them with operating profit are moot questions, questions we discuss at greater length in subsequent chapters.

The techniques for adjusting the reported data in the various estimates of accounting deviation from reality are by no means identical, but the fact that the error in reported data is large and variable (both year to year and company to company) is undeniable.

Efforts to Close the Gap

The results of studies such as those just summarized show without question that something serious is wrong with present accounting practices and the data to which they lead. Efforts to close the gap between the needs of users of accounting data and accounting practice, between the demand for and supply of data, have been proceeding along two lines, neither of which seems to us to resolve the conflict. One approach, espoused by a growing number of accountants and receiving considerable support from the American Accounting Association, has been to urge the publication of reports corrected for changes in the general price level. A second approach can be traced to economists who study and use accountants' reports. They suggest an economic concept of income that is essentially subjective in nature and involves a highly unreal, abstract view of what accountants should do. Even if the economic concept were objectively measurable—and it is not—it would not, as we indicate below and more extensively in Chapter II, serve the more important purposes of either the internal or external users of accounting data. Neither of these approaches seems to us to get to the heart of the problem; neither is very useful for decision-making within the firm; neither

[13] M. Gordon, "The Valuation of Accounts at Current Cost."

is especially useful for the varied outside demands made upon accounting data. While we shall return to these considerations in subsequent chapters, as peripheral matters to the development of our theory of business profit, we must here indicate briefly the difficulties we see in each of the two approaches.

Real Income and the Price Level School

Most studies of the price limitations of accounting data have been stimulated by periods of inflation. The apparent magnitude of the price level error has tended to draw attention to it and the problems related to individual price changes have generally been neglected. It is not surprising, therefore, that the many studies which have been undertaken here and abroad in the postwar period have tended toward agreement on one particular modification of present accounting principles, namely, the correction for changes in the price level.[14] The fact that some of the studies have been published by the American Accounting Association suggests that the modification is receiving serious consideration. We feel that the modification is a necessary one, but hope that the doctor, having cured the hangnail, does not fail to diagnose the pneumonia.

The difference between the two problems, a difference which has long been recognized in the field of economics, merits further analysis. There is the allocation problem, on the one hand, for the analysis of which the economist relies upon differential price movements; there is, on the other hand, the inflation problem, for whose analysis the economist generally relies upon aggregate demand and supply functions. For the accountant, of course, who is attempting to measure the events of a past period, both phenomena are given events. He is not so interested in what caused the phenomena, but rather in how to incorporate these events among his records.

[14] See the three monographs published by the American Accounting Association during 1955–1957, one written by Perry Mason, *Price-Level Changes and Financial Statements: Basic Concepts and Methods,* and two by Ralph Jones, one previously cited and *Effects of Price Level Changes on Business Income, Capital and Taxes.* These followed a 1951 recommendation of the Association's Committee on Accounting Concepts and Standards that "the accounting effects of the changing value of the dollar should be made the subject of intensive research and experimentation." *Accounting Review* 26 (October, 1951), p. 469.

We have argued above that the overriding function to be served by his records is the evaluation of past decisions. For this purpose, we shall now argue, it is a record of individual price changes that should be incorporated in the accounts. A modification for changes in the price level can contribute little to this function. The essential decision-making function of management is the allocation of resources, and to further this purpose, management needs a knowledge of relative prices, of expectations of individual price movements. Expectations of price level changes may influence his expectations of individual price movements, but it is the latter which determine his decision as to how best to allocate resources.

Further, if his expectations of individual price movements are correct, then the relative profits the firm can make by alternative resource allocations are entirely unaffected by movements in the price level. The latter variable will in this case affect only the absolute, real profit the firm makes, and this is of importance, not for decision-making purposes, but primarily for tax purposes. Thus, if management feels that the retention of profits will serve the best interests of owners better than its disposition in the form of dividends, changes in the price level will not in themselves affect the correctness of this decision.

Business decisions, then, are based largely upon expectations of individual price movements and relationships among these individual prices. The evaluation of past decisions requires comparable data. The accounting problem becomes one of recording and relating to each other these particular price changes as they occur. Without these data the evaluation of business decisions must be an extremely loose procedure. First of all, management must be aware of the limitations of accounting data for this purpose. Secondly, management must go outside the accounting records in order to evaluate even the particular course of action which the firm is following. Outsiders, too, who attempt to weigh the relative profitability of different firms on the basis of reported data need reports which are modified to include the effects of individual price changes, not reports which incorporate simply the effects of changes in the general price level.

The inadequacy of the price level modification for the evaluation of business decisions is easily explained. A general adjustment for changes in the price level is not a departure from historic cost at all. It simply involves a restatement of historic cost in units of the same purchasing power; the historic cost principle is not affected by this adjustment; only the units in which historic cost is measured are changed.

Although there are genuine reasons for supporting a price level modification, it is unfortunate that at one time or another three misleading arguments have been used, whether implicitly or explicitly, in support of this approach: (1) correcting for individual price changes is a poor substitute for the price level adjustment; (2) all prices generally move together and therefore, by correcting for some general index of prices, an effective correction for changes in the prices of individual assets and liabilities is achieved as well; (3) a general price level adjustment which puts all items in the same purchasing power may prevent the dissipation of real capital.

1. Are the adjustments substitutes?

In our opinion none of these arguments is sound. The first argument is perhaps most clearly without basis; yet the discussion over price dispersion and the price level has been muddled on this point. Too often adjustments for specific price changes and adjustments for changes in the price level have been treated as an "either-or" proposition. A. L. Bell states, ". . . the problem was whether to use a general measure such as the Wholesale Price Index or one of the many specialized indexes," and proceeds to argue along these lines.[15] Warner also asks "which index should be applied to the accounts," and treats corrections for price dispersion as an alternative to corrections for changes in the price level.[16] Both types of correction are necessary in our view for any accounting system to be regarded as complete. In fact unless individual price changes are recognized first, it is an incorrect operating profit that is being adjusted for changes in the price level. And it is operating profit for which most firms are striving, for the enlargement of which most decisions are made.

[15] *Op. cit.*, p. 49.

[16] G. H. Warner, "Depreciation on a Current Basis," p. 630.

It is these decisions that operating profit, appropriately defined, and the events it summarizes, should test.[17]

2. Do all prices move together?

The second argument rests on a false premise. Prices obviously do not move together in a dynamic economy. Mills documented this characteristic years ago.[18] He constructed an index of the dispersion of price movements from year to year, the figure given for any year representing a percentage deviation from the general price index (preceding year = 100) that was exceeded by approximately 50 per cent of the individual price movements. Thus from 1919 to 1920 the price level rose to 111.0 while 50 per cent of the individual price movements involved differed from 111.0 by more than 15.7 per cent. For the 36-year period, 1891–1926, these indexes of dispersion averaged 9.8 per cent, ranging from a low of 6.8 per cent in 1905 to a high of 18.3 per cent in 1921.[19]

Mills made similar computations using 1891 as a fixed base. The scatter of price movements over a long period of time is naturally greater than the scatter on a year-to-year basis. By 1921, for example, 50 per cent of the price movements differed from the average price movement by more than 23.3 per cent.[20] Cumulative dispersion is of paramount importance in assessing the error involved in depreciation charges, an error that exists even after adjustment for changes in the price level itself.

---

[17] Not all accountants by any means have fallen into this trap. Corbin (*loc. cit.*) discusses them as separate and independent adjustments, though he argues that corrections for price dispersion should not affect the operating statement. Jones in his *Effects of Price Level Changes on Business Income, Capital and Taxes*, previously cited (p. 76) and Mason (*op. cit.*, pp. 12–13) both recognize that the two adjustments are complementary.

[18] F. C. Mills, *The Behavior of Prices.*

[19] *Ibid.*, p. 259. The measures given are based on the unweighted geometric mean of price relatives (wholesale prices), the number of price relatives used in different years varying from 195 to 391. Weighting did not alter the dispersion indexes appreciably. An examination of 44 components of the wholesale price index reveals that from April, 1956 to April, 1957, while the index rose from 113.6 to 117.1, nine of the component indexes fell and four stayed the same.

[20] *Loc. cit.* Measures based on the unweighted arithmetic mean showed greater dispersion, the index of dispersion standing as high as 62.2 in 1916. The range of price dispersion is, of course, much greater than these indexes reveal.

More recent price movements have behaved in a similar fashion. Figure 1 shows the Bureau of Labor Statistics index of consumer goods prices and the general wholesale price index

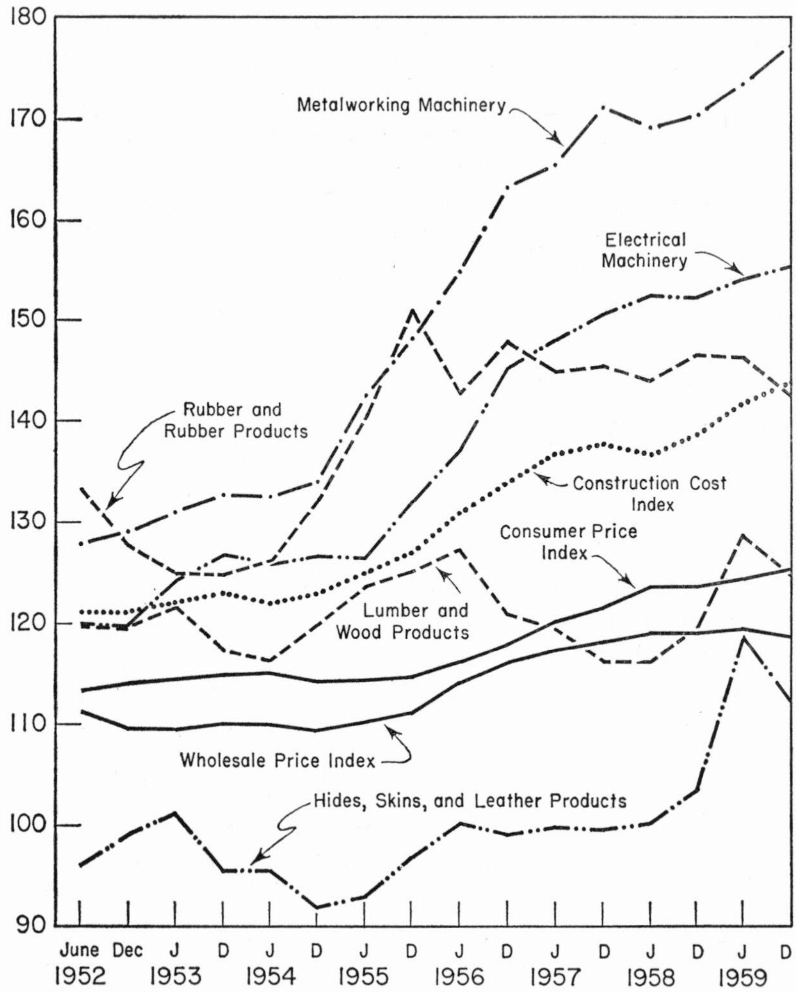

Figure 1. Relative prices of consumer goods and various categories of producer goods, 1952–1959.

ranged against a number of special indexes, some related to fixed assets of manufacturing establishments, some to other special categories of producer and consumer goods. Since the base period for all of the indexes is 1947–1949 = 100, it is clear that between then and 1951, the Korean War period, heavy equipment rose in price considerably more than did the general average of prices for the economy as a whole. But then consider a period of relative calm, that between 1952 and 1959. The consumer price index changed very little and the wholesale price index still less. But construction costs and the prices of electrical and metalworking machinery, both related to the value of fixed assets of manufacturing firms, rose rapidly and rather unevenly. On the other hand, the prices of many less durable products, which are in part used as raw materials by manufacturing establishments (some subcategories are shown by dotted lines in figure 1), typically behave much more erratically, and during the 1950's those prices did not increase nearly as markedly as construction and machinery.

Even this cursory study of price movements in the United States is sufficient to indicate that there is marked dispersion of individual prices around the movement of the norm. Any correction of asset values on the basis of the consumer price index during the period 1951–1959 would have left the accounts of a firm still far from a realistic statement of market value, and it is quite possible that such a correction at various points in the middle of this period would even have been, for many firms, a move away from greater truthfulness rather than toward it.[21]

3. *Does the price level adjustment permit the maintenance of real capital?*

The third argument, that a general price level correction permits the maintenance of real capital in a dynamic economy, really rests heavily on the second. Jones justifies the purchasing power adjustment as the relevant correction in the following way:

On one point there is practically unanimous agreement; namely, that during periods of marked price level change, the customary financial statements lose some of the economic significance which they have during periods of monetary stability. It is true, of course, that

[21] The studies by Jones for the American Accounting Association, as well as almost all others, covered the period of rapid increases in the general price level up to 1951. In such periods of sharp general inflation, price level adjustments will almost invariably be a step toward truthfulness, the exceptions being those firms whose particular asset and liability values move downward.

even during a long period of price stability, differences between costs and values would develop and that the conventional statements would not satisfy all needs for economic information. In such a period, however, a firm which reported a profit would as a rule be better off at the end of the year than it was at the beginning, and an investor who received a dividend could be reasonably certain that it was actually out of income and not out of capital.[22]

But price level adjustments by themselves can ensure only that a firm will not unwittingly disperse its *real historic cost,* which is quite different from its *real capital.* The latter cannot be determined unless the current values of the firm's assets, not just their historic costs, are recognized. A comparison of real capital at two different dates can only be done by comparing the *current values* at the two dates, one adjusted to the dollar in which the other is stated. The price level correction ignores the fact that capital can be dispersed through changes in individual prices if those relevant to the individual firm rise at a rate slower than the rate of change in the price level. Nor does it recognize that real capital can be augmented if the relationship is reversed.

But let us suppose for a moment a situation in which the price level adjustment applied to historic costs does yield (by accident) a correct measure of changes in the real capital position of a firm. Relative prices of the firm's assets have changed, but in such a way that the weighted average of the changes over the period is accurately revealed by the application of the price level adjustment to the historic costs of assets held at the beginning and end of the period. Suppose further that the adjustment reveals that a scheduled dividend payment out of end-of-period assets will reduce real capital below that held at the beginning of the period. Clearly the fact that a dividend would be distributed out of real capital is a matter of knowledge, not of decision. Adjustment for price level changes in this case reveals the fact, but it does not aid in making the decision as to whether expansion or contraction in real terms is the most profitable thing to do, nor which particular avenue of expansion might be

---

[22] Jones, *Price Level Changes and Financial Statements: Case Studies of Four Companies,* p. 1.

most profitable. A recognition of individual price changes is necessary to help make the expansion decision. A consideration of the effects of relative price movements might reveal that contraction promises the greatest benefit to stockholders.

Other decisions related to the earning of income also require a recognition of individual price changes. What prices to charge, where to locate a plant, what product mix is most profitable, are examples. Finally, these and similar decisions can be made more intelligently if data are available with which similar past decisions can be evaluated.

In short, only one of the defects of existing accounting profit, the last of the three criticisms enumerated earlier in this chapter, can, even under the very best of circumstances, be remedied by the restatement of historic cost figures in real terms, and it will normally be fully remedied only if the other two defects are corrected too. Legitimate claims for the price level adjustment can be summarized as follows: (1) it is normally an important step toward truthfulness in the sense of rendering reality accurately; (2) it does not violate the historic cost principle; (3) it does not violate the realization postulate; (4) it can be objectively applied once agreement has been reached on the price index to be used; and (5) its application for tax purposes would tend to make the income tax more equitable. It is probable that the ardent support of many businessmen for the price level modification can be traced to its anticipated effect on tax payments in periods of generally rising prices.

None of these points, however, relates directly to the evaluation of business decisions. As a means of enabling accounting data to serve this function better, the price level modification alone is a weak improvement over existing data. It is the other two defects of accounting data, both stemming from the neglect of individual price changes, that most need correction, not only to promote the objective of the firm (the making of profit) but also to provide outsiders with more economic information. While taxes are based on some concept of absolute profit, decisions and decision evaluation are based upon relative profitability. To achieve realism in accounting, we must look beyond the efforts of the price level enthusiasts.

Economic Concept of Income

Economists, often by invitation, have been criticizing the accountants' concepts of profit for years.[23] But in attempting to derive an alternative which the accountant might find useful, economists have almost invariably lost track of the objective of accounting measurement.

The concept of income[24] most widely appealed to by economists working in this area is as follows: ". . . a person's income is what he can consume during the week and still expect to be as well off at the end of the week as he was at the beginning."[25] Income in this sense is a welfare concept applicable to any individual regardless of the nature or source of his expected receipts. Such an explanation of income is thoroughly subjective in nature whether viewed as an ex ante or an ex post concept. It is, of course, the latter concept that promises significance for accounting. This is usually interpreted as his actual consumption during the period plus the excess of how well off the individual thinks he is at the end of the period over how well off he thought he was at the beginning of the period.

When the concept is transferred from the individual to the accounting problems of the business firm, someone must do the "thinking," and some measurement of "well-offness," or welfare, must be introduced. The "thinkers" clearly must be the managers, who may or may not be the owners; they comprise the only body of persons sufficiently cohesive and knowledgeable to be able to make any welfare estimate. In the absence of dividend payments and new contributions by stockholders, income is measured

---

[23] Two recent expressions of such criticism can be found in the Study Group on Business Income, *Five Monographs on Business Income* (in which S. Alexander's "Income Measurement in a Dynamic Economy," and S. Fabricant's "Business Costs and Business Income under Changing Price Levels" are particularly germane), and in the Taxation and Research Committee of Certified and Corporate Accountants, *Accounting for Inflation.* G. O. May has, properly we think, criticized the significance of the economists' offerings in "Concepts of Business Income and Their Measurement."

[24] The terms "profit" and "income" are used interchangeably in this chapter, subject to the particular context at issue. In subsequent chapters we show preference for the term "profit" because the concept developed there is quite different from, though related to, the economic concept of income. We recognize, however, that "income" is now a much more widely used term in accounting.

[25] Hicks, *op. cit.,* p. 176.

at the end of the period by adding up the discounted values of all net receipts which the managers then expect to earn on the firm's existing net assets and subtracting from this subjective value a similar computation made at the beginning of the period.[26] It is this ex post difference in subjective values which many economists have argued should be the ideal goal of accounting.[27] Being subjective, this concept is by definition not susceptible to objective measurement. Economists recognize that this deficiency cannot be remedied and suggest only that the change in the market values of a firm's assets is perhaps the best approximation.[28] We shall develop the position in Chapter II that the change in market value, appropriately defined, is much more than an approximation; it is the ideal concept of short-run profit itself; in Chapter III this concept will be modified for long-run purposes.

This much is clear. If the objective of accounting is to aid in the decision-making processes within the firm, specifically to aid in the quest for profit, it is hardly appropriate that the fundamental measure of income should be based on the assumption that all decisions have already been made, which is the premise underlying the ex post subjective value concept. A concept of profit which measures truly and realistically the extent to which past decisions have been right or wrong and thus aids in the formulation of new ones is required. And since rightness or wrongness must, eventually, be checked in the market place, it is changes in market values of one kind or another which should dominate accounting objectives.

---

[26] The development of this concept, stated here in extremely simple terms, has been largely the work of Erik Lindahl, *Studies in the Theory of Money and Capital*, pp. 74–111, and Hicks, *op. cit.*, pp. 171–188.

[27] N. Buchanan defines the accounting ideal in this way and regards accounting profit as containing "certain aberrations from this . . . 'ideal,'" (*The Economics of Corporate Enterprise*, p. 213). Joel Dean takes the same view in his *Managerial Economics*, pp. 13–14. S. Alexander has said, ". . . the gap must be bridged between the objective measure . . . and the subjective measure, which is really the final desire," (*op. cit.*, p. 203).

[28] This suggestion is implicit in Hicks (*op. cit.*), Buchanan (*op. cit.*), and S. Alexander (*op. cit.*). Dean states it explicitly in "Measurement of Real Economic Earnings of a Machinery Manufacturer," p. 257. The same position is taken in *Accounting for Inflation*, previously cited, p. 62.

Differential Price Movements and the Theory of Business Profit

We offer in subsequent chapters two concepts of profit which depend for their significance on the recognition of specific price changes. One concept, which we call *realizable profit,* is based on the measurement of opportunity costs and is in our view the ideal profit concept for short-run purposes; the other concept, called *business profit,* requires the accumulation of current cost data and has important advantages over the former when the horizon is extended to the long run. These advantages coupled with the practical consideration that business profit violates fewer accepted accounting principles than does realizable profit, lead us to develop it in more detail. Specifically we modify the concept to incorporate price level changes and suggest some techniques involving year-end adjustments by which the relevant data can be accumulated as a supplement to historic cost data.

The basic idea of current cost data can hardly be said to be new.[29] Our contribution we feel lies in: (1) the theoretical basis

[29] Such a measurement of profit or income was, for example, advocated by Ronald Edwards in 1938. See his series of articles in *The Accountant* of that year, republished in W. T. Baxter, *Studies in Accounting,* pp. 227–320. It has been advocated many times before and since. A rather comprehensive effort to work out the techniques appears in *Accounting for Inflation,* previously cited. Perhaps the strongest advocate in the United States is Willard Graham whose efforts date from 1934. His more recent article, "The Effect of Changing Price Levels on the Determination, Reporting, and Interpretation of Income," has aroused considerable discussion.

There is also a substantial German literature on the subject, especially following the hyperinflation period of the early 1920's. One of the most interesting and thoughtful of these works is F. Schmidt, *Die organische Tageswertbilanz,* which contains a bibliography of other German works on the subject, mainly in the 1920's. Schmidt tries to show why individual firms must consider their operations in terms of changes in the economy as a whole (thus "*organische*"). This involves taking account of present values ("*Tageswertbilanz*" may be loosely translated as "present-value outlook"). On its balance sheet, he argues, a firm should report all its assets and liabilities in terms of present market values; changes in proprietorship or the equity account would thus include *all* capital gains, both those which have been realized and those which have not yet been realized (see, for example, the statement at the top of p. 227, ". . . before selling, it is an unrealized gain and should be included as such . . . ," as well as the discussion on pp. 278–295). In the profit and loss account he argues that profits of the firm must be seen as originating in three different ways (pp. 51–60): (1) gains from changing the form of goods (manufacturing); (2) gains from changing the place of goods (distribution); and (3) gains from holding assets which change in provided for the concept (*a*) in Chapter II where a related short-run concept of profit, namely, realizable profit, is derived from and reconciled with the economic theory of profit maximization and (*b*) in Chapter III, where this concept and the related theory are modified to conform to the requirements of long-run analyses; (2) the breakdown of such a measure in Chapter IV into its various components which can be recombined in several ways so as to yield other profit concepts thus increasing substantially the versatility of accounting data (after all, the concept of profit which is most useful in making maximization decisions may not be best for tax purposes, and the one best for tax purposes may not be best for decisions on the distribution of dividends); and (3) the detailed derivation of such a measure, with its component parts, in Chapters V–VIII, showing general procedures which could be followed, coupled with a comparison of these procedures with present accounting practices.

One problem remains. Even if our justification is sound, our flexible concepts pedagogically useful, and our procedures logical and consistent, can the framework be applied with the degree of objectivity needed to win acceptance by practicing accountants? Even if the answer to this question is "No," there seems to us to be considerable merit in setting forth an ideal, both to indicate what the goal of accounting really should be as well as to show clearly and unmistakably how far short of that goal existing accounting practices leave us. But we believe that the computation of business profit is within reach, and this we try

price over time (speculative gains). But there is confusion on the part of the author both as to *what* is to be done in the accounts and *how* it is to be done. Nowhere is a full system elaborated. One key element which would appear to be missing is a concept of "current operating profit." Manufacturing operations are to be kept strictly on a historic cost basis; changes in the current cost of inputs are nowhere discussed. In our terminology, gains realized through use of assets whose price has risen while held by the firm are, in Schmidt's framework, included as part of manufacturing or operating profit. Speculative gains would thus presumably be a mixture of realizable gains accruing during the period less those realized through use in this period, although they may have accrued in past periods. In the only illustration of how his system might be employed, Schmidt includes as speculative gains only those arising from changes in security prices (pp. 241–248). While Schmidt's work therefore leaves a great many questions unanswered, and makes little or no effort to take account of changes in the price level, in contrast to changes in individual prices, it is an interesting early attempt to get at some of the basic issues involved.

to show in Chapters V–VII. In fact, many businesses are already making some of the necessary calculations for internal decision-making purposes, and other calculations, on an aggregate level, are being perfomed regularly by government statisticians. As to the problem of objectivity when it comes to publishing reports such as we have in mind, there is no reason, it seems to us, why accountants should not follow a principle of maximum objectivity in performing certain functions (in deriving certain data) and be permitted to use well-informed judgment in performing other functions (in deriving other sets of data), particularly if those supplement rather than supplant the former.

PART ONE *Development of the Theory*

II *Core of the Theory:*

PROFIT MAXIMIZATION AND THE EVALUATION OF BUSINESS DECISIONS

As we have tried to show in Chapter I, the crucial responsibility of management in a dynamic economy is the making of decisions in the face of uncertainty. Luck may swell the profits of a firm but in business circles profit is regarded, and properly so, as a return for above-average decision-making ability.[1] Decisions, by definition, relate to future actions. Profit decisions are directed at choosing a course of action for the firm that will yield maximum (or at least some) profit. Profit as an objective of the firm (economic profit) is therefore both future and anticipated—future relative to the time of the decision, anticipated because otherwise it could not be the object of decision.

[1] Some economists hold the position that pure profit is the element attributable only to luck. Profit in this sense is unexpected and unanticipated, and clearly cannot be the *object* of maximization efforts. See J. Fred Weston, "A Generalized Uncertainty Theory of Profit," where this view is developed along lines first suggested by F. H. Knight, *Risk, Uncertainty and Profit.*

In making a decision on a future profit-oriented course of action for the firm, management forms expectations about future events which are to occur over a considerable time span ahead. Profit for a particular future period is simply a shorthand expression for the net effect of the events which are expected to occur in that period, given the firm's adopted plan of operation. These events comprise quantities, prices, and costs (and changes therein) of goods produced and sold, of assets and liabilities held, of factors used in production. Expectations about future events may be broken down in great detail for the early portion of an operating plan, perhaps in the form of budgets, of estimated sales, or of standard (expected) costs.[2] For smaller firms, however, these expectations are likely to be subjectively held rather than explicitly stated.

As a means of evaluation, records of the actual events of a period can be compared to those events which were expected to take place. The evaluation of the expectational errors so disclosed should enable management (1) *to control actual events* and, where they are unfavorable (undue waste or pilferage of materials, for example), to make them conform more closely to expected events; and (2) *to formulate new expectations* and perhaps to modify the plan of operation itself. This relationship between expected and actual profit suggests that their components or dimensions should be symmetrical except for the time perspective. *Past profit* could then be said to consist of two elements, *expected profit* and *unexpected profit,* or windfalls, the latter representing decision-making errors whose careful interpretation should serve to improve the decision-making process.[3]

---

[2] The following general procedure, reported in 1940 by A. G. Hart in *Anticipations, Uncertainty, and Dynamic Planning,* p. 82n, appears to be a fairly typical planning and budgeting procedure today: "At R. H. Macy and Co. estimates of sales for each department are reduced to writing as single-valued estimates for each of the next four weeks. At the end of each week its expansion is reviewed, estimates for the next three weeks revised and an estimate for the fourth week framed."

[3] The assumption, often implicit in economic theory, of constant managerial ability is satisfactory for short-run purposes but is clearly misleading when longer run problems are analyzed. Hart, for example, whose analysis of expectations has been invaluable to us (*op. cit.,* pp. 83–87), nevertheless appears to overlook changes in managerial ability.

P. W. S. Andrews in *Manufacturing Business,* p. 129, has also pointed to the

The fundamental character of the accounting limitations illustrated in the previous chapter can be viewed in terms of a lack of symmetry between present accounting and economic concepts of profit. A reconciliation of the two concepts will require (1) a reconstruction of the generally accepted economic concept of profit for the firm and (2) considerable modification of the present accounting concept of profit. This chapter is concerned largely with the first problem and will proceed in four steps. First, the nature of a firm's profit-making decisions will be reviewed briefly; second, the limitations of economic profit for the evaluation of business decisions will be examined; third, a concept of *realizable profit* will be developed and shown to be consistent with logical decision-making; finally, it will be shown that this concept is objective and not subjective in nature and is therefore not encumbered by the same limitations as economic profit when used for the evaluation of business decisions.[4]

One point merits renewed emphasis before proceeding. The essential differences in symmetry between existing economic and accounting concepts of profit are not related to changes in the price level, but rather to changes in specific prices. To make this clear, a stable price level is assumed throughout this chapter, To simplify the theory presented, we shall, second, assume that all goods produced are sold and, third, that the market value of assets (in sale) equals their current cost (to purchase). All three of these assumptions are examined, and the theory consequently modified, in Chapters III and IV.

Economic Plan of the Firm

Nature of Profit Maximization

A business firm attempts to hold at any moment in time that array of assets and equities that promises to yield the greatest profit. Assets represent the tools which, wisely used in conjunc-

---

assumption of constant managerial ability as an error in economic theory. "Where economic theory appears to go wrong is that it regards the capacity of the business men as being 'given' in the same way as the fertility of a 'given' field. . . ."

[4] The modifications in the accounting concept of profit currently in use which are suggested by the profit concept developed in this and the following chapter will be presented in Chapter IV. The consideration of the practical difficulties in the way of developing the additional data necessary to compute business profit in the accounting records is postponed to Chapters V–VII.

tion with factors purchased later, will yield a profit; equities represent the current means of financing the tools. In its efforts to maximize profit the business firm must determine how large a box of tools to hold, how it is to be financed, and what kinds of tools the box should contain. Thus the three key problems of any business concern are as follows: It may increase the total value of its assets by assuming responsibility for additional equities (the expansion problem), but it must also decide at any moment in time in what form to hold its total resources (the composition problem), and its total equities (the financing problem). In actuality, of course, each business firm in some fashion solves all of these problems simultaneously and continuously.

If the firm's total resources are given (there is no expansion problem) and the owners of the firm have contributed all of the capital (there is no financial problem), the task of determining the kinds of assets and their proportions to each other (the composition problem) remains. At any moment in time the price relations among assets of different kinds are given so that, in whatever form a given amount of resources is put, the total market value of the firm's aggregate assets is unchanged.[5] It is clear then that market value is not a useful criterion for selecting one particular composition of assets in preference to all others. A comparison of market values of alternative asset arrangements would indicate that it is immaterial which asset composition is selected. And indeed this would be so if no expectations about the future were entertained within the firm.

Because the management of a firm does entertain expectations about the future, each asset arrangement or plan of operation signifies a series of expected dividends including, as a "final dividend," the expected market value of the assets remaining in

[5] By the market value of any asset we mean its quantity multiplied by the price of the item established in the market in which the item is usually traded. Market imperfections may mean that a firm's *buying price* for an asset differs from its *selling price*. An automobile or a machine purchased at one price can often be immediately sold in the same market only at a lower price. We assume in this chapter that such market imperfections are nonexistent so that market value is not an ambiguous concept. Changes in technology and the aging of assets may mean that no market exists for some assets. We shall abstract from this problem also until the simpler theory has been exposited. These important, practical complications will be introduced and examined in some detail in Chapter III and subsequent chapters.

the possession of the firm on the horizon date. These alternative dividend streams, each associated with a different asset composition, may differ from one another, and management will value some more highly than others. The firm's valuation of each dividend stream is a *subjective value* and represents the value to the firm of a particular asset arrangement as a box of profit-making tools. It is the inequality of these subjective values that enables the firm to select one asset arrangement in preference to others at any given moment in time. If the firm seeks to maximize profit, it is clear that the firm should select that composition of assets which, in the eyes of management, has the greatest subjective value.

Any realistic view of profit maximization in this sense must accept as a necessary complication its long-run nature. A firm for which a continuous long life is contemplated cannot afford to maximize its profit over a span of a single month or even a single year because the profit of one period is intimately related to the profits of other periods. A short-sighted firm, say, an automobile manufacturer, that acts to maximize this year's profit by using less costly construction materials whose poor quality will go undetected for a time would find subsequent yearly profits severely reduced as customers became antagonized. Any short-run conception of profit maximization is at odds with the long-run profit maximization which is typical of the going concern.

It would be meaningless, on the other hand, to suggest that the long run is "forever." A firm's specific activities cannot be shaped for the indefinite future so long as that future is uncertain. The point beyond which projections cannot be made is the *expectational horizon*. The managerial ability to project (or to formulate expectations) differs with the activities involved and with the knowledge brought to the particular problem, but one author suggests that the business decision horizon usually lies ten to twelve years beyond the present.[6] The existence of a horizon does not mean that a firm must plan for liquidation at that point, but rather that expected activities beyond that point are so shapeless that returns above normal interest on the market value of assets then held cannot be contemplated.

[6] B. S. Keirstead, *An Essay in the Theory of Profits and Income Distribution*, p. 37.

It should also be recognized that the kinds of activities the firm may expect to undertake in the future in order to maximize profits are not homogeneous. This suggests that for the evaluation of business decisions the accounts kept should be classified according to the activity undertaken. Most business firms are already organized in this fashion. Both the work and the accounts may well be organized along product lines, by stage of production, and by function.

Another type of distinction which is not always so clearly drawn is assigned a leading role in our next chapter. The purposive profit-making activities of a firm can be conveniently divided into (1) those that yield a profit by combining or transforming factors of production into products whose sale value exceeds the value of the factors, and (2) those that yield a gain because the prices of assets rise (or prices of liabilities fall) while such assets (or liabilities) are in possession of the firm. In the first instance profit is developed by *using* factors; in the second it results from *holding* factors or products.[7] Profit through use is probably of greater significance for most firms and clearly is the more desirable social objective. Both accounting and economic theories of the firm focus on this aspect of gain. Holding, or speculative, activities are important, nevertheless, because this type of gain can also be the object of a firm's maximizing efforts. The natures of these two types of activity and the decisions involved, however, are so different, though related, that their separation is vital for decision evaluation. Confusing the gain from one with the gain from the other, we shall argue, may mislead management into embarking on unprofitable ventures.

How subjective values are actually formulated is a matter of some conjecture. The logic of the problem, however, is straightforward. Once expectations of the amounts and timing of dividend payments are formulated and a *target* (or *adequate*) *rate of interest* is selected for the firm, the subjective value of a group of assets is that amount which, if presently put out at the target rate of interest, could yield the expected dividend pattern. The

---

[7] Individual changes in the prices of a firm's liabilities are relatively unimportant and will be neglected throughout this chapter. Accounting principles for handling such changes can be easily derived from those suggested for asset price changes, as shown in Chapter VII.

technique for determining subjective values involves discounting, but the more complex problems concern the estimation of the dividend pattern and the determination of the target rate of interest.[8]

Subjective Value as a Criterion in Business Decisions

We have seen that, when markets are perfect, the market value of a firm's total assets is unaffected by the substitution of one asset composition for another. The choice among alternative asset arrangements is made on the basis of subjective values. The subjective value of, at least, the selected asset structure must equal or exceed the market value of the assets involved or it would pay to liquidate the firm by selling its assets and to invest the proceeds at the market rate of interest.

It is quite likely, however, that the firm could be sold as an entity at a price in excess of the sum of the market values of the individual assets. This would indicate that outsiders also visualize the firm as a producer of dividends and value the stream they foresee above the market value of the individual assets. This excess of the market value of a firm as a whole over the market value of its assets is the *market value of goodwill* (hereafter referred to as *objective goodwill*). The excess of subjective value over the total market value of individual assets we shall call *subjective goodwill.*[9]

It follows (1) that subjective goodwill must exceed objective goodwill or the ownership of the firm will change hands; (2) that subjective goodwill must be positive or the firm will go out of business; (3) with given resources a firm should select that plan whose subjective value (and therefore whose subjective good-

[8] The technique of discounting is reviewed in Appendix A of this chapter. Though a knowledge of it would be helpful throughout this chapter, a willingness to accept a few computations on faith should be sufficient for the nonprofessional reader to understand the principles involved.

A discussion of the more complex factors in determining subjective values can be found in Erich Schneider, *Pricing and Equilibrium,* pp. 161 ff., from which the term "target rate of interest" has been borrowed. The target rate of interest is the minimum rate the firm is willing to accept on funds it plans to invest. This is often interpreted as the rate that could be earned on investment outside the firm, the opportunity cost to the firm. This may or may not be equal to the borrowing rate to the firm.

[9] Goodwill reflects expected profitability whether this stems from monopoly position, efficiency, or other factors.

will) is the greatest; and (4) if the firm can borrow at the target rate of interest so that resources are not otherwise limited, that plan with the maximum subjective goodwill is the most profitable. It can be seen that (3) is a special case of (4). It is the maximization of subjective goodwill that is the general criterion for choice among alternatives.

Subjective Profit and Evaluation of Business Decisions

A firm's plan of operation entails a pattern of expected dividends (or net receipts). From this pattern is derived the subjective value of the firm's assets. Given the market value of the firm's total assets, the firm will choose that composition of assets which has the greatest subjective value, and therefore the greatest subjective goodwill.

But maximization is a continuous process. Although the firm plans for a considerable period into the future, these plans are usually flexible and are subject to modification as expectations or circumstances change. Making these modifications is the principal function of the management of a going concern. Periodic measurements of profit should assist management in making these modifications by bringing to light deviations of actual profit from expected profit. It is a tempting path, and one that has not been infrequently followed, to argue that, because the profit which is maximized is subjective in nature, the ex post profit which is to be compared with it must also be subjective in nature. We feel that this procedure is basically incorrect. An examination of its principal defects, however, will lead us directly to a concept of profit which is both useful and objective.

Expected Subjective Profit

The subjective value of a firm's assets represents how well off the firm is in the eyes of its management. A sensible definition of expected profit is immediately suggested. It is the amount that could be paid out as dividends in any period without impairing subjective value.[10] This amount we shall call subjective profit because it can be derived directly from a knowledge of subjective value and the target rate of interest.

---

[10] Comparable definitions of economic profit can be found in J. R. Hicks, *Value and Capital*, pp. 161–188, and Erik Lindahl, *Studies in the Theory of Money and Capital*, pp. 74–111.

Suppose that a firm is organized now and is to operate for three years. Its limited life permits us to reduce the arithmetic to manageable proportions without impairing basic principles or conclusions. The firm's resources are limited to $10,000. After surveying many opportunities, it adopts a plan calling for the payment of $10,000 to purchase a machine whose use is expected to enable the firm to pay dividends at the end of each year of $4,000, $7,000, and $8,000, respectively; i.e., these are the net cash receipts expected from use of the machine. After the last dividend, the machine is expected to be worthless and the firm will retire from business. The target rate of interest is 5 per cent.[11]

Given the stream of receipts and the rate of interest, we can compute the subjective value, V_0, of the asset. It is $17,070.[12] It is expected that at the end of the first period and after the payment of the first dividend the asset will have a subjective value, V_1, of $13,923.[13] Therefore, a moment before the dividend of $4,000 is scheduled to be paid, the subjective value of the firm's total assets should be $13,923 + $4,000, or $17,923. These data and similar data for the remaining periods represent a summary of the firm's plan of operation.

PLAN OF OPERATION

	End of period			
	0	1	2	3
Subjective value (before dividend payments) . . .		$17,923	$14,619	$8,000
Dividends		4,000	7,000	8,000
		$853	$696	$381
Subjective value (after dividend payments) . . .	$17,070	$13,923	$ 7,619	0

[11] Developing the example in relation to a particular fixed asset is not necessary, but it does simplify computations. In subsequent chapters we will show that the principles developed are applicable to inventories and other assets as well.

[12] $V_0 = \frac{\$4,000}{1.05} + \frac{\$7,000}{1.05^2} + \frac{\$8,000}{1.05^3} = \$3,809 + \$6,350 + \$6,911 = \$17,070.$

[13] $V_1 = \frac{\$7,000}{1.05} + \frac{\$8,000}{1.05^2}.$

By the end of the first period the present will have moved one period closer to the remaining dividends.

During the first period, subjective value is expected to increase by \$853 (see first diagonal arrow in the plan of operation). Clearly this is the amount the firm could pay in dividends without depleting its subjective value. It is the firm's subjective profit. It can be computed in another fashion as the interest on the subjective value at the beginning of the period ($.05 \cdot \$17{,}070 = \$853$).[14] The expected subjective profit of a firm in *any* period can be defined then as interest at the target rate on the subjective value of the firm's assets at the beginning of the period.

Defined in this way the subjective profit expected to accrue to a firm during a particular period is simply the expected increase in subjective value that would occur if no dividends were paid.[15] If the firm wished, it could arrange its activities so that an amount equal to this increase, say, \$853, could be paid as a periodic dividend forever. This could be accomplished by buying equivalent risk securities (or other assets) with any excess of annual receipts over the established dividend and drawing on the interest and principal of these securities when receipts from the use of the machine were insufficient to support the dividend. The securities or other assets must earn interest at the target rate. The data in table 1 illustrate the operation of such a plan using the receipt data from the example discussed above.

A further illustration of subjective profit is given in figure 2. Initially the firm has a machine having a market value of \$17,070. The payment of a dividend of \$853 at the end of the first period permits the firm to maintain its subjective value by replacing the

---

[14] This should not be surprising because the subjective value at the beginning of the period was initially determined by discounting \$17,923 at the target rate of interest for one period. Letting D stand for dividend we have

$$D_1 + V_1 = \$4{,}000 + \left[\frac{\$7{,}000}{1.05} + \frac{\$8{,}000}{1.05^2}\right] = \$17{,}923.$$

But as

$$V_0 = \frac{D_1 + V_1}{1.05}, \quad D_1 + V_1 = V_0\,(1.05);$$

i.e., $V_1 + D_1$ is equal to V_0 accumulated at the target rate of interest for one period. The difference between the two amounts is simply the interest.

[15] Even if the receipts during a particular period were expected to be zero, this profit would arise simply because, by passing through such a period, the present is moved closer to subsequent receipts and the firm considers itself to be better off because of this fact.

TABLE 1

AN OPERATING PLAN DESIGNED TO PRESERVE SUBJECTIVE VALUE

End of period	Cash receipts			Subjective value of firm's total assets before distribution of receipts	Cash disbursements		Subjective values after distribution		
t	From machine (1)	From securities (2)	Total (3)	(4)	Dividends (5)	Securities (6)	Of securities (7)	Of machine (8)	Total (9)
0	...	...	...	$17,070	...	...	...	$17,070	$17,070
1	$4,000	...	$4,000	17,923	$853	$3,147	$ 3,147	13,923	17,070
2	7,000	$157	7,157	17,923	853	6,304	9,451	7,619	17,070
3	8,000	472	8,472	17,923	853	7,619	17,070	...	17,070
4, etc.	...	853	853	17,923	853	...	17,070	...	17,070

decline in subjective value of the firm's machine with the market value of securities (which equals their subjective value). Subsequent declines in the subjective value of the machine are similarly replaced by market values. The characteristics of subjective profit, then, are three in number: (1) It is subjective in nature; (2) it permits the maintenance of subjective value; and (3) it permits the conversion of subjective values into market values.

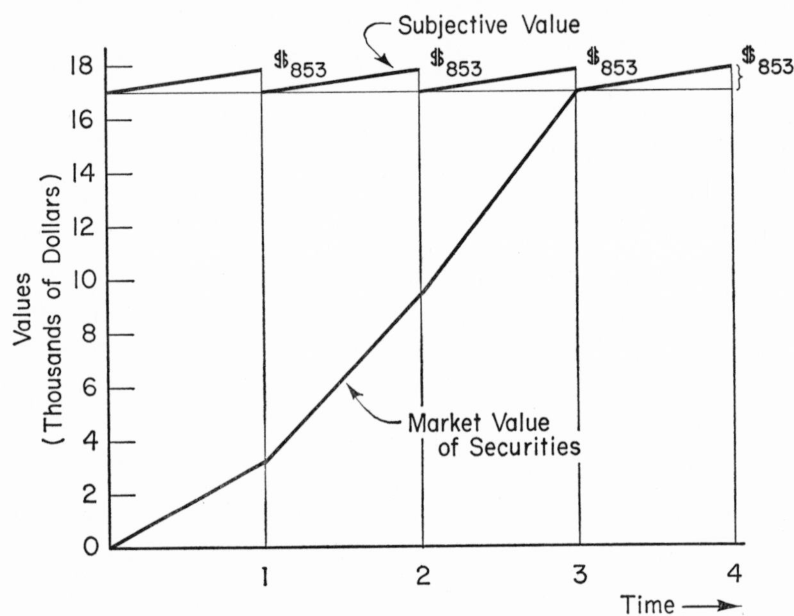

Figure 2. Payment of dividends equal to subjective profit maintains subjective value.

The word "permits" is used advisedly. If the firm elects to pay a higher dividend than its subjective profit, say, the $4,000 we assumed initially, as opposed to $853, it must pay for the dissipation of its subjective value by accepting a lower subjective profit in the future, a profit computed on the basis of the new (lower) subjective value.

Subjective Profit of a Past Period

Let V_1 stand for the subjective value expected to obtain at the end of the first period of a plan of operation before any dividends are paid for that period. Then anticipated subjective profit, S^a, is defined as follows:

$$S^a = iV_0 = V_1 - V_0,$$

where all values are those which are expected at the beginning of the period. It is probable that, when the period has passed, expectations will not prove to have been entirely correct. Suppose that, after the first period has passed but before the dividend has been paid, the subjective value then assigned to the firm's plan of operation differs from the expected value by the amount c. Then past subjective profit for this period, S^p, will differ from the subjective profit originally anticipated for this period, S^a, by c, i.e.,

$$S^p = S^a + c = (V_1 + c) - V_0.$$

We have apparently succeeded in comparing past and expected subjective profits. As indicated in Chapter I, some economists have argued that the measurement of past subjective profit is the ideal goal of accounting. Indeed, if the purpose of accounting is limited to the historical measurement of how much better off a firm, through its managers, feels itself to be at the end of a period as compared to the beginning, there can be no argument. If, however, accounting is to serve the purpose of aiding management in the formulation of decisions by clarifying errors in past expectations, the measurement of past subjective profit (and the isolation of its deviation from its expected counterpart) suffers from a major defect. The subjective value attached to the firm's assets at the end of the period is based upon new expectations concerning such things as the interest rate, the uses to which the assets can be put, and price-cost relationships; i.e., it implies that the original plan of operation has already been revised. Clearly the difference between subjective value at the end of the period as expected in the old plan and a new subjective value based upon a revised plan cannot be used as an aid in formulating the revised plan itself. Subjective profit according to our interpretation of the principal managerial purpose of accounting must be discarded as the ideal concept for accounting measurement because (1) it cannot be measured objectively and (2) even its subjective measurement normally cannot be accomplished until the firm's plan of operation has already been revised.[16]

An Alternative Formulation: Realizable Profit

It requires little elaboration to make the point that management does not request subordinates to submit for objective valuation expectations of how they will feel one period hence. Rather, management requests expectations of the events of the forthcoming period (and often of subsequent periods as well). These expectations can be verified or disproved by the hard facts once the period has passed; one need not probe into the nebulous question, "Do you now feel as you thought you would feel about the still futuristic aspects of the selected course of action?" Not that such information is not useful in the formation of decisions but rather that such subjective feelings cannot now be tested against past events; they can only be tested against future events. The error in expected subjective profit includes too much for the effective objective evaluation of decisions. But if that part of the error which relates to the events of the period just ended can be effectively isolated from that part which relates to expectations of still future events, a useful step towards objective evaluation has been taken.

The subjective value of a firm represents a list of *subjective* events. It is the market value of a firm's assets, more particularly changes therein, that represents *objective* events. The measurement of changes in market value can be accomplished, at least theoretically, on an objective basis and is not dependent on the subjective estimates management or its subordinates might choose to report. If it could be shown that a concept of profit based on the expected change in market value was consistent with a rational profit maximization process and that its ex post counterpart revealed errors in expectations that could be reconciled with errors in subjective profit, a symmetrical definition of future and past profit would be achieved that would also meet the accountant's crucial requirement of objectivity. The formu-

[16] G. O. May has put it this way, "The economists, in general, seem to conceive income as an accretion to economic power between two points in time; a concept that would have to be implemented by discounting expectations; a concept that could not possibly be implemented by accounting means," "Income Accounting and Social Revolution," pp. 36–37.

lation of such a concept of profit is our immediate objective. Its careful delineation and modification is the subject of Chapter III.

Expected Realizable Profit

We shall define *expected realizable profit* as the size of the dividend a firm could plan to pay at the end of a period without impairing the market value of its assets.[17] To interpret the firm's plan of operation in these terms requires a knowledge of expected market values. In the example used to illustrate subjective profit, expected dividends were \$4,000, \$7,000, and \$8,000 at the end of three consecutive periods. The cost or market value of the firm's assets at the beginning of the plan was \$10,000. Let us add to our data expected market values for the firm's machine at the end of each of the three periods, \$7,000, \$3,000, and zero, respectively. At the end of each period before dividends have been paid, the market value of the firm's *total* assets must include both the market value of the machine and the cash held for dividend payment. These totals are \$11,000, \$10,000, and \$8,000, respectively.

These data are arranged below to bring out clearly the nature of realizable profit as the hypothetical dividend that could be paid without impairing total market value of the firm's assets. Realizable profit is indicated along the diagonal arrows as the increase over the period in the market value of the firm's total assets. For example, the largest dividend that could be paid at the end of the first period without reducing the market value of the assets below their value at the beginning of the period is \$1,000. This is total realizable profit for the period. We do not have enough information at hand to divide this total into its components, operating profit and capital gains. This problem will be discussed in the next chapter.

[17] Throughout this discussion objective goodwill is assumed to be zero. There is no conceptual difficulty, however, in including changes in objective goodwill along with changes in the market value of the firm's assets. In general, however, the market for goodwill is a slumbering one, awakening only occasionally when bona fide offers for the firm as a whole (or a major part of it) are made; at other times, for all intents and purposes, the market is nonexistent and there exists no other means for estimating this value. (The value of a corporation's stock on the market is not a reliable gauge of the firm's value as a going concern because so many other factors are involved. Stocks of banking concerns, for example, are notoriously underpriced according to the occasional going-concern market values that come to light.)

TABLE 2

AN OPERATING PLAN DESIGNED TO PRESERVE MARKET VALUE

End of period t	Cash receipts		Values before distribution of receipts					Cash disbursements		Values after distribution		
			Market values									
	From machine (1)	From securities (2)	Cash (3)	Machine (4)	Securities (5)	Total (6)	Subjective value (7)	Dividends (8)[a]	Securities (9)	Market value (10)	Subjective value (11)[b]	Excess (11) – (10) (12)
0	...	...	...	$10,000	...	$10,000	$17,070	...	...	$10,000	$17,070	$7,070
1	$4,000	...	$4,000	7,000	...	11,000	17,923	$1,000	$3,000	10,000	16,923	6,923
2	7,000	$150	7,150	3,000	$ 3,000	13,150	17,769	3,150	4,000	10,000	14,619	4,619
3	8,000	350	8,350	...	7,000	15,350	15,350	5,350	3,000	10,000	10,000	...
4, etc.	...	500	500	...	10,000	10,500	10,500	500	...	10,000	10,000	...

[a] Column $(8)_t$ = Column $(6)_t$ − Column $(10)_{t-1}$.

[b] Column $(11)_t = (1 + i)$ Column $(11)_{t-1}$ − Column $(8)_t$, where i = the rate of interest.

PLAN OF OPERATION IN TERMS OF A SET OF EXPECTED MARKET VALUES

	End of period			
	0	1	2	3
		$1,000 ↗	$3,000 ↗	$5,000 ↗
Total market value (before dividend payments) . . .		$11,000	$10,000	$8,000
Dividends		4,000	7,000	8,000
Total market value (after dividend payments) . . .	$10,000	$ 7,000	$ 3,000	0

The nature of realizable profit can perhaps be brought out most clearly by assuming that the dividend paid is exactly equal to the realizable profit of each period. Any excess of receipts over realizable profit is assumed to be used for the purchase of securites earning the target rate of interest. Data for such an operating plan are given for our single machine enterprise in table 2, and are summarized in figure 3. It will be noted that realizable profit has three principal characteristics: (1) It is objective in nature; (2) it is an accurate measure of changes in the market value of the

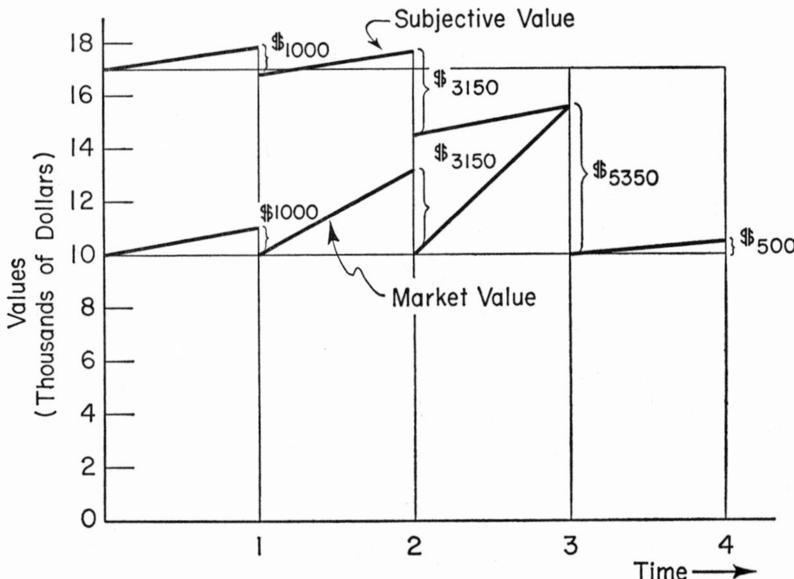

Figure 3. Payment of dividends equal to realizable profit maintains market value.

firm;[18] and (3) its use for determining the value of dividend payments permits the conversion of any excess of subjective value over market value into market values to be distributed as dividends over the life of the plan.[19]

Conversion of Subjective Goodwill into Market Value

The relationship between realizable and subjective profit can be described in terms of the expected conversion of goodwill into market value. Subjective goodwill, the excess of subjective value over market value, exists because the market does not share the expectations on which the firm is operating. If these subjective expectations are correct, however, this goodwill will be converted into market value by the end of the plan; the market will then recognize the correctness of the subjective expectations by sharing them.

The attempt to maximize profit involves a choice of that alternative course of action which has the largest subjective goodwill. To enlarge subjective goodwill enlarges the possibility of greater profit in terms of market values in the future. The accomplishment of profit maximization, on the other hand, is the result of a continuous effort to be "justified" by the market, i.e., to convert that subjective goodwill into some form of market value. The test of success, and therefore the logical criterion for the evaluation of business decisions, is the extent to which the achieved increments in market value approximate the increases originally anticipated.

The operation of the plan, therefore, can be viewed as having two aspects in each period, the earning of subjective profit and the conversion of some subjective goodwill into market value. As the firm's managers are already convinced that subjective goodwill represents a real value, its conversion into market value does not affect their sense of well-being; it is subjective profit that represents the increase in their notion of well-being. But the conversion of subjective goodwill into market value as the plan progresses does represent an element in realizable profit because

[18] And, if deflated to real dollars, the redefined profit would permit the maintenance of real capital.

[19] The question may arise as to whether streams of anticipated realizable profits can be used as a basis for deriving subjective values as a means of making rational decisions. This point is examined rigorously in Appendix B of this chapter; the question receives an affirmative answer.

a market value now exists which did not exist before, because the market judges the firm to be that much better off.

We can view realizable profit, then, in terms of the following equation:

Realizable Profit = Subjective Profit + Reduction in Subjective Goodwill

This relationship is illustrated below for the case in which all receipts are paid out as dividends.

	End of period			
	0	1	2	3
Dividends	...	$ 4,000	$7,000	$8,000
Subjective value after dividends	$17,070	13,923	7,619	0
Market value after dividends	10,000	7,000	3,000	0
Subjective goodwill	$ 7,070	$ 6,923	$4,619	0
Realizable profit		$ 1,000	$3,000	$5,000
Subjective profit		853	696	381
Reduction in subjective goodwill		$ 147	$2,304	$4,619

While in our example subjective goodwill is reduced in each period, this is not a necessary, nor perhaps even a usual, condition. If realizable profit is smaller than subjective profit in a particular period (a new firm may plan to sell at a loss in order to build up a future demand for its product), subjective goodwill would be expected to increase during that period. The sacrifice of market value would be willingly accommodated only if it were compensated for by the increase in subjective goodwill.

It might be thought that the amounts by which subjective goodwill are altered in each period depend on the particular dividend pattern adopted by the firm. This is not the case. Consider figures 4a, b, and c, which are based on the data in tables 1 and 2 and on the numerical example above. Figure 4a is drawn on the assumption that dividend payments are equal to subjective profit, i.e., they are such as to maintain subjective value. It is assumed in figure 4b, on the other hand, that dividends equal realizable profit, i.e., that market value is maintained over time. In figure 4c all receipts are paid out as dividends. In each case the amount of subjective goodwill converted into market value in three periods is $147, $2,304, and $4,619, respectively. In figure 4a, the converted goodwill takes the form of an increase in the market value of the firm's assets, dividend payments being just equal to subjective profit. In figure 4b, the market value into

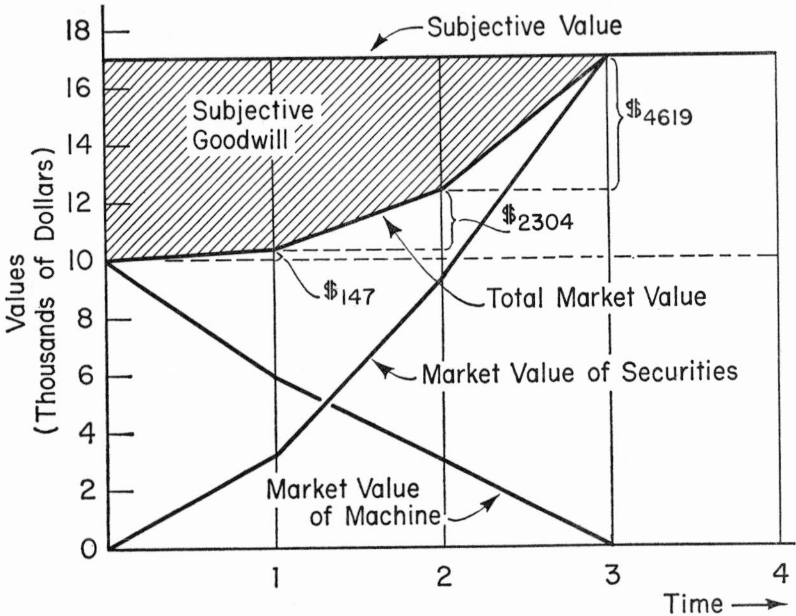

Figure 4a. Conversion of subjective goodwill into market value: under the assumption that dividend payments equal subjective profit.

which goodwill is converted is paid out in dividends along with the market value equivalent of subjective profit; dividends equal realizable profit. In figure 4c converted goodwill again appears in the dividend flow, which is now so large as to dissipate entirely the market value of the firm's assets over the period of planned operation.

So long as the pattern of machine receipts is not disturbed, the amount of subjective goodwill converted into market value in each period is unaffected by the dividend pattern selected. In

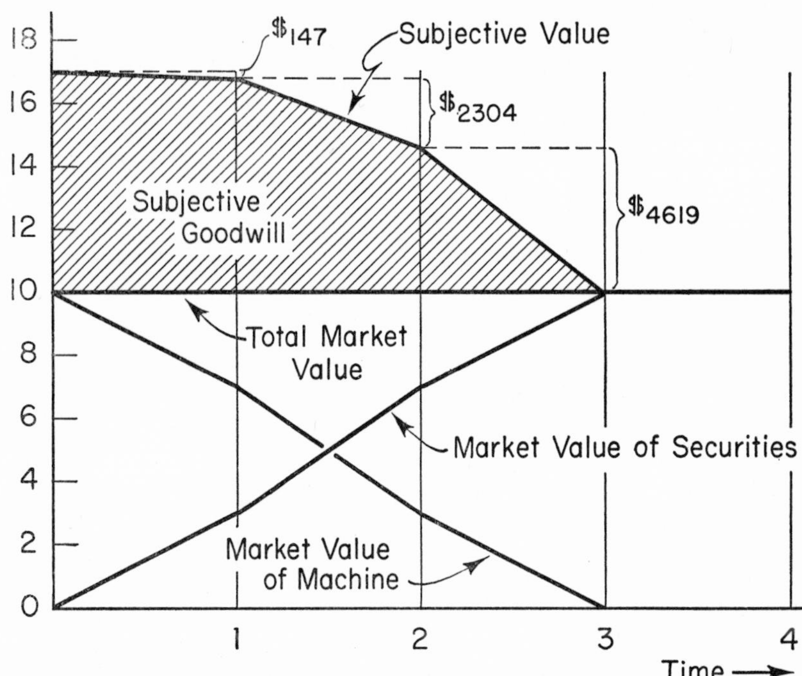

Figure 4b. Conversion of subjective goodwill into market value: under the assumption that dividend payments equal realizable profit.

our plan we have assumed that the firm invests retained receipts in securities whose market value and subjective value are equal since they earn the target rate of interest. No new goodwill can therefore result from the reinvestment of retained receipts.

REALIZABLE PROFIT AND EVALUATION OF EXPECTATIONS

Relationship between ex post Realizable and Subjective Profit

It remains to be shown that the errors in expectations revealed by ex post measures of realizable profit are not only objective in nature but useful in the evaluation of business decisions.

The relationship between subjective profit and realizable profit in their expected versions has been shown to be

$$\text{Expected Subjective Profit} = \text{Expected Realizable Profit} - \text{Expected Reduction in Subjective Goodwill.}$$

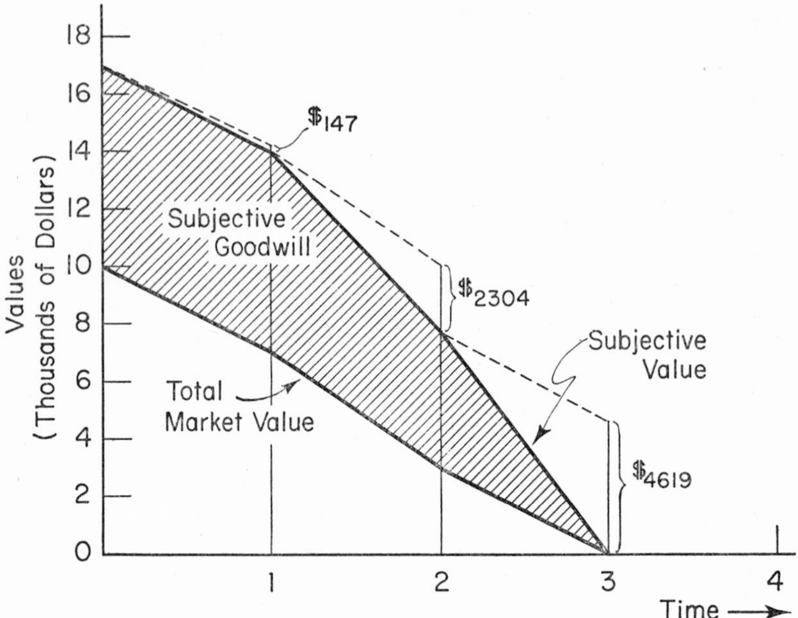

Figure 4c. Conversion of subjective goodwill into market value: under the assumption that all receipts are paid as dividends.

The subjective profit of a past period can be similarly defined.

$$\text{Past Subjective Profit} = \text{Past Realizable Profit} - \text{Past Reduction in Subjective Goodwill.}$$

If one equation is subtracted from the other, we obtain a definition of *unexpected subjective profit* in terms of unexpected realizable profit and the unexpected change in subjective goodwill. Unexpected subjective profit, defined as *c*, is now broken down into two components: *b*, the unexpected element in the actual change in market value, and *d*, the unexpected element in the actual change in subjective goodwill. Thus

$$\text{Unexpected Subjective Profit} = \text{Unexpected Change in Market Value} + \text{Unexpected Change in Subjective Goodwill}$$

$$c = b + d$$

The unexpected change in subjective goodwill, *d*, is quite straightforward. Subjective goodwill is the value at any moment of all excess profits (realizable profits less interest at the target rate on market value) expected to arise in subsequent periods.[20] An unexpected change in subjective goodwill means that the value now assigned to these excess profits is different from what it was expected to be according to the original plan of operation. We have two views of the excess profits likely to arise after the end of the first period—the expectations entertained at the beginning and those entertained at the end of the period. Any difference between these views does not represent a deviation of actual events from expected events but rather a change from one set of expectations to another. Whether the new set is correct can be verified only by comparison with the actual events of still future periods. It is this element in past subjective profit that destroys its usefulness in evaluating expectations; this element cannot yet be evaluated against objective events.

It is then the unexpected element in past realizable profit that indicates how actual events of a period differ from the events expected to occur in that period. The realizable profit expected to arise during a period is simply the expected increase in market value, M, of the firm's total assets before dividend payments, i.e., $M_1 - M_0$.[21] As market value at the beginning of the plan is known, the unexpected element, b, in actual realizable profit for the period must indicate a deviation of actual market value at the end of the period from the market value expected to exist by then. Actual market value at the end of the period must be $M_1 + b$. The deviation of actual from expected realizable profit is a measure of net *windfalls*, a term that indicates their unexpected, or surprise, characteristic. Windfalls, which should not be confused with capital gains or losses, include the unexpected elements of both operating profit and capital gains. Separating windfalls into these two elements, which is necessary if they are to aid successfully in the evaluation of business decisions, is deferred to the next chapter. For effective use the further breakdown of windfalls into even finer components, perhaps by divi-

[20] See Appendix B of this chapter.

[21] Excluding increases in asset value because of new contributions by stockholders and creditors.

sion of the firm, plant, department, product, process, or product, is necessary; indeed, much of standard costing is directed toward just this end.

General Significance of Realizable Profit

We are now in a better position to examine carefully how the evaluation of past expectations can aid management in formulating new ones. We can imagine the firm's plan of operation as including a series of projected realizable profits, the early ones specified in considerably more detail than later ones. When the actual realizable profit of the first period is computed and analyzed, it can be compared in detail with the expectations embodied in the plan. The deviations so disclosed represent errors in those expectations in the plan that relate to this first period. What is the significance of these errors?

Two things are immediately clear. First, errors in expectations of events of this period need not affect expectations of still future events. A firm that sold more of its product in this period than it had expected to sell may decide that this was a temporary phenomenon and will not reappear in future years. Nevertheless, while errors in expectations may be interpreted in this way, the importance of isolating the errors so that interpretation can take place is not diminished.

Second, expectations related to still future events may change although no errors in the plan for the current period have been disclosed. This possibility simply indicates that accounting for those courses of action adopted by the firm in its plan does not furnish all the data on which business decisions are based. Outside data may lead management to expect a general fall in national income and employment and thus a reduction in future sales even though current sales are equal to or even greater than the amount originally expected; a new patent granted to a competitor may force management to revise its expectations of future sales of its product despite a currently successful year; an alternative course of action discarded by the firm last year may now appear more profitable than the one adopted although that one so far has been as profitable as expected.

When errors in expectations are interpreted as more than temporary deviations from the original plan, the firm's management has two alternatives, to alter its expectations of the events of future periods or to attempt to alter the events themselves to accord with old expectations. If the deviation of actual events from expected events is the result of some factor beyond the control of the firm, perhaps higher raw material prices or reduced sales because of increased competition, the firm can only adapt to the new situation. Its expectations of sales, cost of sales, etc., according to existing selling and production techniques must be altered. As a result, the firm may find it advisable to alter its selling technique, say, by increasing advertising, or its technique of production, perhaps by substituting one material for another. On the other hand, an unfavorable deviation of actual events from expected events over which management has some control may result in attempts to reshape the events themselves. Suppose, for example, that the material cost of a particular product is higher than expected but prices have not deviated from expectations. If investigation discloses that material is being wasted or pilfered, steps can be taken to correct the situation.

Important as such results may be, the analysis of deviations of actual events from expected events may be significant for the evaluation of management itself. A comparison of the operating profit of this firm with the operating profit of other firms may reveal whether the actual profit of this firm is above or below average. But as one part of determining whether the firm's actual performance is the consequence of managerial ability or of luck, its actual profit must be divided into expected and unexpected elements.[22] The luck element, that profit or loss attributable to deviations of actual events from expected events, should not be credited to management; these deviations, by definition, were not anticipated by management.

Genuine managerial skill should be reflected in a consistently good correlation between expected and actual events, not only for those events related to the adopted plan but also for those

[22] It will be recalled that it is not the realizable profit of any one period that a firm tries to maximize. Low profits for a time may be purposive; the firm may currently be selling at low prices because it is felt that by attracting customers now, higher profits in the future will result, profits that will more than offset those currently sacrified. If one wishes to speak of maximizing short-run profit in any meaningful sense, he must refer to subjective profit, which is unique in this respect.

events associated with discarded alternatives. If events are consistently unfavorable, management is optimistic. If deviations are erratic and large, profits and losses are probably the result of luck. Management selects a course of action on the basis of expectations related to many alternatives. If the realization of managerial expectations is generally erratic, it could select the best alternative only by pure chance.[23]

Top management can use the same techniques to evaluate the performance of lesser executives and management teams.[24] An awareness of the nature of errors in expectations on all levels is a first step toward improving managerial ability, and the accumulation of this kind of information should aid in improving the decision-making process itself.[25] In a dynamic economy, a firm's profits may hinge on such improvement. Profits, in the long run, should go generally to those firms whose managerial ability is relatively high. But as most firms are attempting constantly to raise the level of managerial ability, a continuously successful firm must increase the proficiency of its decision-making process at least as rapidly as others.

Levels of Decision Evaluation

The emphasis we have placed on price and profit data in this and the preceding chapter should not be misunderstood. The evaluation of many decisions and activities can be undertaken without such data. But as the importance of the decision or activity increases, that is, as the level of responsibility of the decision-maker increases, the importance of price and profit data in summarizing the current events of a period grows rapidly.

Some expectations relate to quantity data alone and can be evaluated in those terms. A purchasing agent who estimates de-

---

[23] These considerations undoubtedly play a role in the market's evaluation of managerial ability in different firms, an evaluation that is very important in determining relative prices on the stock market. R. F. Harrod has made the point that managerial ability may be capitalized in this fashion, in which case the return earned by the firm is no longer profit; it has been transformed into rent. See "Theory of Profit," in *Economic Essays,* pp. 188–207.

[24] Peter Drucker emphasizes the importance of such evaluations in his *Concept of the Corporation.*

[25] The usefulness of these evaluation techniques is not limited to cases where profit maximization is the principal aim. The financial aspects of any plan can be similarly evaluated.

livery dates following the placement of an order may find that his performance is partly evaluated on the accuracy of these kinds of expectations; attempts to minimize inventories may be partly evaluated by the sizes of inventories actually carried; a foreman who feels he can increase efficiency by reducing the physical waste of raw materials may be evaluated by comparing his performance with his expectations; the performance of a salesman may be judged in part by how closely the actual volume of his sales corresponds to his projection; and the performance of a man in charge of an assembly line may be assessed, in part at least, by the volume of production that rolls off the line. Often such evaluations may masquerade as a kind of value assessment. Thus a salesman may be given product prices and asked to estimate his volume of sales in dollar terms; efforts to minimize inventories or to prevent the physical waste of raw materials may also be evaluated by attaching given dollar prices to the physical quantities involved. These kinds of decision evaluation clearly rest solely on quantity data. The decision or decision-maker being judged is given no control over prices and, therefore, cannot be held responsible for deviations in prices, but only for deviations in quantities.

The role of a decision-maker is expanded as soon as he is given some responsibility for price as well as for quantity. The manager of a retail outlet for a large firm might conceivably be asked to maximize his dollar sales; a purchasing agent might be asked to minimize storage costs; a foreman might be asked to minimize his labor bill or his material costs; or a department manager might be given the output he is to produce and be requested to minimize the total cost of that output. Evaluation based on such partial values may be quite effective for the unit involved, but it must be made clear that the impact of these activities on the total profit of the firm may be adverse unless the prices and outputs fixed to the subordinate decision-maker are carefully selected by higher management.

Even greater authority may be given to managers of departments, divisions, or subsidiaries. Such people and their staffs may have the responsibility to maximize profit for that part of the business in their care. The latitude given these managers may vary considerably, however, depending upon the amount of data which is specified to them by higher management. A person in charge of one step of an integrated process may have specified for him his input prices and his output prices and be asked to maximize his profit given these facts. He may vary his product mix and his input mix, but his freedom to vary prices would be limited to supplementary materials and labor. Nevertheless, his decision-making ability may be partly evaluated in terms of the extent to which his actual profit meets his expectations, and by how well these profits compare with those made in similar operations whether elsewhere within the firm or in other firms. The use in the evaluation process of accounting data based upon current prices becomes extremely important.

When we reach the level of the firm itself and are concerned with the evaluation of top managerial decisions, current price data in conjunction with quantity data are essential. It is at this level that prices given to lesser managers are determined. Decisions on the effectiveness of these judgments cannot be made without the aid of current quantity and price data. If such data are not to be found in the accounting records themselves, the evaluation must either be abandoned or based upon data obtained outside the accounting records. Of course, many of the prices recorded in the accounts are current prices. It is not mere conjecture that, if this were not the case, accounting would serve management less well than it does. But many of the factors of production used by a company in a particular period are entered on the records at historic cost, and most of the assets of the business firm are carried in these terms as well. If a management has purchased a particular asset primarily for speculative reasons, the kind of data presently collected in the accounts will not aid management in evaluating its own decision as price events unfold. Other false judgments can be traced to comparisons over time made on the basis of operating profit figures which are obtained by subtracting factors of production valued at historic cost from sales made at current prices. As a basis for evaluation, such figures may be even more misleading if a management or the owners of a firm judge the effectiveness of internal decisions by comparing company profit with the profits reported by other companies in the same industry. And the risk of false judgments may be enlarged further if particular departments and divisions of a firm are compared with each other or with similar departments and divisions in other firms.

When we move outside the firm itself, the evaluation of business decisions is equally significant. Here it is not a question of comparing actual events with a plan, for of course the plan cannot ordinarily be made known to outsiders. Rather, it is a question of making judgments on the basis of apparent increments in market value. This kind of evaluation may have even greater social significance than the internal judgment of a firm's decisions. Security analysts, owners of business firms, and potential entrepreneurs are continuously comparing one company with another, one industry with another, and on the basis of this kind of evaluation, making decisions which are important determinants of the allocation of capital. Economists who use such data to study relative profitability, to identify profits as related to efficiency or as related to monopoly, or to measure income generated in particular companies or industries, are performing essentially the same function though in a more indirect manner. They may draw conclusions on such things as the desirability of a tariff, the effectiveness of antitrust laws, the impact of taxes on business incentives, the real costs of farm or business subsidies, and the effects of administered prices. Economists and others often go beyond these kinds of studies. They analyze industry divisions such as service, manufacturing, farming, and mining; they develop national income data for the economy as a whole; they undertake many types of international comparisons. The effectiveness of these studies can be no better than the data on which they are based. It is for this reason that we urge the accounting profession, not to abandon the kind of data now collected, but rather to expand its range of collecting activities so that more comprehensive data can be made available not only to the management of a business firm but also to interested outsiders.

Appendix A: Determination of Subjective Values

How a managerial group actually formulates subjective values for alternative plans of operation is a matter of some conjecture. That it is done is undeniable, however, because otherwise there would be no economic basis for preferring one asset arrangement to another. A technique for determining subjective values that is logically defensible has been developed by economists. It is improbable that businessmen attain the precision this technique implies, but it does suggest the nature of the relationships that the businessman must employ if a profit decision is to stand the test of time.[26]

Of two different sums of money (dividends) receivable at the same time, a business firm interested in maximizing profit should prefer the larger. Similarly, if two equal sums are receivable on different dates, the firm should prefer the earlier one. If, however, a smaller sum is receivable at the earlier date, a simple comparison of the amounts or of the dates is not sufficient to determine the preference. The time disadvantage of the larger receipt may offset its advantage in size. A comparison of such alternatives can be made only if the two alternatives can be restated in such a way that the difference between them is limited to one dimension. An example may help to explain the nature of the process.

Suppose that a firm can always invest its funds to earn interest at 4 per cent per year, say, in government bonds or a savings bank, and is currently faced with a choice between two other courses of action each requiring an immediate expenditure of $95,000. Course *A* promises to return $100,000 at the end of one year but cannot be repeated; course *B* promises $110,000 at the end of three years and is not repeatable; no risk is involved in either alternative; no premium is attached to liquidity per se. The alternatives are depicted in the following diagram:

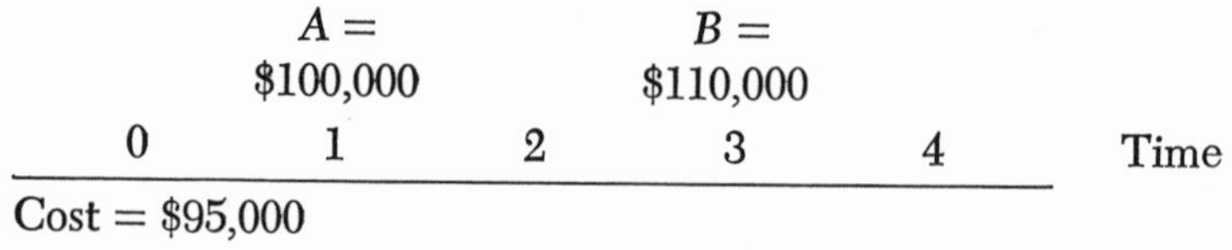

	A = $100,000		*B* = $110,000		
0	1	2	3	4	Time
Cost = $95,000					

[26] In the presentation to follow, consideration is limited to those decisions which relate to the holding of assets for their income-yielding properties; if an asset is desired for consumption, other principles are involved.

The manager of the firm might reason as follows: "If I choose course *A*, then I can deposit \$100,000 in the bank at the end of one year where it will earn interest at the rate of 4% per year. At the end of the second year I will have \$104,000 (\$100,000 plus .04 · \$100,000), which I can leave in the bank for another year. At the end of the third year I will have \$108,160 (\$104,000 plus .04 · \$104,000). But this is clearly less than the \$110,000 I would have at the end of the third year if I choose course *B*. Therefore, course *B* is the preferable one."

This line of reasoning involves an *accumulation process;* after accumulation to the same future point in time the course equivalents (A'' and B in the diagram below) differ only in amount, the larger of which is to be preferred. This procedure leads to the proper choice where it can be applied.

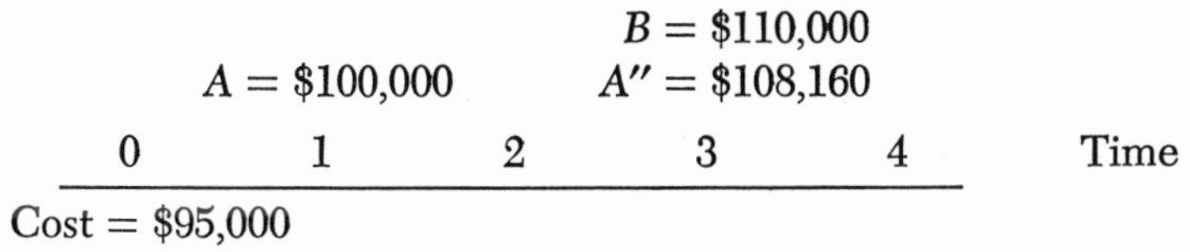

			$B = \$110,000$		
	$A = \$100,000$		$A'' = \$108,160$		
0	1	2	3	4	Time
Cost = \$95,000					

Suppose, however, that the firm is considering a third alternative, course *C*. For the same cost, course *C* promises to return \$3,900 each year forever. Accumulation does not lend itself to the solution of this problem because the accumulation of course *C* to any definite date must be incomplete. Further, accumulation always yields *future* values whereas the subjective values we have mentioned are related to the present.

If we use the *discounting process* both of these difficulties disappear. Instead of finding an equivalent amount for each alternative at some future time, we determine an equivalent amount A', B', C') at the present. In the case of course A, for example, we determine how much money, A', would have to be deposited in the bank now so that with interest of $.04A'$ it will amount to \$100,000 at the end of one year, i.e.,

$$A' + .04A' = \$100,000, \quad \text{or}$$

$$1.04A' = \$100,000 \quad \text{and}$$

$$A' = \frac{\$100,000}{1.04} = \$\ 96,154.$$

This amount is the subjective value of course *A*; it represents the largest amount that the firm would be willing to pay for it or, once acquired, the smallest amount for which the firm would be willing to sell it. The reasoning is important and lies at the basis of the following generalization: any receipt, A, has a value a year before its due date of $A/(1+i)$, where i is the rate of interest the manager expects to be obtainable in the market during that period.

This formula permits the computing of the subjective value of course B. Due at the end of the third year, it must be worth $B/(1+i)$ a year earlier, i.e., at the end of the second year. Dividing this amount by $(1+i)$ and dividing the result by $(1+i)$ determines B's value at the present. Each division by $(1+i)$ moves the value of any receipt one period closer to the present. The present subjective value of B, if 4 per cent is the appropriate interest rate, is,

$$B' = \frac{\$110{,}000}{(1.04)^3} = \$97{,}790$$

Course B is shown to be preferable to course A.

The present value of a stream of receipts is simply the sum of the present values of each receipt in the stream. A series of receipts, $a, b, c, \ldots l$, each receipt separated from the others by one year would have a present value of

$$V = \frac{a}{1+i} + \frac{b}{(1+i)^2} + \frac{c}{(1+i)^3} + \cdots + \frac{l}{(1+i)^n} \qquad (1)$$

where l stands for the last receipt and n for its distance in time. A close examination of this equation will reveal that any receipt is presently worth less (1) the smaller its size, (2) the more distant its date, and (3) the higher the rate of interest. If each periodic receipt, R, is equal to every other one and the series is expected to continue forever, it can be shown that this equation simplifies to

$$V = \frac{R}{i}, \qquad (2)$$

that is, the amount V left at interest forever would permit its owner to withdraw the amount $iV = R$ each period. Course C in the example is a series of this kind; it promises \$3,900 each year forever. Clearly it is presently worth \$97,500 at the interest rate of 4 per cent. The technique of discounting as a means of comparing alternative courses of action is illustrated in the following diagram:

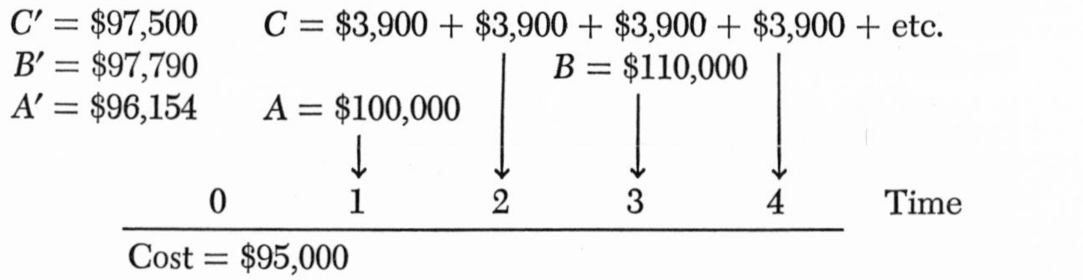

$C' = \$97{,}500$ $C = \$3{,}900 + \$3{,}900 + \$3{,}900 + \$3{,}900 + \text{etc.}$
$B' = \$97{,}790$ $B = \$110{,}000$
$A' = \$96{,}154$ $A = \$100{,}000$

0 1 2 3 4 Time

Cost = \$95,000

Of the subjective values thus determined, B' is the largest and course B, therefore, represents the most profitable course to be pursued by the firm.

We could also determine the perpetual stream of uniform receipts to which each alternative is equivalent and use these as a means of comparison. Course A is presently worth \$96,154. If the firm could realize this amount immediately and deposit it at interest, it would yield $.04 \cdot \$96{,}154$, or \$3,846, each year forever. By similar reasoning course B is equivalent to a perpetual stream of \$3,912 per year, and course C, to a stream of \$3,900 per year.

We have not exhausted the means of comparison. We might compare courses A and B, for example, by accumulating A (or discounting B) to whatever date is necessary to make the two amounts equal, then selecting the course corresponding to the amount which is closer to the present.

Still another technique is the comparison of *rates of return over cost.* Cost is a necessary ingredient of this computation. An amount \$95,000 deposited in the bank would yield 4 per cent. This is the *external rate of return* (earned on investment outside the firm. The \$95,000 invested in course A would also earn interest at some average rate most easily computed in this example by dividing the yearly receipt in A's equivalent perpetual stream, \$3,846, by \$95,000. A's rate of return over cost is seen to be approximately 4.05 per cent, B's is 4.12 per cent, and C's, 4.11 per cent. The course promising the highest rate of return over cost is, of course, preferable.

Another method, often confused with the rate of return over cost, involves a comparison of *internal rates of return.* To compute the internal rate of return for any course of action, no knowledge of the external rate of interest is necessary; we need only know the cost of the asset, *K*, and the anticipated stream of net receipts, *a*, *b*, *c*, . . . *l*. We then ask what rate of return, *r*, will make the present value of that anticipated stream of receipts equal to its cost; we solve the following equations for *r*:

$$K = \frac{a}{1+r} + \frac{b}{(1+r)^2} + \frac{c}{(1+r)^3} + \cdots + \frac{l}{(1+r)^n}. \qquad (3)$$

In the case of a uniform, perpetual stream of receipts, this reduces to

$$K = \frac{R}{r}. \qquad (4)$$

Applying this procedure to our simple examples yields an internal rate of return of 5.26 per cent for course *A*, 5.01 per cent for course *B*, and 4.11 per cent for course *C*.

But a discrepancy is disclosed immediately. While the other methods reveal course *B* to be preferable to the other alternatives, the internal rate of return technique makes course *A* preferable. The results of the three principal methods are set forth below:

Course	Subjective values	Rates of return over cost	Internal rates of return
A	$96,154	4.05%	5.26%
B	97,790	4.12	5.01
C	97,500	4.11	4.11

What distinguishes the internal rate of return technique from the others? Will a firm make errors in its decisions if it relies on one technique rather than another? A clue to the distinguishing factor is the equality for course *C* of the internal rate of return and the rate of return over cost. Course *C* promises a perpetual income stream. Though the other alternatives do not, the internal rate of return technique assumes implicitly that each investment-receipt pattern can be repeated indefinitely.

Suppose, for example, that course *A* was expected to be repeated indefinitely, that at the end of the first year $95,000 of the $100,000 receipt would be used to purchase another machine yielding $100,000 a year hence. The net receipt at the end of the first year is reduced to $5,000. If this pattern is repeated forever the true expected receipt pattern is a uniform, perpetual stream of \$5,000 annually, which has a subjective value (at market rate of interest of 4 per cent) of \$125,000 and a rate of return over cost of \$5,000/\$95,000 = 5.26 per cent. The internal rate of return is simply the rate of return over cost when perpetual replacement (on the same terms) is anticipated.

If the horizon of the entrepreneur is infinite and alternative courses of action involve perpetual replacement, the subjective value and rate of return over cost techniques will yield the same ranking as the internal rate of return method. If the entrepreneur's horizon is limited, and this is probably the more usual case, either of the first two methods is better adapted to the making of sound investment decisions than is the internal rate of return method. Subjective values can be tailored to the managerial horizon; internal rates automatically assume that horizon to be infinite.

The point has often been made that a higher interest rate tends to make less durable assets more profitable than more durable assets, while a lower interest rate tends to stimulate investment in longer-lived assets. It is not always made clear that this effect depends on a limited horizon for the entrepreneur. Thus the subjective value technique reveals course *C* to be preferable at an interest rate of 3 per cent, while course *A* is ranked highest at a rate of 5 per cent.[27] But the internal rates of return are unaffected by changes in the market rate of interest. Therefore, the preferred investment cannot lose its position by virtue of a change in the interest rate. As perpetual replacement is implicitly assumed in this technique, every alternative is assumed to have an infinite life; there are no short-lived alternatives!

The stream of dividends associated with each of our hypothetical alternatives has been assumed to be known. In reality each item in the stream is the subject of estimation by the firm, and this estimation is made in the face of considerable uncertainty. Each item is best described, therefore, as a *certainty equivalent,* an amount which, if certain to be received on the specified date, would satisfy the recipient just as well as the

---

[27] Subjective values at 3% are: *A*, \$97,087; *B*, \$100,666; *C*, \$130,000. Subjective values at 5% are: *A*, \$95,238; *B*, \$95,022; *C*, \$78,000.

less clearly specified "amount" he anticipates with uncertainty.[28]

The determination of the appropriate interest rate to be used in discounting is another complex problem. The external rate of interest used in our examples is appropriate for a firm having unlimited resources. This is not realistic. If a firm's resources are limited, the appropriate target rate of interest would be somewhat higher. For a firm that already holds particular assets, the subjective value of alternative asset compositions (some of which may involve only minor changes in the present structure) would probably be obtained by discounting at the rate expected to be earned by the present asset structure.[29]

Appendix B: A Reconciliation of Realizable Profit and Subjective Value

Our quarrel with the subjective profit concept has been restricted to its use in ex post analysis. There is little question but that rational decision-making must involve a comparison of subjective values. The question may arise, however, as to whether businessmen will make decision-making errors if, accustomed to using a realizable profit concept for ex post purposes, they rely on anticipated realizable profits as a means of deriving the subjective values upon whose comparison decisions are based. It is our purpose in this appendix to show that expected realizable profits can be used in rational decision making.[30]

There is one "cost" that has been omitted in computing real-

[28] The treatment of uncertainty is a complex subject beyond the scope of this volume. See Friedrich and Vera Lutz, *The Theory of Investment of the Firm*, pp. 179–182, for a brief discussion. The two major approaches in this field are reflected in A. G. Hart, *op. cit.*, and G. L. S. Shackle, *Expectation in Economics*. Neither treats the relationship between uncertainty and changes in managerial ability, but Shackle notes it (pp. 1–2).

[29] The full complexity of the problem cannot be indicated here. When money can be borrowed, for example, the borrowing rate may introduce further complications.

[30] A. G. Hart has argued that accounting-type concepts of income cannot be used for decision-making; ". . . the accountant's income concept permits exactly the same anticipated financial history to be interpreted by any of several variant anticipated income schedules, having different discounted values. The discounted-future-income rule cannot be taken seriously unless this ambiguity can be eliminated" (*op. cit.*, p. 90).

izable profit. The firm, by keeping current asset values tied up in its own business, sacrifices the interest that could be earned by converting its assets into cash and investing that amount at the target rate of interest. During the first period of our hypothetical plan, for example, the firm is sacrificing \$500 (.05 · \$10,000) by passing over this possibility in favor of its adopted plan. In the second period \$350 (.05 · \$7,500) is sacrified; \$150 (.05 · \$3,000) is sacrificed in the third period. When these sacrificed earnings are deducted from realizable profit in each period we have left "above-normal" or *excess realizable profit,* the amount by which the periodic profit according to the plan exceeds normal earnings on the amount risked in the plan. These excess profits are computed as follows:

	Period		
	1	2	3
Realizable profit	\$1,000	\$3,000	\$5,000
Less interest sacrificed (5% of market value of assets at beginning of period)	500	350	150
Excess realizable profit	\$ 500	\$2,650	\$4,850

It will be recalled that the amount by which the subjective value of a firm's assets exceeds their market value is called subjective goodwill. As the subjective value of the plan of operation used in our example is \$17,070 at the beginning of the plan and the market value of the asset is \$10,000 at that time, subjective goodwill at the beginning of the plan is \$7,070. The meaning most frequently assigned to subjective goodwill is that it represents the present value of expected "above-normal" profits. We have now defined such profits as excess realizable profits. The present value of these profits should be equal to subjective goodwill if the definition of excess realizable profit is consistent with the profit maximization criterion. This is the case; the present value of these excess profits is subjective goodwill.[31]

The subjective value of a firm's assets can be viewed as the present value of an expected stream of dividends or as the market

[31] Subjective goodwill $= \frac{\$500}{1.05} + \frac{\$2,650}{1.05^2} + \frac{\$4,850}{1.05^3} = \$476 + \$2,404 + \$4,190 =$ \$7,070.

value of the assets plus the present value of expected excess realizable profits. The significance of this relationship is: The business firm whose managers think in terms of "profits" will arrive at rational decisions if these profits are appropriately defined as "excess realizable profits." The business firm that is contemplating several alternative courses of action can legitimately establish projections of profit in each case and on the basis of these projections can make a rational choice.

The principle can be generalized. The subjective value of an expected stream of receipts is given by the following equation:

$$V_0 = \frac{D_1}{1+i} + \frac{D_2}{(1+i)^2} + \frac{D_3}{(1+i)^3} + \cdots + \frac{M_n}{(1+i)^n}, \qquad (1)$$

where V_0 is subjective value, the D_j's ($j = 1, 2, 3, \ldots, n$-1) are the expected dividends, M_n is the expected market value of assets on the horizon date, and i is the target rate of interest. If the market value of the firm's assets is presently M_0, the subjective goodwill associated with the operation of the plan is simply $V_0 - M_0$. We must show that the present value of an anticipated stream of excess realizable profits yields this amount.

Realizable profit, B, in period t has been defined as

$$B_t = (M_t + D_t) - M_{t-1}. \qquad (2)$$

Excess realizable profit, E, is obtained by subtracting interest on market value from this amount. Thus

$$E_t = (M_t + D_t) - (1+i)\, M_{t-1}. \qquad (3)$$

The stream of anticipated excess realizable profits will have a present value given by the following equation:

$$G_0 = \frac{M_1 + D_1 - (1+i)\, M_0}{1+i} + \frac{M_2 + D_2 - (1+i)\, M_1}{(1+i)^2} + \cdots + \frac{M_n - (1+i)\, M_{n-1}}{(1+i)^n}, \qquad (4)$$

which, upon rearrangement and use of equation (1), becomes

$$G_0 = V_0 - M_0 + \frac{M_1}{1+i} - \frac{M_1}{1+i} + \frac{M_2}{(1+i)^2} - \frac{M_2}{(1+i)^2} + \frac{M_3}{(1+i)^3} - \cdots - \frac{M_{n-1}}{(1+i)^{n-1}}. \qquad (5)$$

All terms but the first two cancel; the present value of an anticipated stream of excess realizable profits equals subjective goodwill. Hart's objection to accounting income as a basis for decision-making (cited above) would thus seem to be overcome by the excess realizable profit concept.

As all of the expected market values except the final one drop out of the equation, it is clear that any one pattern of expected market values may yield the same subjective goodwill as another so long as expected dividends and the final market value are unaffected.[32] It seems as though needless information is used, albeit harmlesly. This is not the case, however. Which of the many expected market values is the final market value for any particular asset or group of assets depends upon, among other things, the stream of market values. The lifetime which yields the largest goodwill can itself be determined only by comparing alternative lifetimes using as a final receipt in each case the market value expected on the relevant date. These expected market values form an integral part of the necessary data for decision-making. It must be remembered also that assets may be purchased specifically because a rise in market values is expected.

[32] Suppose that the expected pattern of dividend payments in our hypothetical example remained the same but the pattern of expected market values was different except for the original cost. The subjective value of the assets would be the same, $17,070, and so would subjective goodwill, $7,070. Different patterns of realizable profits and excess realizable profits would now be expected. The present value of the stream of expected excess realizable profits under such assumptions yields the same subjective goodwill as in our example.

Take the following case as an example:

	End of Period			
	0	1	2	3
Market value before dividends		$14,500	$13,000	$ 8,000
Dividends		4,000	7,000	8,000
Market value after dividends	$10,000	$10,500	$ 6,000	0
Realizable profit		$ 4,500	$ 2,500	$ 2,000
Interest sacrificed		500	525	300
Excess realizable profit		$ 4,000	$ 1,975	$ 1,700

Subjective goodwill $= \frac{\$4,000}{1.05} + \frac{\$1,975}{1.05^2} + \frac{\$1,700}{1.05^3} = \$3,810 + \$1,791 + \$1,469 =$ $7,070, as before.

III *The Theory Extended:*

OPERATING VERSUS HOLDING ACTIVITIES AND THE PROBLEM OF MARKET VALUES

The discerning reader will have noticed that the theory developed in Chapter II is essentially short-run in nature. It deals mainly with the evaluation of those business decisions that concern the use to which existing assets are put. When the horizon of the business concern is extended to include replacement and chains of replacement, some modification of the short-run theory is in order.

The nature of the required modification is intimately related to the way in which "market value," a term used rather loosely in Chapter II, is defined. A necessary background for the modification of the theory is therefore a careful development of various concepts of value. Any full array of value concepts should include the effects of changes in the price level, but to sharpen the fundamental distinction between such effects and those caused by differential price movements, the impact of the price level will not be introduced until the latter part of Chapter IV, after the more basic questions related to price dispersion have been discussed.

In this chapter, we shall utilize several value concepts to define, in an accounting framework, two concepts of profit. One of these concepts is *realizable profit,* the concept consistent with the theory advanced in the preceding chapter. The other concept is *business profit,* which is especially significant in our view for the evaluation of long-run decisions and for many of the external uses to which accounting data are put. After defining the two profit concepts, we shall compare them in the theoretical settings of the short and the long run, and shall introduce as well certain practical considerations. Although both profit concepts have a sound claim to incorporation into the accounting records, subsequent chapters are written largely in terms of business profit.

Concepts of Value and Cost

Dual Flow of Assets through Production Stages and Time Periods

The business firm can be viewed as a receptacle into which factors of production, or inputs, flow and out of which outputs flow. On the other hand, if emphasis is placed on a particular time period during which the firm operates, we can conceive of inputs flowing into the time period and of outputs flowing out of the time period. The operations of a business firm can be described in terms of these two concurrent flows.

The first, the vertical or production flow, relates to the movement of inputs from their acquisition to their sale as outputs, that is, to the movement of inputs through the various stages of production within the business firm. The second flow, the horizontal or holding flow, relates to the movement of inputs (and "inputs" is used here in the broad sense of including all the assets of the business firm) from one moment in time to another, that is, over the period of time for which a measurement is attempted.

This two-way flow of inputs is depicted in figure 5. Time is measured on the horizontal axis, but of the firm's total life span only the current fiscal period has been pictured; the figure refers to but one arbitrarily selected segment of a continuous flow over time. The firm's asset size is depicted vertically but the reader is asked to imagine this as being composed of successive layers of more nearly finished product. The vertical flow represents, therefore, raw inputs being steadily processed until final output is emitted from the firm by sale to outsiders. The total of the inputs with which the firm can work within the time period

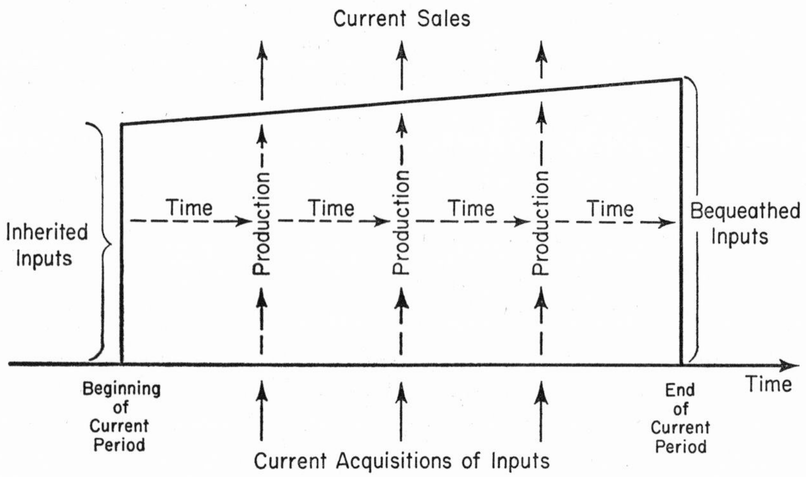

Figure 5. The two-way flow of inputs.

specified includes those inherited from the previous period and those acquired during the current period. The total of the outputs of the business firm in the same period includes the amounts of output currently sold and the amounts of inputs which are bequeathed to the firm in its succeeding period of activity.

These two flows are really simultaneous. The value of the assets held by the firm changes as production alters *asset form* and as time alters *asset date*. If examples of this simultaneity are needed, consider the cases of trees and wine in which the vertical and horizontal flows are not only concurrent but inseparable. Nevertheless, we shall find it useful to draw a sharp distinction between changes in value which result from production and changes in value which result from the passage of time. Changes in form (including changes in location) are characteristic of the vertical flow of assets. We visualize production as taking place in a series of timeless stages. On the other hand, any input may be held over any length of time, however short, before it enters the next stage of production.

Distinction between Operating Profit and Holding Gains

The activities of the business firm in a particular time period resemble an escalator which has the ability to move to one side as well as upward. Any gains which accrue to the firm as a result of horizontal movements, or *holding activities*, are *capital gains*. Any gains made by the firm as a result of vertical movements, or *operating activities*, are *operating profits*.

These two kinds of gains are often the result of quite different sets of decisions. The business firm usually has considerable freedom in deciding what quantity of assets to hold over time at any or all stages of the production process and what quantity of assets to commit to the production process itself. The opportunity to make profit through holding activities, that is, by holding assets while their prices rise, is probably not such an important alternative for most business firms as is the opportunity to make profits through operating activities, that is, by using asset services and other inputs in the production and sale of a product or service. The difference between the forces motivating the business firm to make profit by one means rather than by another and the difference between the events on which the two methods of making profit depend require that the two kinds of gain be carefully separated if the two types of decision involved are to be meaningfully evaluated.

Even if the primary or sole objective of the business firm is to make a profit through its operating activities alone, it is still necessary to isolate the effects of holding activities, incidental though they may be. If this is not done, the effects of these holding activities will be confused with the effects of the firm's operating activities, making any meaningful evaluation of the firm's production decisions difficult if not impossible. Suppose, for example, that a firm expects to make $100 in the absence of price changes by pushing a group of inputs through the production process to final sale. If, during the period necessary for production to take place, the prices of the firm's inputs (already acquired) and outputs rise, the final profit reported according to present accounting procedures will be partly a result of holding activities and only partly a result of operating activity. The apparently favorable result of the production decision may lead the firm to make similar production decisions for the future. In this case, however, price changes may not occur, and gains from holding activities will not inflate reported operating profit.

The Dimensions of Value

How the line is drawn between operating profit and capital gains depends upon the way in which revenues and costs, and assets and liabilities are valued. When values are assigned to such things, at least three dimensions should be carefully stated. Specifying these dimensions and indicating the ways in which they can be combined will serve to make clear the ambiguous nature of value. The dimensions we shall consider are (1) the form (and place) of the thing being valued, (2) the date of the price used in valuation, and (3) the market from which the price is obtained.[1]

Assume for the moment that the asset we wish to value is semi-finished so far as the production process of the firm is concerned. The asset in question could be described and valued in its present form, say, a frame for a chair, and there is a certain logical appeal about this approach. But instead of describing the asset in terms of its existing characteristics, we could describe it in terms of the list of inputs which were combined by the firm in bringing the asset to its present state, such as wood, labor, rivets, etc. A third possibility would be to describe the asset as the output it is ultimately expected to become less the additional inputs which

[1] The quantity of the item being valued must also be specified, but we assume that this dimension can be unequivocably stated. Another dimension to be considered is the objectivity of the value. But objectivity, or its antithesis, is closely related to the dimensions mentioned in the text.

have yet to be combined with the asset, for example, an easy chair less springs, cloth, padding, labor, etc. While there are other ways in which the form of an asset could be described, these three would appear to have special relevance. The description of an asset in terms of its *initial form* to the firm, that is, as a list of inputs, is characteristic of accounting valuation. The valuation of an asset in terms of its *ultimate form* or in terms of its *present form* is more characteristic of the economic approach to valuation.

In whichever way an asset is described for valuation purposes, the related prices must carry dates before the values can have significance to those who read the reported data. Thus the list of inputs which the firm used in bringing the asset to its present state can be assigned prices which are past, current, or future. The price assigned to the asset in its present form could also carry a past, current, or future date; and the prices assigned to the asset in its ultimate form (and to the inputs which must be deducted) could also bear past, current, or future dates.

The combination of the three form descriptions with the three time specifications yields nine possible values for a particular asset. The possibilities are by no means exhausted, however. A current, past, or future price for an asset can be obtained from many different markets. These markets can be divided into two kinds, the markets in which the firm could buy the asset in its specified form and at the specified time and the markets in which the firm could sell the asset in its specified form and at the specified time. The prices obtained in markets of the first group we shall call *entry prices;* the prices obtained in markets in the second group we shall call *exit prices.* Given the knowledge which the firm has of its entry markets and its exit markets, it is perhaps not unreasonable to assume that the only significant entry price is the lowest known to the firm, while the only significant exit price is the highest known to the firm.

It is still necessary to show that a difference between entry prices and exit prices is likely to exist at least for some important assets. A convenient approach to this problem is to list the conditions under which entry prices and exit prices could be expected to be the same. These conditions are the following: (1) there must exist a large number of identical assets traded on one market so that market prices are known for both new and used assets; (2) the firm must have nondiscriminatory access to both the selling and buying sides of that market; and (3) there must be no transportation or installation costs involved in either the purchase or the sale of the particular asset.

The terms on which a firm can buy and sell identical assets are often different. A firm may buy a new truck at one price but an immediate decision to sell may not return to the firm the full purchase price. The difference can be regarded as a payment for the additional selling and transfer services necessary to resell the truck to another final buyer, services which the firm itself is not equipped to furnish. Such payments to people whose function it is to make markets—stockbrokers and real estate brokers are other examples—create a difference between buying and selling prices. To the extent that a market is controlled (whether by the strength of brokers, buyers, or sellers) the difference between buying and selling prices to the firm is likely to be greater because it may then include a monopoly payment.

Exit prices are likely to differ from entry prices whenever transportation and installation costs are important elements. The best selling price a firm could get for an asset is the price the prospective buyer would have to pay the manufacturer or wholesaler, including delivery and installation in his plant, less the costs of removal from the seller's plant, transportation to buyer, and installation in buyer's plant. This amount is likely to be less than the firm's lowest buying price (manufacturer's cost plus transportation and installation) because the firm in selling must bear the cost of removal, delivery, and installation for the buyer.[2]

Many of the raw materials purchased by the firm on a week-to-week or a month-to-month basis will meet the first two listed conditions. Even for these assets, however, there are likely to be some transportation or installation costs which will make the

[2] Suppose that *A*'s current buying price of a machine from manufacturer *M* is $58,000 ($50,000 invoice cost plus $8,000 for transportation and installation). *A*'s current selling price of this (new) machine depends upon buyer *B*'s location with respect to *M* and *A*. *B* will not pay more than the cost to buy from *M* including transportation and installation. Suppose this cost is $56,000 ($50,000 plus $6,000). If the cost of removing the machine from *A*'s plant, delivering it to *B*, and installing it there is $9,000, the best net price *A* can get for this machine is $47,000 ($56,000 – $9,000), substantially less than *A*'s current buying price.

installed costs to the firm greater than the net amounts the firm could recover if it turned around and sold these assets immediately. For other assets, particularly fixed assets, even the first two conditions may not be met. Many fixed assets are not traded regularly on markets; many fixed assets are unique in nature, being one or a few of a kind, and their exit prices are not easily obtainable; and markets for many used assets are at best sporadic in nature. Market perfection is not a commonplace characteristic.

Given a difference between entry and exit prices, we have eighteen possible value concepts. We shall concern ourselves, however, with only six of these possibilities, three based on exit prices and three based on entry prices. The possibilities selected for discussion are italicized in the list of eighteen presented in table 3. The concepts are presented for an asset having a present

TABLE 3

An Array of Value Concepts

Value date, market \ Form and place of asset	Initial inputs	Present form	Ultimate form
Past, entry	*historic costs*	discarded alternatives	irrelevant
Past, exit	discarded alternatives	discarded alternatives	irrelevant
Current, entry	*current costs*	*present costs*	irrelevant
Current, exit	irrelevant	*opportunity costs*	*current values*
Future, entry	possible replacement costs	possible replacement costs	irrelevant
Future, exit	irrelevant	possible selling values	*expected values*

form which differs both from the initial inputs of which it is composed and from the ultimate form it is expected to take. Let us consider the asset first as a list of inputs.

The entry prices actually paid for these inputs represent their historic costs. Past exit prices represent prices which could have been obtained for these inputs had the firm chosen to do so. The entry prices prevailing currently for the specified inputs represent the current costs of those inputs. Because those inputs have already been combined into an asset having a different form, the exit prices currently prevailing for those inputs are not relevant. Entry prices expected to prevail in the future for the specified inputs represent possible replacement costs. The exit prices expected to prevail in the future are irrelevant for the same reason that current exit prices are irrelevant.

The six values applicable to the asset in its present form can be similarly analyzed. Past entry prices are at best discarded alternatives; while the asset could have been purchased in its present form, it was not. Similarly past exit prices represent prices which could have been realized through the sale of the asset in the past; such a sale was not made. We have appropriated the term "present cost" to mean the cost at the present time of acquiring the asset in its present form by direct purchase in the appropriate market. An excess of current cost over present cost would indicate that the firm's method of production is not as efficient as that used by competitive firms. We shall have more to say later about the relationship between these two concepts. The opportunity cost of the asset represents the best exit value that could be obtained for the asset if it were sold at the present time. The price the firm would expect to pay in the future for the asset in its present form represents a possible replacement cost. The firm could acquire the asset in the future by purchasing it directly rather than by producing it internally. The prices which could be obtained in the future for the asset in its present form represent possible selling values. If these selling values are high enough, the firm may simply hold the asset in its present form in the hope of obtaining a capital gain.

Of the values assignable to the asset in its ultimate form only two have particular significance. The price at which finished products can currently be sold has primary significance as a means of valuing assets which are in fact sold during the current period. The values expected to be obtained for assets sold in the future represent the data from which subjective values are derived.

The six concepts which will merit further discussion as we go along in this chapter are summarized below:

Exit values:

1. *Expected values*—values expected to be received in the future for output sold according to the firm's planned course of action.
2. *Current values*—values actually realized during the current period for goods or services sold.
3. *Opportunity costs*—values that could currently be realized if assets (whether finished goods, semifinished goods, or raw materials) were sold (without further processing) outside the firm at the best prices immediately obtainable.

Entry values:

1. *Present cost*—the cost currently of acquiring the asset being valued.
2. *Current cost*—the cost currently of acquiring the inputs which the firm used to produce the asset being valued.
3. *Historic cost*—the cost at time of acquisition of the inputs which the firm in fact used to produce the asset being valued.

The fundamental difference between the use of entry and exit prices as means for valuing assets lies in the different answers they imply for the following question: At what stage of the process of production and sale should exit values assume dominance in the valuation of assets? The use of entry values as a basis of asset valuation implies that all assets should be valued on an entry basis until they actually leave the firm as the result of sale. It follows that no operating profit would be recognized in the accounts, if an entry value basis is utilized, until sale has been consummated. This view is consistent with the accounting concept of a firm's operations; it is a version of the sale or realization criterion for defining operating profit. The use of entry values as the dominant basis for valuation implies also that only current values will have significance as exit values.

The use of exit values, other than current values as defined above, as a principal means for valuing assets suggests that these exit values should dominate the accounting records from the original acquisition of inputs to the final sale of outputs. Such a treatment requires that operating profit be recognized as soon as the exit value of assets at one stage of production exceeds the sum of the exit values of all inputs (whether raw material inputs or intermediate products) used in moving the asset from the preceding stage of production. This view of operating profit utilizes the production, realizable, or accrual criterion for recognizing operating profit. If all stages of production must be completed before title to final goods is passed to a customer, no operating profit will be related to the actual sale of the final product. The sale of the final product will represent an exchange of one asset for another, the value of both on the books of the firm being the same.

We intend now to develop two views of operating profit, one based on entry values and one based on exit values, and to consider their implications for the balance sheet and the measurement of capital gains.

Realizable Profit and Its Components

When operating profit and capital gains are defined in terms of the production or realizable criterion, we are dealing with the profit concept around which the simplified theory of Chapter II was built.

Opportunity Cost: The Basis for Valuation

The choice of an exit value is not a complicated problem. Current values are not meaningful because only assets sold can be so valued and the realizable criterion requires that exit values be applied to all assets. In the special case of assets sold, either of the other two concepts of exit value should yield values equal to those given by the current value concept.

The choice then is between expected values and opportunity costs. Expected values represent amounts which the firm anticipates receiving when goods are sold in the future on the date on which sale is expected to take place according to the firm's plan of action. It is clearly possible to value existing assets on the basis of these expected values. An inventory of finished goods, for example, might be valued by subtracting from the expected selling value of those goods, those selling and distribution costs which the firm expects to incur before final sale of the goods. By a similar subtraction process, values for assets falling further back in the production process could be derived from the series of values expected to be received eventually through the use and disposal of those assets. We can conceive of the asset being valued as providing a future stream of receipts each item of which must be reduced by the amount of expected additional costs necessary to obtain that receipt. The stream of net expected values so obtained is still future in time, and thus each item in the stream must be discounted before it can be treated as an element in present valuations.

The procedure we have described is, of course, precisely the way in which subjective values would be derived for assets. In Chapter II, however, it was shown that subjective values cannot serve efficiently as a basis for accounting valuations for the very reason that they do not represent strictly current events of the period under consideration. Values relating to expected future events cannot be used as a means of evaluating past expectations about current events.

Opportunity cost, then, is the significant valuation basis for the keeping of records in terms of exit values. It is a value current in date and one which can be applied, at least in theory, to all of the assets of the firm. It is also objective in nature and therefore meets all the requirements of market value discussed in Chapter II. The profit concept developed on this basis we have called realizable profit. Let us outline its characteristics more carefully.

Production Moments and Holding Intervals

We assume as before that production is timeless and only holding activities take time. We can imagine that each fiscal period can be broken up into a large number of *holding intervals* preceding each of which is a *production moment* during which actual production takes place. The total assets of the business firm are considered to progress through each production moment. It should be clear, however, that all of the assets of the business firm need not undergo change during the so-called production moment. In fact, it is probable that during any production moment very few of the firm's assets will actually undergo change. Cash, most liquid assets, and many of the firm's fixed assets will not enter into the physical production process at all. As production is timeless, we can say that the opportunity cost of those assets not directly involved in the production process will be the same at the end of the production moment as it was at the beginning. Therefore, any operating profit resulting from the production moment under consideration is attributable entirely to those assets which undergo physical production. Under these conditions *realizable operating profit* can be defined as the excess of the opportunity cost of the firm's total assets at the end of the production moment over the opportunity cost of the firm's total assets at the beginning of the production moment.

As a production moment is followed by a holding interval, the opportunity cost of the firm's total assets at the end of a production moment must be equal to the opportunity cost of the firm's total assets at the beginning of the succeeding holding interval. During the holding interval no production takes place. Therefore, if at the end of a holding interval the opportunity cost of a firm's total assets exceeds the opportunity cost of these assets at the beginning of the holding interval, the increase can be attributed only to the net effect of price changes on the values of those assets. This newly defined total asset value now represents the value of resources committed to production in the next production moment. This procedure can be repeated for any number of production moments and holding intervals into which it seems desirable to divide the given fiscal period.

The Realizable Profit Matrix

To make these relationships clear, let us adopt the following letters as basic symbols:

A Assets
p Production moment
h Holding interval
b Beginning of the fiscal period
e End of the fiscal period
o Opportunity cost

The symbols p, h, b, and e all have to do with the horizontal and vertical flow of assets through the fiscal period, and are used as prescripts or subscripts. When p or h is used as a prescript, it indicates inputs; when used as a subscript, it indicates outputs. Therefore we have the following:

${}_pA$ Inputs of a production moment
A_p Outputs of a production moment
${}_hA$ Inputs of a holding interval
A_h Outputs of a holding interval

(As indicated above, $A_p = {}_hA$ at the end of any production moment and $A_h = {}_pA$ at the end of any holding interval.)

${}_bA$ The firm's inherited inputs (its assets at the beginning of the fiscal period) which are assumed to enter immediately a production moment (${}_bA$ is therefore a particular ${}_pA$ value)

A_e The firm's bequeathed inputs (its assets at the end of the fiscal period) (A_e is therefore a particular A_h value)

Supercripts have to do with the method of valuing the assets. Thus, we have, for example,

${}_bA^o$ Opportunity cost of the firm's inherited inputs

Finally, we use the following symbols to denote profit concepts:

ROP Realizable operating profit
RCG Realizable capital gains
RP Realizable profit, the sum of *ROP* and *RCG*

With the aid of these symbols, the splintering of the fiscal period into production moments and holding intervals is depicted in figure 6. We suppose the concurrent flows through the firm and through the fiscal period to take place in a series of successive production moments and holding intervals. The period begins with a list of the firm's assets valued at their opportunity cost on that date; it ends with a list of the firm's assets valued at the opportunity cost prevailing at the end of the period. The excess of the latter figure over the former represents the *realizable profit* earned by the firm during the particular fiscal period. Thus

$$RP = A_e{}^o - {}_bA^o. \quad (1)$$

Further the realizable operating profit for any particular production moment at time (t) can be defined as

$$ROP_{(t)} = A_{p(t)}{}^o - {}_pA_{(t)}{}^o. \quad (2)$$

And finally the capital gains accruing to the firm over any particular holding interval ending at time t can be defined as

$$RCG_{(t)} = A_{h(t)}{}^o - {}_hA_{(t-1)}{}^o. \quad (3)$$

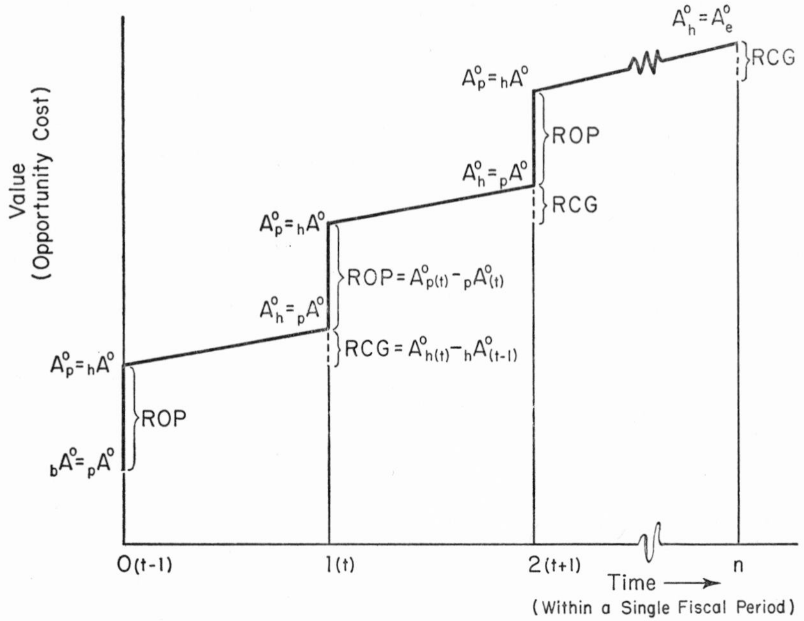

Figure 6. Production moments and holding intervals for a single fiscal period.

It follows that the total realizable operating profit earned by the firm over the specific fiscal period involving $(n-1)$ production moments is given by

$$ROP = \sum_{0}^{n-1} A_p{}^o - \sum_{0}^{n-1} {}_pA^o. \tag{4}$$

This defines the total realizable operating profit of the firm as the excess of the total value of assets held at the end of all production moments over the total value of the assets introduced into all production moments. For reasons which will become obvious it is desirable to restate equation (4) in such a way that the initial endowment of assets, which directly enter the first production moment, is separately stated. Let us therefore separate the second term in equation (4) into two parts, one of which will be the value of inherited inputs, ${}_bA^o$, while the other will be the value of all intermediate inputs of the fiscal period. It should be noted that the term "intermediate" is used here with reference to the time period, not with reference to the stages of the production process. We can now rewrite equation (4) as follows:

$$ROP = \sum_{0}^{n-1} A_p{}^o - \sum_{1}^{n-1} {}_pA^o - {}_bA^o. \tag{5}$$

The total realizable capital gains which accrue to the firm over the entire fiscal period can be defined in similar fashion as the excess of asset values at the end of holding periods over the asset values at the beginning of holding periods where asset values in both cases are defined in terms of the opportunity costs prevailing at the moment of valuation. Thus we have by summing equation (3):

$$RCG = \sum_{1}^{n} A_h{}^o - \sum_{0}^{n-1} {}_hA^o. \tag{6}$$

It will be useful in this case to separate the first term of equation (6) into two elements, one of which will be the total value of the firm's assets at the end of the fiscal period. The remainder of the first term of equation (6) will be the output of all intermediate holding periods. Equation (6) becomes:

$$RCG = A_e{}^o + \sum_{1}^{n-1} A_h{}^o - \sum_{0}^{n-1} {}_hA^o. \tag{7}$$

We can now summarize the realizable profit concept, which is based on opportunity cost as a valuation technique, in the following matrix form:

The Realizable Profit Matrix

$$\begin{array}{lllllr}
0 + & \sum_{0}^{n-1} A_p{}^o - & \sum_{1}^{n-1} {}_pA^o - & {}_bA^o & = ROP & (5) \\
A_e{}^o - & \sum_{0}^{n-1} {}_hA^o + & \sum_{1}^{n-1} A_h{}^o + & 0 & = RCG & (7) \\
\hline
A_e{}^o + & 0 \quad + & 0 & - {}_bA^o & = \Delta A = RP & (1)
\end{array}$$

As the outputs of all production moments are equal to the inputs of all holding intervals, the vertical equation in the second column,

$$\sum_{0}^{n-1} A_p{}^o - \sum_{0}^{n-1} {}_hA^o,$$

must equal zero. Furthermore, because the inputs of all intermediate holding periods are equal to the outputs of all intermediate holding periods, the vertical equation in the third column,

$$\sum_{1}^{n-1} A_h{}^o - \sum_{1}^{n-1} {}_pA^o,$$

must also equal zero. The sum of the realizable profit equation and the realizable capital gains equation is therefore $A_e^o - {}_bA^o$. This amount is the change in the value of the firm's assets from the beginning to the end of the fiscal period under consideration and represents realizable profit. It should be noted that the system of equations does not provide for any new contributions of capital by the owners of the business or for any withdrawals of capital by the owners of the business.

Treatment of Sales and Acquisitions

There is, however, another omission which may appear at first sight to be even more startling. We have developed in a fairly rigorous framework a definition of realizable operating profit and realizable capital gains without at any time making reference to sales of product or to acquisitions of inputs. The omission of final sales from our calculations is relatively easy to justify. Profit is considered to be earned and is recorded as assets move through the several stages of production. In the normal course of events all stages of production (the last of which might be the loading of product aboard a freight car or the completion and mailing of an invoice) are completed before title to the goods passes from the producer to the customer. If this is so, all operating profit will have been recorded before the sale takes place. It is reasonable to assume that the opportunity cost of the goods merges with their sales price. Thus the sale of goods merely represents the exchange of one asset for another both of which are carried at the same value on the books of the firm.

The current acquisition of inputs brings with it another complication. The mere acquisition of inputs is not a stage in the production process and the purchase of an input cannot be regarded as a signal for the recording of profit. But unlike goods sold, the opportunity cost of goods purchased need not be equal to the assets exchanged for them. We must assume, of course, that the current cost of inputs at the time of acquisition is equal to the asset values exchanged for the input. But we cannot assume that the current cost of these inputs is equal to their opportunity cost. Because of various market imperfections the opportunity cost of at least some assets will differ from the current cost of those assets to the firm. Opportunity cost may be either higher or lower than current cost. If it is higher, the seller of the asset may not have access to the market from which the buying firm's opportunity cost is obtained, as in the case of a retailer buying from a wholesaler. It is probably true for plant and equipment items and for many raw materials that opportunity costs will be less than current costs. A firm that buys a truck for x dollars, for example, could probably resell it immediately only at a price somewhat below x dollars. This differential is simply evidence of the imperfection of the automobile market. A firm cannot buy and sell at the same price in this market because it does not have the institutional characteristics by which sellers are identified.

The initial gain or loss which becomes realizable upon the acquisition of inputs should be recorded immediately on the books if one is following the hypothesis that exit values, namely, opportunity costs, should dominate the accounts from acquisition through the final sale of product. This initial gain or loss could be included with gains or losses from holding activities, although a strong case could be made for setting up a separate account in which to record initial gains and losses of this sort. But the general acceptance of opportunity cost accounting is not so imminent that refinements of this sort need receive further attention at this time.

Characteristics of Realizable Profit Summarized

Our discussion of the opportunity cost basis for record-keeping has been pursued largely in terms of the identification of operating profit. The implications of this method for the comparative balance sheet are the following. All assets (and liabilities) held at the beginning of the fiscal period must be valued at the opportunity costs of those assets (and liabilities) on that date. The gains resulting from all prior production moments and holding intervals (less dividends plus new contributions of capital) are included in the net assets shown on this balance sheet. These values represent the amount which the firm is risking in the succeeding fiscal period. The values recorded at the end of the fiscal period will reflect the opportunity costs prevailing at that time. If the price level has been constant, these two balance sheets can be directly compared. The change in net asset value which has occurred over the period is a measure of the total realizable profit which has been earned by the firm during the period under consideration.

It should be noted in conclusion that the opportunity cost basis for record-keeping relies on only one concept of value, namely, opportunity cost. In defining operating profit it is the opportunity cost of assets at the beginning of a production moment which is subtracted from the opportunity cost of assets at the end of a production moment. Operating profit arises because at least some of the assets of the firm have changed their form (or place) during the production moment. Operating profit is attributable solely to this change in form.

Capital gains, on the other hand, result from holding activities alone. The amount of the gain is determined by subtracting the opportunity cost of the assets at the beginning of the holding interval from the opportunity cost of the same assets at the end of the holding interval. Except for the initial acquisition of inputs, capital gains result from changes in date. The same value concept is applied to the same asset at two different points in time; any difference which is noted is a capital gain.

The opportunity cost basis for record-keeping has this unique characteristic: except for the initial acquisition of inputs, all gains and losses can be attributed either to changes in form or to changes in date and none can be attributed to changes in the method of valuation itself. The profit concept which results from the application of the opportunity cost principle is consistent with that developed in Chapter II. It is tempting to discuss its limitations at this point, but there may be some economy in first presenting what is in our view its major competitor. We shall then be in a position to compare the two rival concepts and to see in what way the theory presented in Chapter II requires modification.

Business Profit and Its Components

Production and Time Dimensions of the Realization Criterion

If we adopt the proposition that entry values should dominate the accounting records until final sale is consummated, we are adopting what might be called the accounting view of business operation. It should be emphasized that we have defined the realization criterion in terms of the vertical, or production, flow through the firm, and not with respect to the horizontal, or holding, flow. This definition is not sacred and does not appear to be even usual in the accounting literature. Much of what has been written on the realization principle might however be clearer if its production and time dimensions were carefully defined. When we say that entry values will be used as a basis for valuation until final sale, we are simply saying that the prices to be used in valuing assets at different stages of production are to be derived from prices prevailing in those markets from which the firm gets its inputs. We might alternatively emphasize the time flow by defining the realization criterion as follows: Historically dated prices will be used as a basis for valuation until a current price is realized. There are, therefore, two dimensions to the realization criterion, a production dimension and a time dimension.

The possible profit concepts to which different combinations of these criteria lead are presented in table 4. The traditional

TABLE 4

A COMPARISON OF REALIZATION AND REALIZABLE CRITERIA

	Entry values (realization principle: production basis)	Exit values (realizable principle: production basis)
Historic values (realization principle: time basis)	accounting profit	historic values
Current values (realizable principle: time basis)	business profit	realizable profit

accounting concept of profit is dependent on the use of both facets of the realization criterion; it is applied on a time basis as well as on a production basis. On the other hand, realizable profit, which was developed above, does not employ the realization criterion in either of its dimensions, but rather depends upon the application of the realizable criterion both on a time basis and on a production basis.

The business profit concept which we now develop is based upon the application of the realization criterion on a production basis and on the use of the realizable principle over time. Entry values are used as a basis for valuation of assets on hand, but these entry values carry current dates; all assets are carried at current cost but no gains from production are recognized until final sale.[3]

Current Cost: The Basis for Valuation

This discussion suggests that we are preparing a case for the matching of current (exit) values with current (entry) costs as a means of defining operating profit. The alternative exit values shown in table 3 can be rather quickly discarded as means of arriving at any kind of realized profit; the alternative entry values, however, cannot be so summarily dismissed. Let us examine the other entry and exit values bearing in mind that we are judging them against the following criteria:

1. The events recorded in the accounts must be objective events of the current period alone.
2. Operating profit must be carefully separated from capital gains.
3. The events recorded must relate to the actual activities of the firm.

Expected value must again be dismissed as a basis for valuation on the revenue side, in this case for two reasons. In the first place, as before, valuations derived from expected values are essentially subjective in nature. In the second place, this method of valuation would yield values for the assets of the firm whether those assets are sold or not. But entry values are to be used as the

[3] It is also possible, although we shall not take time to do so, to develop a profit concept which would be based upon the application of the realization criterion on a time basis but which would use the realizable criterion on a production basis. We would use in this case exit values as a basis for valuation but these exit values would carry historically defined dates until an exit value became realized.

basis for valuation until sale; clearly, expected values are inconsistent with this approach.

Opportunity cost, too, must be discarded primarily for the second reason given above; opportunity cost as a method of valuation is not limited to the assets sold by the firm. To determine profits on a realization basis so far as production is concerned, therefore, we are left with current value as a basis for the valuation of revenue. Current values, by definition, apply only to goods sold by the firm.

The elimination of the other two concepts of entry values merits further discussion. Historic costs, like expected values, have a usefulness of their own; but, in common with expected values, historic costs cannot be used as a means of recording current events. Specifically, historic costs represent current events of the period in which assets were acquired. One might go further and attach a pretense of currency to historic costs by accumulating them to the present, but accumulated historic costs are no more a representation of current events than are discounted expected values. They may, as we shall see, provide a useful basis for taxation but once the period of acquisition has passed, historic costs lose their significance for the evaluation of business decisions. Equally important, the direct matching of historic costs with current values does not permit the proper separation of this total gain into operating and holding components.

The choice between current cost and present cost cannot be so clearly established. It will be recalled that, whereas the current cost of an asset is the sum of the current costs of the contained inputs, the present cost of an asset is the price the firm would have to pay to purchase the asset in its present form. If the production process which created the asset is in current use by the firm, the use of present cost would imply the abandonment of the production facet of the realization criterion. If the asset being valued is a good in process or a finished good, for example, the cost to purchase it from a competitive firm would presumably exceed the current cost of the asset. The valuation of the asset at present cost would therefore imply the recognition of some operating profit prior to final sale. Further, if this market is perfect in the sense that the firm can buy or sell its asset in the market at but one price, present cost is identical to opportunity cost. The use of present cost as a basis for valuation would in this case yield the same result as the use of opportunity cost; i.e., the profit measured would be realizable profit.

It might be argued that present cost should be adopted as a method of valuation for a good in process or a finished product if it is less than current cost. But if the production process is in current use by the firm, the present cost of the asset is not a valid measure of the productive resources of the economy which the firm is actually using. It is true that an excess of the current cost of an asset over its present cost should be a signal to management to abandon the production process currently in use, but if all assets were valued at present cost, this signal would never be apparent. When assets have been produced by a process in current use, current cost is a better summary of actual events than is present cost.

There is one case in which adherence to current cost is troublesome, namely, the case in which there has been abandonment of the process originally employed in making the asset being valued. A good example of this situation is a fixed asset which was originally constructed by the firm itself rather than being purchased from another firm. The firm either no longer constructs its own fixed assets or utilizes a different method of production. In this situation the sum of the current costs of the inputs of the outmoded process of production is not a relevant summary of current events. The present cost of the asset (if the asset is now purchased) or the current cost of the inputs now used in producing the asset would be preferable to the current cost associated with the outmoded production technique. The cost selected should be that which most closely approximates the current process of production (or purchase). In the event that a fixed asset is no longer produced by the firm and is also no longer produced by other firms, the present cost of the asset in a second-hand market is perhaps the best approximation of current cost available.

Values based on current cost (with the modifications just noted) would appear to be the best measure of the productive resources being used by the firm in its existing process of production. *Current operating profit,* the gain related to the production and sale of output, results from the matching of current costs with current values.

The use of current cost as a basis for the valuation of the firm's assets until those assets are sold has certain implications for the balance sheet. Each asset on the balance sheet at the beginning of the period is valued by summing the current costs of all of the inputs which the firm uses in bringing the asset to its present state. Assets at the end of the period are valued in similar fashion using the current costs prevailing at that time. What significance is to be attached to an excess of current cost at the end of the period over current cost at the beginning of the period for a particular asset which has not been used in production? It cannot be called a realizable capital gain because the excess is a difference between entry values, not exit values. A realizable capital gain would imply that it could be realized by selling the asset. When current cost figures are being used, it is not at all clear that a sale of the asset would convert the excess current cost into a realized value.

An increase in the current cost of assets held represents instead a *cost saving*. Imagine a firm to acquire an asset early in the fiscal period and to hold this asset over one holding period before it enters production and is sold. Assume further that the asset was originally acquired for $100 but that its current cost at the time it enters the production period is $120. Assume also that other inputs used in conjunction with this one have a current cost of $30 and that the resulting production is immediately sold for $175. Current operating profit is to be defined as the excess of the current value of goods sold over the current cost of the related inputs. In this simplified example current operating profit is $175 – $150, or $25. This is not, however, the only gain realized by the firm. The firm has used up an input having a current cost of $120 for which it had to pay originally $100. The difference of $20 represents a cost saving, a saving attributable to the fact that the input used was acquired in advance of use. This saving is attributable to holding activities in exactly the same way that realizable capital gains were attributable to holding activities in the opportunity cost case.

In the example given, the cost saving is both realizable and realized; it not only arose in the current period but it was also realized in the current period. For present purposes we shall deal with cost savings on a realizable basis and shall appropriate the term "business profit" to mean the sum of current operating profit and realizable cost savings.

The Business Profit Matrix

The symbols used in developing the realizable profit matrix will stand us in good stead here. As opportunity costs are no longer relevant for valuation, however, two other superscripts must be substituted to represent values. They are:

- r Current values of goods sold
- c Current costs of the inputs contained in the goods sold

It is also necessary to distinguish between assets sold, A_s^r, and assets unsold, A_u^c, the former being valued at selling prices and the latter at current cost. We shall designate the related inputs in the two cases by the symbols $_sA^c$ and $_uA^c$, respectively, both being valued at current cost. The inputs and outputs of holding intervals will be designated by $_hA^c$ and A_h^c, respectively.

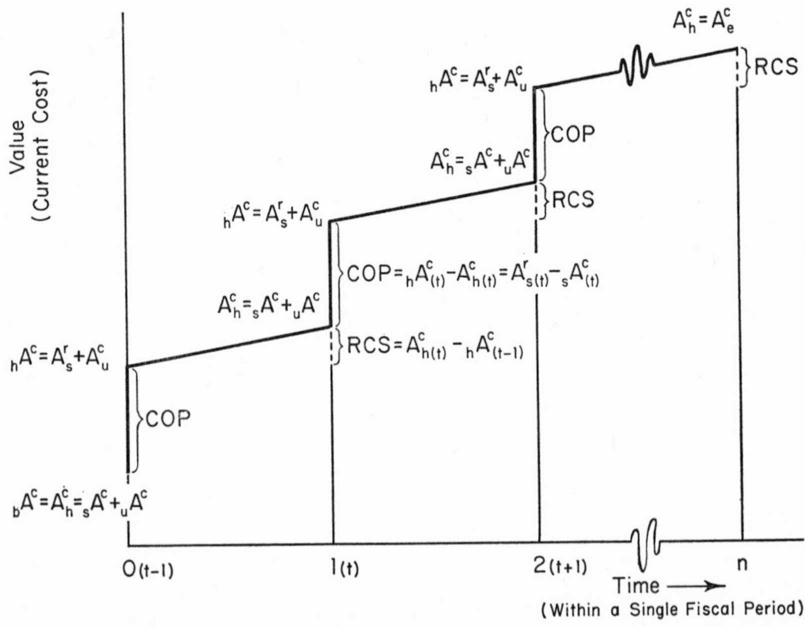

Figure 7. Sale moments and holding intervals for a single fiscal period.

As operating profit is related to the sale of assets and not to their production, we need deal only with sale moments and holding intervals. An illustration of a fiscal period divided into several such parts is presented in figure 7. We assume the firm to start the period with an inheritance of assets valued at current cost, ${}_bA^c$, and to end the period with another set of assets valued also at current cost, A_e^c. No dividend payments or capital contributions have occurred. Business profit, BP, can be defined as follows:

$$BP = A_e^c - {}_bA^c. \tag{8}$$

We wish to divide this amount into current operating profit and realizable cost savings. It can be seen in figure 7 that at the end of any sale moment the total value of the firm's assets (the inputs of the following holding interval) must include receipts from the sale of assets, A_s^r, plus the value of assets remaining unsold, A_u^c.

$${}_hA_{(t)}{}^c = A_{s(t)}{}^r + A_{u(t)}{}^c. \tag{9}$$

The form which the receipts from sales take is unimportant. Neither does the immediate use of such receipts for the current acquisition of inputs affect the equation because the current cost of such acquisitions must just equal the receipts-from-sales exchanged for them.

It can also be seen in the figure that at the beginning of any sale moment the total value of the firm's assets (those assets held at the end of the last holding interval) can be identified as (1) inputs destined for immediate sale, ${}_sA^c$, or as (2) inputs not to be sold, ${}_uA^c$.

$$A_{h(t)}{}^c = {}_sA_{(t)}{}^c + {}_uA_{(t)}{}^c. \tag{10}$$

When (10) is subtracted from (9) we have current operating profit for a particular sale moment.

$$\begin{aligned} COP_{(t)} &= {}_hA_{(t)}{}^c - A_{h(t)}{}^c \\ &= (A_{s(t)}{}^r - {}_sA_{(t)}{}^c) + (A_{u(t)}{}^c - {}_uA_{(t)}{}^c). \end{aligned} \tag{11}$$

But the inputs of a sale moment which are not sold must be equal to the unsold outputs because unsold outputs are valued at the current cost of all the inputs contained therein. Thus (11) simplifies to

$$COP_{(t)} = A_{s(t)}{}^r - {}_sA_{(t)}{}^c. \tag{12}$$

The current operating profit earned throughout the fiscal period can be defined, then, as follows:

$$COP = \sum_{0}^{n-1} A_s{}^r - \sum_{0}^{n-1} {}_sA^c. \tag{13}$$

Identifying those assets held at the beginning of the fiscal period which are immediately sold as ${}_{bs}A^c$, we have

$$COP = \sum_{0}^{n-1} A_s{}^r - \sum_{1}^{n-1} {}_sA^c - {}_{bs}A^c. \tag{14}$$

In order to keep account of unsold assets, let us sum the last term of equation (11) for all sale moments, identifying separately those initial assets not immediately sold as ${}_{bu}A^c$. We have

$$\text{Profit on unsold assets} = \sum_{0}^{n-1} A_u{}^c - \sum_{1}^{n-1} {}_uA^c - {}_{bu}A^c = 0. \tag{15}$$

Realizable cost savings for a particular holding interval are simply the excess of the current cost of assets at the end of the interval over their current cost at the beginning, that is

$$RCS_{(t)} = A_{h(t)}{}^c - {}_hA_{(t-1)}{}^c. \tag{16}$$

Summing all holding intervals and segregating those assets held at the end of the fiscal period, $A_e{}^c$, yields

$$RCS = \mathrm{A}_e{}^c + \sum_{1}^{n-1} A_h{}^c - \sum_{0}^{n-1} {}_hA^c. \tag{17}$$

Using the appropriate equations we can now define business profit and its components in matrix form as follows:

The Business Profit Matrix

$$
\begin{array}{lllllll}
0 & + \sum_{0}^{n-1} A_s{}^r & - \sum_{1}^{n-1} {}_sA^c & - {}_{bs}A^c & = COP & & (14) \\
0 & + \sum_{0}^{n-1} A_u{}^c & - \sum_{1}^{n-1} {}_uA^c & - {}_{bu}A^c & = 0 & & (15) \\
A_e{}^c & - \sum_{0}^{n-1} {}_hA^c & + \sum_{1}^{n-1} A_h{}^c & + 0 & = RCS & & (17) \\
\hline
A_e{}^c + & 0 & + \quad 0 & - {}_bA^c & = \Delta A = BP & & (8)
\end{array}
$$

The first vertical equation adding to zero states that receipts from sales plus the value of unsold assets equals the total value of assets which enter holding intervals. The second vertical equation adding to zero states that assets held at the end of holding intervals are the inputs contained in assets sold and unsold.

Characteristics of Business Profit Summarized

It can be noted by way of summary that the business profit concept requires no knowledge of production while the realizable profit concept requires no knowledge of sales. Production itself generates no profit in the current cost approach because outputs are valued as the sum of the current costs of contained inputs. Profit arises when an exit value is substituted for an entry value, when a sale price is substituted for the current cost of the inputs sold. This change in the method of valuation lies at the heart of current operating profit while realizable operating profit depends mainly on the change in the form of the asset being valued.

The realizable capital gains which are a part of total realizable profit and the realizable cost savings which are a part of business profit, on the other hand, have more in common. Each depends on the passage of time, on a change in the date on which valuation takes place. But the first depends on changes in opportunity cost from one point in time to another, while the second depends on changes in current costs. The two gains may be equal even when opportunity costs differ from current costs at every point in time. The necessary requirement is equality between the changes in the two costs over time.

THE CONCEPTS COMPARED AND THE THEORY EXTENDED

In what follows no attempt is made to make a strong case for one or the other of the profit concepts presented above. To the contrary, it is our feeling that a strong case can be made for the incorporation of both sets of data in the accounting records. Perhaps in some utopian future the advantages of both profit concepts will be recognized in this way. In the meanwhile a less ambitious role seems warranted, namely, the selection of one of these profit concepts for development in the accounting records, perhaps initially as addenda to the historic cost data presently accumulated.

It probably goes without saying that the two profit concepts serve somewhat different purposes. A choice between the two concepts therefore depends upon which purposes are given the highest priority and upon certain practical considerations such as the wide acceptance of traditional accounting principles.

Comparison in Terms of Internal Uses

Realizable profit is the amount the firm makes in a particular period as a result of using or holding its assets within the firm rather than disposing of them outside the firm. At the beginning of any period a firm's endowment of assets would be valued at the highest opportunity cost prevailing at that moment. This figure represents the value the owners of the firm are consigning to the management of the enterprise for use in promoting the firm's activities during the subsequent period. It is the amount of capital that the owners (and creditors) are risking in the business in the short run. As the period proceeds, management uses some of these asset values in an effort to make a profit. Management also buys current inputs, some of which may be added to stock, others of which are used up immediately in the process of production. If the management is successful during the period, the opportunity cost of the firm's assets at the end of the period will exceed the opportunity cost of its assets at the beginning of the period. If this gain, which includes both operating profit and capital gains, exceeds interest on the opportunity cost of the firm's assets at the beginning of the period, the owners were wise to permit the business to operate during the period rather than discontinuing it at the beginning of the period. The existence of a gain informs the owners and others that the short-run cost of operating the business has been covered.

Current operating profit, on the other hand, provides an answer to a different question. It indicates whether or not the current proceeds from the sale of product are sufficient to cover the current cost of the factors of production used in producing that product. The factors of production are valued in this case not at prices which could be obtained by selling them outside the firm but at the prices which would currently have to be paid in order to bring the factors of production into the firm. The existence of a profit for a particular period indicates that the firm is making a positive long-run contribution to the economy; the production process in use by the firm is an effective means for converting resources having one value into an output having a larger value. If this profit exceeds interest on the current cost of the firm's assets at the beginning of the period, the production process of the firm is worth continuing. Current operating profit, therefore, is essentially the long-run profit associated with the existing process of production carried on under existing conditions.

The nature of the long run for which current operating profit is significant can be more carefully specified. Current operating profit is a measure of the amount of current output, in the sense of value added, which is profit. It indicates the excess of the value of output sold over the resources used in producing and selling that output on the assumption that resources and output are flowing in the direction in which they are actually flowing. It does not indicate, as does realizable profit, the excess of what is obtained from one outflow of resources over what could be obtained from another outflow of resources.

The significance of current operating profit may extend to periods other than the current period if certain assumptions are valid. Current operating profit can be used for predictive purposes if the existing production process and the existing conditions under which that process is carried out are expected to continue into the future; current operating profit then indicates the amount that the firm can expect to make in each period over the long run. The assumption that production processes will not change is rather unrealistic, however. A more limited but realistic approach to the problem of prediction would be based upon the following: If a particular production process promises a larger current operating profit in this period than that promised by any other production process, is it reasonable to assume that the production process will also promise higher current operating profits in subsequent periods than alternative processes, even though conditions have changed in those periods?

The answer to this question may often be yes. If the conditions which are expected to be different in the future are external to the firm, these changes may affect one production process as much as another. For example, if it is expected that the demand for the firm's product will fall in the future, it is not unreasonable to expect that the current operating profit associated with each possible production process will fall in the future. If the prices of raw materials are expected to change in the future, these changes too may affect the current operating profit associated with one production process in much the same way as they affect the current operating profits associated with other production processes.

Indeed, rather specific expectations must be held before the relative current operating profits obtainable today from alternative production processes would not be indicative to the firm of the relative current operating profits to be obtained in the future with these same alternatives. If certain raw materials are expected to go down in price while others are expected to rise in price, for example, then a production process which utilizes the material which is expected to become relatively cheaper might be preferred. In the absence of such specific expectations, however, it would seem reasonable to maintain an existing production process unless it can be shown that the production process which is challenging the existing one would provide a higher operating profit in the current period than was in fact earned by the existing process. Under the specified conditions current operating profits would be a useful device for choosing among alternative production processes. In this comparison the current operating profit reported in the accounts would indicate the long-run profit to be realized from using the existing process of production.

In this sense current operating profit evaluates the firm as a going concern. It is probably clear that realizable operating profit cannot perform this function. A positive realizable operating profit (in excess of interest on opportunity cost) indicates only that the firm should be operated in the short run. It does not indicate that the firm's receipts are sufficient to cover its long-run operating costs. The difficulty involved is the following: Realizable operating profit has been constructed essentially on the basis of the theory of a single investment. The horizon of the entrepreneur in this case does not exceed the life of the asset. This artificial restriction of the entrepreneur's horizon rules out the possibility that the entrepreneur might envisage a chain of replacements for a particular machine or a continuing existence for the going concern. Thus, while realizable operating profit indicates whether or not the firm should use the particular asset or set of assets rather than liquidating, it indicates very little about whether or not the production process is worth extending beyond the life of the particular asset. We have then a short-run concept of profit and a long-run concept of profit. We can perhaps clarify a bit more the relative usefulness of these concepts.

A business firm should not even consider abandoning one particular production process for another unless the other can be shown to utilize the resources of the firm to better advantage. For most going concerns, therefore, the current operating profit associated with the existing process of production is quite meaningful; any alternative production process must successfully challenge the existing one before it can be adopted.

A comparison of current operating profits is one way in which the appropriate decision can be indicated. If there is no way in which the long-run use of the firm's assets can be justified, realizable profit assumes significance. Once a decision has been made to abandon the firm's assets, the precise date on which abandonment should take place cannot be determined in terms of current operating profit because that figure is based on the assumption that the process will not be abandoned. A reversion to realizable operating profit and the related capital gains, if any, would better serve this purpose. When realizable profit falls below interest on opportunity cost (and is not expected to exceed it in the future), the date of abandonment has arrived.

We have distinguished in this discussion between the abandonment of a production process and the abandonment of the related assets. Realizable profit may indicate when the assets themselves should be abandoned by the firm, but the abandonment of a particular use of those assets can better be determined on the basis of current operating profit. So long as there is some use to which the assets can be put within the firm and which will yield a positive current operating profit (in excess of interest), the measurement of realizable profit serves a secondary purpose.

As we have formulated it, realizable profit is based on the assumption that the only alternative to operating the business in the way in which it is being operated is to discontinue the business. If realizable profit were to be modified to take account of the shiftability of assets within the firm, as among departments, for example, or of the possibility of using assets within the firm in ways different from those actually adopted, different opportunity costs would have to be introduced. Thus the opportunity cost of a machine in a very particular use may be the present value of quasi-rents that could be earned by putting the machine to a different use. Similarly, the opportunity cost of an asset to one department of the firm may be the present value of the stream of quasi-rents which could be realized in another department of the firm. If top management were to use opportunity costs as a means of evaluating the decisions of a departmental manager, these kinds of opportunity costs would be more relevant than the opportunity cost of the asset to the firm itself, that is, the amount obtainable by sale of the asset outside the firm. Such considerations would dictate, however, that a different opportunity cost be used for each level of decision. Obviously, such records would be extremely difficult to maintain. More important from a theoretical point of view, however, is the fact that many of these opportunity costs are subjective in nature. On the other hand, the current cost of the firm's resources is objectively given and probably not subject to substantial variation from one department to another or from one use to another. So long, then, as the liquidation of the firm's assets is not imminent, current cost data would appear to be more useful to the firm than opportunity cost data.

For certain firms or industries, however, a reversion to opportunity cost might yield more useful data. This may be the case for declining firms or for firms in declining industries and specifically for firms in which the decision has already been made to discontinue the long-run use of the assets of the firm. This means that the continued operation of these assets in whatever use is insufficient to cover their current cost; the assets will in fact be abandoned as soon as opportunity cost itself cannot be recovered.

The current cost associated with railroading may be a case in point. While the necessary data are not available, one might guess that the operating revenues of railroads are insufficient to cover their current costs. Given efficient management, continuing losses on a current cost basis indicate that there is no long-run future for the present method of operation. These losses indicate also the social cost of continuing to operate them on the basis on which they are being operated; i.e., they would indicate the subsidy which would have to be paid to railroads in order for them to continue operation in the long run.

Given losses on a current cost basis, one must turn to opportunity costs to determine whether there is any short-run future for the production process being used. If losses are being made on an opportunity cost basis also, even the continued short-run operation of the process is a social rather than an economic question. If left to themselves, the profit-maximizing railroad owners would liquidate. A question society must answer is whether the increase in social welfare to be obtained from the continued short-run operation of the railroads is worth the necessary subsidy. Opportunity cost data would at least indicate this problem.[4]

Comparison in Terms of External Uses

In touching on subsidy problems we have already strayed into a discussion of the value of these concepts for external users of data. A few other external uses merit consideration also. Let us take first the allocation of capital among firms and industries on the basis of reported profits.[5] To the extent that securities are purchased on the basis of long-run considerations, the reporting of profit on a current operating profit basis would appear to be preferable to the reporting of profit on a realizable operating profit basis. A firm which reports a larger realizable profit than another firm may be employing assets whose opportunity costs are extremely low relative to their current costs. If this is the case, the current operating profits which the two firms would report might be reversed in relative size as compared with their realizable operating profits. If the potential investor believes that the large realizable profit of the one firm is indicative of its long-run operating profit possibilities, he would put his capital into the wrong firm.

The water would be muddied even further if some firms re-

---

[4] Discussions with Professor W. T. Baxter aided immeasurably in clarifying this point.

[5] It should be clear that in this case, as in many of the others we discuss, the assumption is made that current reported profits can be projected into the future or at least can serve as an index number for such projections.

ported on a current operating profit basis while other firms reported on a realizable operating profit basis. A firm might report a positive realizable operating profit while its current operating profit is negative. Comparisons of the profits of different firms would be extremely hazardous. Something like this situation may be reflected currently in the reported profits of railroads as compared to those of manufacturing firms. Many of the assets of railroads have been written down over the course of several bankruptcies to figures which may represent opportunity costs. The assets of manufacturing firms, on the other hand, may be carried at figures which are at least closer approximations to current cost. There is, after all, much to be said for uniform reporting.

Potential entrants into an industry, whether new firms or existing firms operating in other industries, have a major interest in reported accounting data. Elementary economic theory suggests that potential entrants should respond to relatively high profits. But as potential entrants have yet to acquire their resources, relatively high realizable profits are not of much value to them. Current operating profit, the excess of the value of output over the current cost of the related inputs, would be a much more useful figure for potential entrepreneurs in assessing the relative profitabilities of different lines of business. Just as we would like to have money capital allocated to those existing firms which are most profitable, so we would like new firms to add to the real capital invested in those industries which are most profitable. If the various firms in the different industries represent all of the existing economical production functions, current operating profits should indicate their relative profitabilities. Presumably a potential entrant who has yet to acquire his resources will select those kinds and combinations of resources which offer the largest current operating profit. If the potential entrant has a new production process to try out, the current operating profits obtainable with existing production methods would represent valid standards against which he would compare the expected profitability of his new method. Current operating profits are superior to realizable operating profits as data for the new firm.

The measurement of national income and output is premised

on the existing flow of resources. Opportunity costs to the individual firm again have little significance. Profit in the national income accounts is more appropriately measured as the excess of the value of output generated by the existing flow of resources over the current cost of those resources. The concept of value added suggests immediately that the values assigned at any particular stage of a production process are vectored values, that is, values based upon the existing flow of resources into the firm rather than values based upon a hypothetical outflow of those resources. As the national income accounts are currently designed, cost savings due to price changes would be excluded. Current operating profit by itself is the ideal measure of value added by the business sector in the formulation of national income accounts.[6]

It seems fairly clear that the external users of accounting data should prefer current operating profit figures to realizable operating profit figures. The point of view of external users of accounting data is not likely to be a dominant influence in the decisions of business firms as to which accounting techniques to prefer. The final decision will likely rest on the uses which business firms feel will be served by the different profit concepts. For this purpose, too, we have seen that current operating profit has much to recommend it although realizable operating profit has certain advantages also.

The Concepts Related

Under certain conditions realizable profit and business profit may turn out to be identical. Such an occurrence cannot be described as general, but the specific conditions under which the identity holds may be meaningful for some firms within the economy. Further, the specification of these conditions may clarify the relationship between the two concepts. The matter of adjusting from one concept to another becomes then a matter of technicality.

---

[6] As a measure of output in the national income accounts sales figures must be adjusted to production figures. If inventories are valued on a current cost basis, however, profit in the national income accounts would not be affected by the adjustment.

It will be recalled that realizable profit is defined as follows:

$$RP = A_e^o - {}_bA^o. \tag{1}$$

Business profit, on the other hand, is given by

$$BP = A_e^c - {}_bA^c. \tag{8}$$

As the physical inventories of goods at the beginning of the period and at the end of the period are not affected by the method of valuation, the excess of realizable profit over business profit can be defined as follows:

$$RP - BP = A_e\,(o_e - c_e) - {}_bA\,({}_bo - {}_bc), \tag{18}$$

where o_e and c_e represent end-of-period prices while ${}_bo$ and ${}_bc$ represent beginning-of-period prices.

Let us divide the stock of assets into two groups: *processed assets,* that is, those assets which have been used in some production within the firm, and *unprocessed* (or *purchased*) *assets,* that is, those assets which have been purchased by the firm but which have not been used in production. Let us designate processed assets, I, and purchased assets, X. The difference between the two profit concepts now becomes:

$$RP - BP = X_e\,(o_e - c_e) - {}_bX\,({}_bo - {}_bc) + I_e\,(o_e - c_e) - {}_bI\,({}_bo - {}_bc). \tag{19}$$

The equation as stated is valid only if the composition of purchased assets at the end of the period is the same as the composition of purchased assets at the beginning of the period. Further, the composition of processed assets at the end of the period must be the same as the composition of processed assets at the beginning of the period. If these conditions do not hold it is not a valid procedure to describe the prices to be attached to each inventory as a kind of weighted average of all of the opportunity costs or the current costs as the case may be.

Another cause of a difference between the two profit figures is the gap between opportunity cost and current cost at the beginning and end of the period. Specifically, if this differential remains unchanged from the beginning of the period to the end of the period, a substantial cause of difference between the profit figures is eliminated. In the short run, changes in this gap may in fact be negligible. In the case of purchased assets the gap represents market imperfections, and transportation and installation costs. Institutional marketing arrangements which restrict the firm's access to both sides of the market at the same price are not likely to change much over a fiscal period. Transportation and installation costs, too, are likely to remain fairly constant. These considerations suggest that for purchased assets at least, the cost gap is not likely to change much from one point in time to another.[7]

To assume that the excess of opportunity cost over current cost for processed assets is unchanged over a particular fiscal period is perhaps less justifiable than in the case of unprocessed assets. The cost gap for such assets may exist for the same reasons that were given above for purchased assets. In addition, however, opportunity cost may differ from current cost in this case because, as the result of production itself, the processed assets can now be sold in a different market than could the inputs which were used in processing the asset. If production has become more efficient during the period, i.e., if fewer inputs are needed in order to produce the same output, opportunity cost is likely to exceed current cost at the end of the period by more than it did at the beginning of the period. If the fiscal period is fairly short, however, changes in efficiency may be negligible. In this event the cost gap for both processed and unprocessed assets should be constant over the fiscal period.

If the cost gap is constant from one moment in time to the next, equation (19) can be rewritten as follows:

$$RP - BP = \Delta X\,(o - c) + \Delta I\,(o - c). \tag{18}$$

It is clear from this equation that the difference between realizable profit and business profit will disappear if, in addition to a constant cost gap and a given composition of assets, the size of the firm is unchanged over the fiscal period.

Let us suppose now that markets are perfect in the sense that the business firm has equal access to both buying and selling sides of the markets in which it deals and transportation and installa-

[7] It is probable that for purchased assets the current cost will exceed the opportunity cost. The current cost of a new car or a new machine delivered and installed at the firm's factory is likely to be greater than the amount the firm could recover if it turned around and sold the machine or car at the best net recoverable price.

tion costs are zero. In this event opportunity costs will equal current costs for all purchased assets. It follows that, even if the size of the stock of purchased assets has changed over the fiscal period, the change cannot create a difference between realizable profit and business profit; opportunity cost equals current cost for these particular assets.

It does not follow, however, that opportunity cost will equal current cost for processed assets. For these assets, opportunity cost can exceed current cost because the assets involved have achieved a higher stage of production and therefore can be sold in different markets. If production during the period has exceeded sales during the period, stocks of processed assets will have increased. In this case realizable profit will exceed business profit by the increase in the processed inventories (by the amount of unsold production) multiplied by the unrealized profit per unit of production, where that unrealized profit is indicated by the excess of opportunity cost over current cost for the processed asset. The difference between a production criterion on the one hand and a sale criterion on the other hand is often described in these rather simplified terms.

If we now make the additional assumption that all production of the period is in fact sold, then realizable profit becomes identical to business profit. It seems reasonable to conclude that for those firms having constant efficiency and size over time and dealing in markets whose institutional characteristics are relatively stable, realizable profit should not differ materially from business profit.

Some Practical Considerations

The discussion of realizable profit and business profit has proceeded so far as though there were no problems involved in accumulating data for either concept. Three not unrelated questions will be mentioned here which will receive more detailed attention in subsequent chapters. (1) Are the necessary raw data available on an objective basis for the construction of either profit concept? While this problem may be serious for certain kinds of assets, we do not feel that it is a major restriction for most assets. (2) Given the raw data, can techniques be devised for accumulating, sorting and combining the data in the accounts whether on a day-to-day basis or as a system of end-of-period adjustments? We feel that this problem can be solved and make some specific suggestions later for accumulating such data as information supplementary to historic cost data. (3) If appropriate techniques can be devised, will the accounting profession be willing to accept them? Our analysis of the two profit concepts should have made it clear that the realizable profit concept represents a more substantial departure from accepted accounting principles than does the business profit concept. This important consideration is a weighty argument in favor of the accumulation of data on a current cost basis, and it is this approach that we intend to take in subsequent chapters.

This choice does not represent a sacrifice of principle for expediency, however. We have seen that for going concerns current cost data may be more meaningful than opportunity cost data. It is also clear that the external users of accounting data are most strongly benefited by the current cost approach. Finally, the problems encountered in accounting for the differences between opportunity cost and current cost are not significantly different from those that must be solved in accounting for the differences between historic costs and current costs.

IV *Consolidation of the Theory:*

BASIC CONCEPTS OF MEASURABLE PROFIT AND THEIR COMPONENTS

In suggesting that accounting data be modified in the direction of business profit, we do not mean to imply that the data necessary for the reporting of other concepts of profit, in particular the traditional accounting profit based on historic cost, should be abandoned. No one concept of profit appears to be most appropriate for all purposes; one that is suitable as a basis of taxation, for example, may not be best for managerial uses; one that excludes capital gains may make sense in the measurement of national income but it may not be appropriate for the owners of a firm.

The fact that accounting data can serve many purposes suggests that it may be a serious mistake to restrict accounts to the kind of data from which but one profit concept can be developed. It is possible, we think, to define several fundamental profit components in such a way that existing record-keeping techniques can be adapted to their collection. If data for these components are made available, several concepts of measurable profit can be constructed by combining them in different ways. Present accounting processes do not yield data on very many profit elements, and as a result, this kind of flexibility does not exist. As a matter of fact, most of the proposed modifications of accounting data are designed to increase the flexibility of the information made available by supplementing presently recorded data with other varieties. What kinds of additional data should be systematically collected in the accounts is, however, still a moot question. We shall advance several suggestions in this and succeeding chapters.

The Components Identified

The basic components with which we shall deal are four in number: current operating profit, realizable cost savings, realized cost savings, and realized capital gains. The first two have already been discussed and little more need be said about them.

Current Operating Profit and Realizable Cost Savings

Current operating profit, representing the excess of the value of output sold during a period over the current cost of the related inputs, is a relatively unambiguous concept. It will be necessary in accounting for realizable cost savings, however, to distinguish between those accumulated cost savings which are currently unrealized and those cost savings which have become realizable during the current period. Only the latter can be counted as a profit element of the current period.

The amount of cost savings which are unrealized at any moment in time is measured by the excess of the current cost of the firm's assets over their historic cost. These cost savings or gains may have first become realizable in any or all of the periods which have elapsed since the asset was first acquired. To obtain the amount of unrealized cost savings as of the end of a particular period, the amount unrealized at the beginning of the period must be increased by the new *realizable cost savings* which have arisen during the period and be reduced by those cost savings which have been realized during the period. It is the new realizable cost savings which are a component of business profit. These cost savings can be determined as the excess of the current cost of assets at the end of a period or at time of use or sale over their current cost at the beginning of the period or at time of purchase if the assets are acquired in that interval. Cost savings which first became realizable in earlier periods are clearly events of those earlier periods and cannot be counted as a part of the business profit of the current period.

The measurement of gains (cost savings) suggested by the new realizable cost savings component is one that emphasizes the genesis of a gain rather than its realization. This approach is necessary if the balance sheet is to register current costs rather than, or in addition to, historic costs. If cost savings are recorded as they arise, i.e., as current costs change, the balance sheet will automatically contain current costs. Recording these events (the development of cost savings) in the accounts at the time they occur is one means of recognizing explicitly the difference between the genesis of a gain and its conversion into a more liquid form.

Realized Cost Savings

It should be emphasized that for the accumulation of data on business profit no components of profit are necessary other than those discussed above. In the process of recording data in this way, however, information on other possible profit components will be recorded almost automatically. We have already noted above, for example, that in order to keep the unrealized cost savings account up to date, those cost savings which are realized during the period must be deducted from the unrealized account. A record of *realized cost savings* is therefore a by-product of the effort to accumulate current cost figures for the balance sheet. What is the nature of these realized cost savings?

Cost savings are realized through the use of assets in production and sale. If the current costs of assets used up in production and sale exceed their historic costs, the firm has realized a gain because the assets were originally purchased at a cost below that currently prevailing. While current operating profit is the excess of selling price over current cost, realized cost savings represent the excess of current cost over historic cost for those inputs used in production and sale.

Gains realized through use in this way should not be confused with operating profit. The gain is attributable to changes in cost which have occurred since the firm first purchased the asset. These gains arose as current cost deviated from historic cost. While the gains are realized through the use of the assets in the firm's operations, they do not have their genesis in operating activities but rather in holding activities.

Gains through use are realized largely on materials that enter into the cost of goods sold and on those asset services whose value is estimated by depreciation charges. For most services purchased directly by the firm, such as the services of labor, the current cost and historic cost coincide and so the opportunity to realize a gain through use does not exist. Take the case, however, where goods are purchased substantially in advance of their use. Specifically, suppose a retailer purchases a good in period 1 for x dollars and that by the end of the period the current cost of this good is $(x + a)$ dollars. A realizable cost savings equal to a has arisen in period 1 and would be counted as a part of business profit in that period. Suppose now that during period 2 the good is sold at a time when its current cost is $(x + a + b)$ dollars. A new realizable cost savings of b dollars has arisen during period 2 and would be included as a part of business profit. On the other hand, we can also identify the amount of cost savings which have been realized during period 2, namely, the amount of $(a + b)$ dollars.

A similar example may clarify gains realized through the use of depreciable assets. A machine with a life of five years may be deemed to depreciate at the rate of 20 per cent per year. If the machine costs $10,000, we can say that it embodies five bundles of asset services, each costing $2,000. If the price of a new machine is $15,000 at the time one of these bundles is used in production, the current cost of this bundle of services is $3,000 (20 per cent of $15,000). A gain of $1,000 has arisen because the firm has held the bundle of services while its value has increased. This gain is realized when the bundle is used in the production and sale of output. The current cost of the bundle of services

($3,000) would be deducted in determining current operating profit; at the same time a cost savings realized through use ($1,000) would be recorded. Depreciation computed in this way we shall call *current cost depreciation;* it is the depreciation rate multiplied by the current cost of the asset.

It should be emphasized that any gains which are realized must first have been realizable gains. These two profit components, realized gains and realizable gains, are, therefore, not additive but rather are substitutes for each other. When gains are recorded as costs change, we are recording the genesis of gains; we are recording them as they arise. When gains are recorded as they are realized, we are recording, in fact, the conversion of gains that already exist into a more liquid form. The genesis of a gain should not be confused with its conversion into liquid form. Both are, however, events of the period in which they take place, and a complete view of the profit-making process would require that both types of events be included in the records. The genesis of the gain would be recorded at the time it occurred; its conversion into liquid form would be recorded upon use of the asset service. A record of both types of gain would be made, but the difference between genesis and conversion would be carefully identified.

Realized Capital Gains

In certain instances the business firm may dispose of some of its assets which would normally have been used up in the regular production and sale of the firm's stock in trade. Such an irregular sale may lead to the realization of a capital gain. If an asset so sold is already carried on the books of the firm at its current cost which in turn is equal to the proceeds realized from the sale of the asset, no additional gain becomes realizable as a result of the sale. But the excess of the proceeds of the sale over the historic cost (depreciated if necessary) of the asset represents a gain which has been realized during the period in which the sale took place. As in the case of realized cost savings, this gain may have arisen in prior periods. When it is realized, however, an entry must be made to record this event. This entry provides data on another possible component of profit, namely, realized capital gains or capital gains realized through the irregular sale of assets.

This profit component has a familiar ring. The capital gains and losses recognized according to current accounting practices are generally of this nature.[1] The irregular sale of any fixed asset at a price that differs from its depreciated historic cost gives rise to this kind of realized gain.

The possible components of money profit can now be summarized:

A. Current operating profit—the excess over a period of the current value of output sold over the current cost of the related inputs.

B. Realizable cost savings—the increase in the current cost of assets while held by the firm during the fiscal period.

C. Realized capital gains—the excess of proceeds over (depreciated) historic costs on the irregular sale or disposal of assets.

D. Realized cost savings—the excess of the current cost over the historic cost of inputs used in producing output sold.

As we have pointed out, these are not all independent components. In particular, *C* and *D* are alternatives to *B* as a way of measuring capital gains (or cost savings).

Three Concepts of Money Profit: Price Level Changes Ignored

Accounting Profit and Its Limitations

The characteristics of accounting profit which were mentioned in Chapter I can now be developed in terms of these components. In determining accounting operating profit, it is the *historic cost* of inputs that is deducted from the current value of output sold. No record of current cost is kept. Therefore, the operating profit that is consistent with accounting principles includes, in addition to current operating profit (component *A*), realized cost savings (component *D*). (In any period the amount of realized cost savings is the difference between the current cost and the historic cost of those inputs related to goods sold.) In accounting operating profit no distinction is drawn between these two elements. Further, assets are carried at depreciated historic cost on the

[1] An exception occurs when large capital losses are recognized, according to the principle of conservatism, before the loss becomes realized. Writing down fixed assets is such a practice.

traditional balance sheet. Hence, no gains are recorded as they arise (component B is excluded from accounting profit). Finally, the excess of the proceeds from the irregular or extraordinary sale of assets over their depreciated historic costs is recorded as a capital gain. It is only these gains realized through irregular sale (component C) that are counted as capital gains in accounting profit. These characteristics of accounting profit can be summarized as follows:

	Profit elements included		
	As operating profit		As capital gains
Accounting profit =	$(A + D)$	+	C

Some limitations of accounting profit as a managerial tool can now be briefly indicated, to be developed further in Chapter VII. Capital gains are counted only when realized. This means that some of the events of past periods, notably price changes and the gains or losses associated with them, are treated as though they were events of the current period. If an asset has been held for five years and then sold, all of the gains and losses arising over the five-year period are credited to the year of sale. Suppose that the asset was held only for speculative gain and that it doubled in price over the five-year period. Does the profit figure for the fifth year indicate that management has been inefficient for four years and successful only in the fifth? Suppose that the asset by the fourth year had tripled in price and had declined in price during the fifth year? The recording of gains when realized permits past events (gains, in this case) to cloud current events (losses, in this case). The evaluation of managerial expectations cannot proceed satisfactorily if events over the whole life of an asset are compared with those events expected to occur in only the current period.

Perhaps of greater importance for managerial purposes, accounting profit confuses those money gains that are realized through use, i.e., realized cost savings, with operating profit. Those gains that have arisen because the firm has held the asset while its price rose not only are credited to the current period but also are counted as operating profit deriving from the use of the asset in production. Large past gains (as well as current gains) from holding an asset are counted as large current gains from using the asset. The difficulty of evaluating the success of a firm's operating activities, as opposed to its holding activities, is increased.[2]

We conclude, then, that in its usefulness for managerial purposes accounting profit suffers from two basic limitations:

1. Gains realized through use are confused with operating profit. That profit which arises through holding assets is therefore counted as though it arises through using them in production.
2. Individual price changes of assets held by the firm are not recorded as they occur. Instead, gains are credited to the period in which they are realized; as a result balance sheet values are based on historic cost, meaningful current costs being excluded.

Because of these limitations the task of evaluating managerial expectations of current events is made unnecessarily difficult. The data management should expect from accounting sources must be developed in other ways unless management is to content itself with guesswork. At best, management must reinterpret accounting data by developing and utilizing nonaccounting sources of data; at worst, management may accept accounting data at face value.

Accounting Principles for Developing Realized Profit

A logical first step toward improving the accounting concept of profit is the reclassification of gains realized through use as cost savings rather than as operating profit. The resulting concept of profit can be called *realized profit.* It differs from accounting profit not in total but in its definition of components. Its measurement entails the application of the following principles:

1. In determining operating profit, inputs should be deducted from the current value of output at their current cost.
2. The difference between the current cost and historic cost of inputs used in production of goods which are sold should be recorded as a realized cost saving.

---

[2] This confusion of realized cost savings with current operating profit leads to comparable difficulties for the statisticians who must base their estimates of the components of national income largely on the data reported by business firms.

Such a measurement would have the advantage of drawing a sharp distinction in the records between current operating profit and realized cost savings. Management could better appraise its operating decisions because the results of current operations would no longer be confused with holding activities. National income statisticians would be able to accumulate aggregate profit figures for the economy with less difficulty and more accuracy. Similar benefits would accrue to financial analysts, creditors, and the public.

The need for restating accounting operating profit in accordance with principle (1) above is widely recognized. The application of principle (1) without principle (2), however, would result in an understatement of total profit when input prices were rising and an overstatement when input prices were falling because gains and losses realized through use would go unrecorded. The outstanding example of this approach is the application in some firms of the LIFO technique for costing inventories and the cost of goods sold. According to this technique, certain inputs (the cost of goods sold) are usually deducted from sales at current cost but no record is kept of the gain or loss arising because current cost differs from historic cost.[3]

It may be argued that the omitted (but realized) gain is a false one because the total current cost must be recovered from sales if the replacement of the physical inputs is to be possible, i.e., the recovery of current cost will just permit the maintenance of a constant physical volume of merchandise. A flaw can be pointed out, however. The existence of the gain is confused with the disposition of the gain. The gain exists and has been realized. The firm can dispose of the gain by paying dividends, by purchasing another kind of merchandise, by buying securities, or in other ways. That it chooses to purchase identical merchandise is to select one of several alternatives. This, or any other choice for that matter, must stand on its own profit possibilities and should not be subsidized by a gain from past activities.[4] But principle

---

[3] A full explanation of this technique is given in Chapter V. There are circumstances under which LIFO does not yield the current cost of goods sold.

[4] Such a subsidy is made available if gains used for replacement purposes are exempt from taxes.

(1) alone, if applied to all inputs, does result in a statement of operating profit on a current cost basis.

Accounting Principles for Developing Business Profit

If measurement is directed towards business profit, a concept whose theoretical justification was explored in the preceding chapter, individual changes in cost must be recorded as they occur. Business profit is defined to include current operating profit (component *A*) and realizable cost savings (component *B*). Its measurement requires data on the price changes of individual (or small groups of) assets and entails the application of the following principles:[5]

1. When price changes increase the value of an asset, realizable cost savings should be recorded. These form the capital gains element of business profit. Similarly, when price changes decrease the value of an asset, realizable capital losses should be recorded. (A debit [credit] should be made at the same time to a value adjustment account. The balance in this account added to an asset's [depreciated] historic cost yields its current cost.)
2. When an asset or asset service is used in production, its current cost should be deducted from the current value of output to determine operating profit. (At the same time the historic cost of the asset or service used should be credited to the asset account, the balance in this account indicating depreciated historic cost of the assets still on hand. The difference between current cost and historic cost of the asset or service used should be credited [if positive, debited if negative] to the asset's value adjustment account.)

When these principles are applied in the accounts, the fundamental accounting equation is modified from a historic cost basis

[5] These principles are applied to the inventory and cost of goods sold problem in Chapter V and to the fixed asset and depreciation problem in Chapter VI. Similar techniques for measuring profit along lines consistent with the concept we have termed business profit are specified in Taxation and Research Committee of the Association of Certified and Corporate Accountants, *Accounting for Inflation*. The title is misleading, however, because the techniques suggested do not account for changes in the *price level* at all but only for changes in individual prices. Of their concept, the authors say, "This treatment does not attempt to maintain original purchasing power but simply to define correctly operating profit by separating out capital losses and capital gains" (p. 93).

to a current cost basis. We have business profit. Barring dividends and new contributions of capital by stockholders, the following relationship holds:[6]

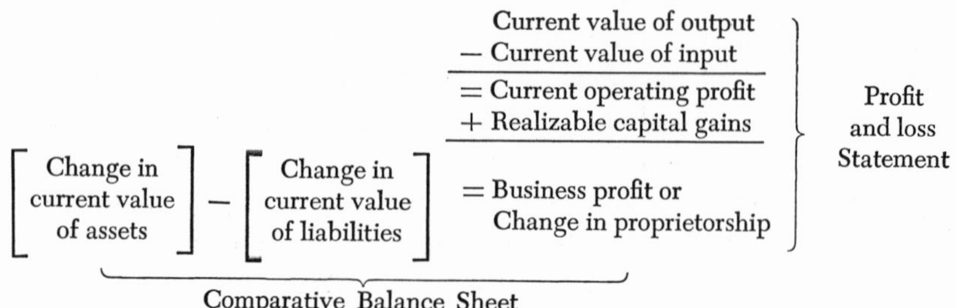

A third principle can be enunciated:

3. The difference between current cost and historic cost of assets or asset services used in production also marks the conversion of what was a realizable gain to a realized gain. This amount should be transferred from the unrealized cost savings account to a realized cost savings account.

Principle (3) applied in the accounts in conjunction with principle (1) yields data for realized profit.

Some Advantages of Flexibility in Accounts

The several advantages of business profit all stem from the measurement of relevant events as they occur. The managerial evaluation of expectations is facilitated because gains of one period are recorded in that period and gains from holding activities are sharply distinguished from current operating profit. Data are available for reporting current values on the balance sheet making this report of greater significance to financial analysts,

---

[6] Compare with the traditional accounting relationship:

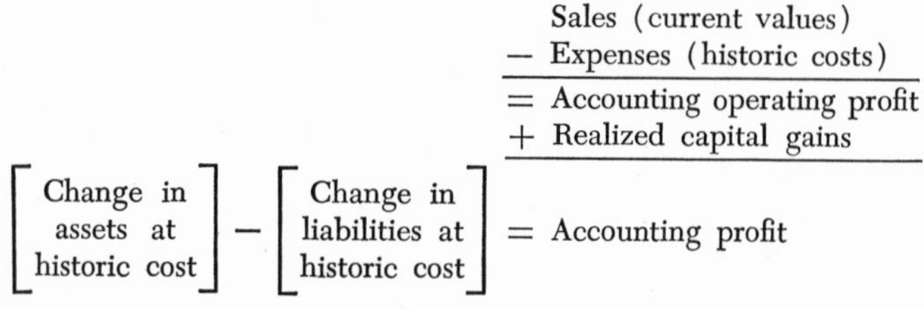

owners, and the public. It would also provide better raw data for measuring the nation's stock of wealth. Finally the collection of the necessary data would make readily available, by the recombination of profit elements, other concepts of profit, thus providing the flexibility that present accounting data lack.

Business profit, as was stated above, includes as separate elements current operating profit (component A) and realizable cost savings (component B). As assets are sold or used up, however, the related realizable savings are realized. A record of this conversion makes possible a statement of realized profit defined as including current operating profit (component A), and gains realized both through use and through sale (components D and C). By combining components A and D, accounting operating profit can be obtained. The definitions of these three profit concepts are given below to facilitate comparison:

	Profit elements included		
	As operating profit		As capital gains (or cost savings)
1. Accounting profit =	$(A + D)$	+	C
2. Realized profit =	A	+	$(C + D)$
3. Business profit =	A	+	B

The advantages of flexibility derive from the fact that no single concept serves all purposes best. Thus, while business profit is ideal for managerial purposes, its use as a basis for taxation can be criticized. Taxes must be paid in cash. Suppose, however, that current operating profit is zero in a particular period but a large realizable gain has resulted from price changes. This cost saving may be locked up in the form of machinery or plant and, if the firm's cash position is low, the firm may be forced to sell some of its machinery in order to get the cash necessary to pay taxes on its gain. Such a situation might often work a hardship on business firms (and on the economy as a whole if resources are misallocated on this account). Operating profit usually has an immediate effect on a firm's cash position; realizable cost savings may not.

Realized profit clearly has advantages for purposes of tax collection because gains are not counted until they are converted into a liquid form. This concept is not far removed from present tax policy.[7] Ideally, perhaps, tax assessment should be related to realizable gains and tax payment to those gains that are realized. A tax liability computed on the basis of business profit would then be carried on the books until tax payments, computed on realized profit, were made.[8]

Another advantage of flexibility has already been indicated. Managerial decisions aimed at profiting from operating activities are essentially different from those aimed at speculative gains. The separation of these profit elements is desirable from a managerial point of view, and also for tax purposes if it is believed that the different elements should be taxed at different rates. This separation also facilitates the aggregation of current operating profit for national income purposes.

Modifications Introduced for Price Level Changes

Changes in the price level introduce two difficulties into the measurement and interpretation of accounting data. Business profit measures the increase over a period in the firm's command over money values. This increase does not represent an equal change in the firm's current real investment (purchasing power)

[7] Capital gains realized through use are, however, taxed as an element of operating profit at regular rates, not at capital gains rates. It might be argued, despite current practice, that capital gains realized through use should not be taxed at all if used for replacement purposes, because replacement might not be possible if some of the gain must be paid immediately to the government. In the case of assets sold, traded, or exchanged for the purpose of acquiring other comparable assets, the tax on any gain is postponed. Thus, if an individual purchased a house for $10,000 and sold it for $15,000 in order to buy another house for $15,000 (or more), the tax on the $5,000 gain is postponed. The exchange is regarded as a means of continuing the same investment. This rationale is not applied to capital gains realized through use even though the proceeds are used to continue an investment, say, in merchandise.

A tax concession when capital gains or cost savings are used for replacement purposes gives replacement an advantage over other uses of the gain, however, and is difficult to justify on economic grounds. For some discussion of this issue see E. O. Edwards, "Depreciation Policy under Changing Price Levels," pp. 271–272, and Nils Västhagen, *De fria avskrivningarna 1938–1951,* pp. 28–37.

[8] On similar grounds it can be argued that tax liability should be related to profit on an accrued basis and tax payment to profit on a cash basis. Since for most firms the difference is negligible, the collection of taxes on accrued profits is not unrealistic. In cases where the difference is great, such as installment sales where receipts lag well behind sales, tax adjustments are permitted.

unless the price level has been constant over the period.[9] Maintaining the money value of a firm's assets (a zero business profit) when the price level is rising represents a decrease in the purchasing power controlled by the firm (a negative real profit). The first problem created by changes in the price level is to determine how much of money profit represents an increase in the current purchasing power of the firm. Its solution has significance for tax, dividend, and wage polices particularly. The levying of taxes on money profits when prices are rising means that a part of the firm's original real investment is being taxed; a firm may be paying taxes even though its real investment has decreased over the period. If management is misled by money profits, it may bring about the same result by paying dividends that deplete the firm's real investment. Or management, on the basis of high money profits, may contract to pay higher wages even though the firm's real profit is small or negative.[10]

The second difficulty concerns intertemporal comparisons. A solution to the first problem enables us to state by how much a firm's purchasing power has increased in current dollars, i.e., to determine how much of current money profit represents an increase in current purchasing power. To compare such an increase for one period with the increase in another period requires a further consideration of price level changes. An increase in purchasing power of $100 in a period when prices are high does not mean the same thing as an increase in purchasing power of $100 when prices are low; the latter increase is really the greater. In order to compare them, each of these increases must be stated in terms of dollars having the same purchasing power. If the price level in the first period is twice that in the second, the real profit of $100 in the first period is worth only $50 in terms of second period dollars. Similarly, the real profit of $100 in the second period is worth $200 in first period dollars.

These two problems can be viewed as (1) determining the

[9] The term "purchasing power" can be substituted for "real investment" at this juncture only if current cost and opportunity cost are identical or if realizable profit is substituted for business profit. In the discussion that follows, however, we shall use the terms interchangeably.

[10] An excellent discussion of these effects can be found in L. H. Kimmel, *Depreciation Policy and Postwar Expansion* (Washington: Brookings Institution, 1946). Some studies of the specific magnitudes involved were cited in Chapter I.

number of current dollars that represents an increase in current purchasing power, and (2) deflating these amounts for different periods so that the dollar sign has the same meaning. The second problem is not difficult to solve if a satisfactory solution to the first can be found.

Real and Fictional Elements of Capital Gains and Cost Savings

Current operating profit requires no adjustment for changes in the price level on the first count. This element of profit is by definition an increase in current purchasing power; it is the excess of the current purchasing power represented by the current value of output over the current purchasing power represented by the current value of input. It measures the increase in current purchasing power that results from the firm's operating activities. It is the results of a firm's holding activities, capital gains (and cost savings) whether realizable or realized, that must be adjusted for price level changes.

Assume for a moment that current operating profit is zero and that the prices of a firm's assets have risen over the period in proportion to the change in the price level. The money capital gain that has arisen (from specific price changes) is entirely fictional; no part of it represents an increase in the current purchasing power of the firm. The larger money value of the firm's assets has the same purchasing power as before.

When the prices of assets do not move proportionally to the price level, some of the capital gains will be real. If asset prices rise but the price level is constant, all of the capital gain is real, none of it is fictional; the current purchasing power of the firm has increased by the amount of the money capital gain. But when this is not the case, cost savings and capital gains must be separated into real and fictional elements.

Realizable gains are easily handled. Some gain (or loss) is necessary simply to maintain purchasing power. This portion of any money gain is a fictional gain; the balance is a real gain (money gains = fictional gains + real gains). A few examples may clarify the computation. If asset prices have risen by 50 per cent while the price level has risen by 20 per cent, two-fifths of the resulting money gain is fictional and three-fifths of the gain is real. If asset prices have not changed, a zero money gain includes a fictional gain of 20 per cent of the asset's money value (the gain necessary if purchasing power were to be maintained) and an equal real loss of purchasing power incurred from holding (say) cash while the price level rises. If the price level falls, say, by 20 per cent, while asset prices rise, say, by 50 per cent, a loss of money value equal to 20 per cent of the asset's money value at the beginning of the period could have been suffered without any loss of purchasing power. This is a fictional loss. As a money gain equal to 50 per cent of asset value has been enjoyed, the total real gain is the sum of the money gain and the fictional loss (real gains = money gains + fictional losses); both represent increases in current purchasing power.

Gains realized through sale are real to the extent that the sales price of the asset exceeds its historic cost adjusted for price level changes since its purchase. If the price level has risen by 50 per cent over this period, an asset sold for $180 which cost $100 yields a real gain of $30, a fictional gain of $50.

Gains realized through use are determined by the same principle, though the computation may appear to be more complicated. For depreciable assets it is again convenient to regard an asset as a collection of bundles of asset services each having a historic cost equal to the depreciation rate for its period of use multiplied by the asset's historic cost.[11] The historic cost of one bundle of services adjusted for the price level change up to its time of use is called *purchasing power cost.* It is equal to historic cost multiplied by the ratio of the present price level index to the price level index at time of purchase. We now have three types of depreciation charge, (1) current cost depreciation, (2) purchasing power cost depreciation, and (3) historic cost depreciation, and the following relationships:

Cost Saving = (1) − (3).
Real cost saving = (1) − (2).
Fictional cost saving = (2) − (3).

The real saving or gain can be explained in this fashion: Purchasing power cost represents the purchasing power (measured in present-day dollars) sacrificed in acquiring the asset. The cost of

[11] Historic cost net of expected scrap value, of course.

using the asset is its current cost, the amount now sacrificed by using the asset instead of not using it. The difference between these two figures represents the real gain or loss to the firm from holding the asset.

The relationship between realizable and realized gains may be clarified by use of a simple example.[12] Suppose that a machine purchased for $10,000 immediately rises in price to $15,000 while the price level rises by 30 per cent, and both stay at their new levels throughout the asset's five-year life. The realizable capital gain of $5,000 has two elements, a real gain of $2,000 ($15,000 – $13,000) and a fictional gain of $3,000 ($13,000 – $10,000). Each of these would be realized as the asset is used over the five years, the first at the rate of $400 per year, the second at the rate of $600 per year. The firm originally sacrificed in money terms $10,000 worth of goods and services in order to buy the machine, or $2,000 for each of five bundles of asset services. At the new price level the goods and services sacrificed would cost $13,000, or $2,600 for each bundle of asset services acquired. These amounts indicate in today's dollars the real purchasing power sunk in the machine or in its services; it is purchasing power cost to the firm; recovering $2,600 whether through the sale or use of one bundle of services would represent no real improvement in the firm's position. The current cost of the asset's services for one year, $3,000, exceeds purchasing power cost by $400, and this amount represents the realization of a real gain. The excess of purchasing power cost, $2,600, over the historic cost of a year's services, $2,000, represents a realized but purely fictional gain.

Modified Concepts of Measurable Profit

The profit elements listed for money profits can now be expanded to include the modifications introduced for price level changes. We have the following list:

- A. Current operating profit
- B. Realizable cost savings
    1. Real
    2. Fictional

[12] Compare with the example used in the early pages of this chapter to illustrate realized cost savings in the absence of changes in the price level.

C. Capital gains realized through sale
   1. Real
   2. Fictional
D. Capital gains realized through use (realized cost savings)
   1. Real
   2. Fictional

The number of possible profit concepts has now been multiplied. We shall examine only those that can be obtained by adjusting each of the three money concepts discussed earlier for changes in the price level. The adjustment requires in each case only the elimination of the fictional element in capital gains. The redefined concepts are as follows:

		Real operating profit		Real capital gains
1. Real accounting profit	=	$(A + D_1)$	+	C_1
2. Real realized profit	=	A	+	$(C_1 + D_1)$
3. Real business profit	=	A	+	B_1

If the desirability of eliminating fictional gains from profit is admitted, an additional limitation of accounting profit as it is presently constituted is revealed. It does not recognize changes in the general price level. Many critics of accounting data would be content with the adjustment of accounting profit to a real basis although this would not correct its other limitations.[13] Real accounting profit results if (1) the purchasing power cost of inputs is deducted from the current value of output in determining operating profit and (2) gains from asset sales are computed as the difference between selling value and purchasing power cost. By the first procedure, operating profit automatically includes real gains realized through use (excess of current cost over purchasing power cost) and excludes the fictional element. The ap-

[13] G. O. May's proposal of a technique for accounting for depreciation is an example of this approach. See his "Proposal for Depreciation of Current Costs," Appendix V of *Business Income and Price Levels: An Accounting Study*, pp. 105–109. The reference to current costs in the title should not be confused with current cost as we have used it in this book. May's current cost is our purchasing power cost.

plication of the second principle yields real gains realized through sale.[14]

Real realized profit would in many respects be useful as a basis for tax payment. It has the advantages of its money counterpart and also excludes fictional gains from the tax base. The exemption of fictional gains from a tax on income is clearly equitable if the principle could be universally applied. If it were to be applied only to the income of business firms, while individuals continued to pay taxes on money income, it could be argued that it would be more equitable to disallow the change to a real income base for business firms.[15]

The significance of real business profit lies primarily in the desirability of measuring the increase in real purchasing power over which the firm exercises control. This is of value to management in the evaluation of expectations because it incorporates the effects of another event, changes in the price level. An unprofitable decision might well be the result of anticipating changes in the price level incorrectly.[16] The measurement of real business profit is of special importance, however, if management is misled by money profits to pay large dividends or if labor unions use money profits alone as an argument for higher real wages.

Intertemporal Comparisons

A brief example will suffice on the theoretical adjustment necessary for intertemporal comparisons. Assume that the real business profit for a firm was \$5,000 in 1946, \$5,500 in 1951, and \$6,000 in 1953, and that an index of the price level based on 1947 = 100 is 90, 115, and 120 in the respective years. These profit figures can be compared by stating them in the dollars of 1946, 1947, 1951, or 1953 (or any other year for which an index

[14] This technique is basic to the extended system proposed by H. W. Sweeney, *Stabilized Accounting,* but he accounts also for unrealized gains on money assets (and liabilities) such as cash and accounts receivable.

[15] See E. Cary Brown, *Effects of Taxation: Depreciation Adjustments for Price Changes,* pp. 100–101, where this argument is well expressed.

[16] Montgomery Ward's decision to hold large amounts of liquid assets at the end of World War II was apparently in anticipation of the real gains that would accrue when the price level fell as it did shortly after World War I. That Sears, Roebuck & Co. outdistanced Montgomery Ward in the immediate postwar period can perhaps be attributed in part to the errors in the expectations on which Ward's decision was based.

number is available). Each profit figure is multiplied by the ratio of the index number for the year in whose dollars the comparison is to be made to the index number for the year in which the profit was made. In 1953 dollars, for example, the 1951 profit is $5,739 (120/115 · $5,500), and the 1946 profit is $6,667 (120/90 · $5,000), as compared to a 1953 profit of $6,000.[17]

Summary of Profit Concepts

The relationships among the concepts discussed and the deviations of each from real business profit are summarized in table 5. All of these concepts represent measurable opportunities. Which one accounting should adopt as its profit definition depends not only on the flexibility of the resulting data and its usefulness for managerial, tax, and other purposes, but also on the cost and difficulty of preparing the data.[18]

All of the concepts of profit we have discussed would be identical under so-called stationary state conditions. When population, tastes, resources, and technology are given, it is reasonable to expect all prices to be constant. Capital gains disappear, price level changes vanish, and the most plaguing problems of measurement in a dynamic economy are dissipated; the measurement of the accounting concept of profit yields accurate data. It follows that the accounting concept may be a fairly efficient one in a dynamic economy also if such an economy is characterized by relatively stable prices.[19] It is not surprising, therefore, that pressures to modify the accounting concept appear and grow in strength during periods when price and price level changes are important and recede and vanish when price movements diminish in size and frequency.

The period since before World War II has been one of profound change in the United States economy and one symptom of this change has been relatively unstable prices. In the postwar years, then, numerous suggestions for modifying traditional ac-

---

[17] Intertemporal comparisons of this sort are of significance largely when used in conjunction with other data such as the size of the firm, profits in other firms, national income, and interest rates.

[18] These matters are considered in Chapters V–IX.

[19] Even when the price level is stable, however, individual price changes may introduce serious discrepancies between accounting and business profit.

TABLE 5

RELATIONSHIPS AMONG CONCEPTS OF MEASURABLE PROFIT

	Inclusions[a]							Deviations from real business profit		
		Real gains			Fictional gains					
			Realized by			Realized by				
	Current operating profit	Realizable (gains arising in this period)	Use	Sale	Realizable (gains arising in this period)	Use	Sale	Excludes accrued but unrealized real gains	Includes fictional gains	Confuses gains realized through use with operating profit
1. Accounting profit........	O		O	C		O	C	X	X	X
2. Real accounting profit....	O		O	C				X		X
3. Realized profit...........	O		C	C		C	C	X	X	
4. Real realized profit.......	O		C	C				X		
5. Business profit...........	O	C			C				X	
6. Real business profit.......	O	C								

[a] O = Included as operating profit. C = Included as capital gains (and losses) or cost savings.

counting techniques have been proposed and a few have been attempted in practice. But change in the field of accounting is understandably, and often wisely, slow. We must turn to the question of what type of specific changes in accounting practices might be required if firms are to provide the data which the theory of Part One suggests might be useful and important.

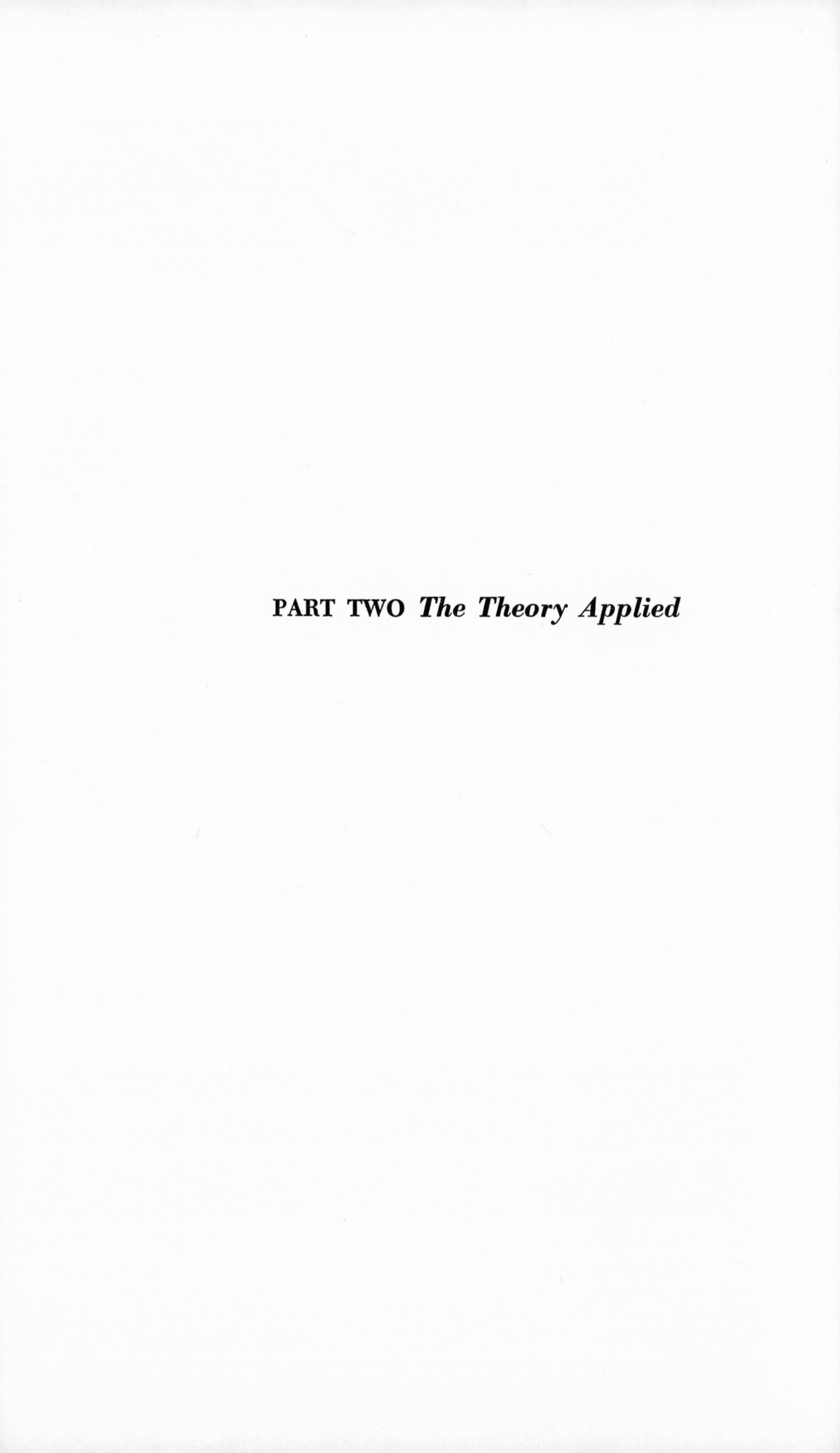

PART TWO *The Theory Applied*

V *Application to Inventories:*

DETERMINING CURRENT COST OF MATERIALS USED

Thus far we have presented a theory of income measurement. We have said nothing explicitly about how such a framework might be handled in the accounts, and only a little about the significance of the resulting data. Our task in the next four chapters is, therefore, a twofold one: (1) to demonstrate techniques for accumulating the desired data, and (2) to analyze more carefully the significance of the resulting statements of profit and position for management, owners, and interested outsiders. The development of techniques runs through all four of the chapters, but as Chapters V and VI are concerned with the two special problems of determining the cost of materials used and depreciation expense, considerations of significance are not treated fully until Chapter VII, in which we first develop full statements of profit and position in money terms, and Chapter VIII, in which we derive data for the presentation of statements in real terms.

The central problem of technique is to devise a system which will keep track of both current and historic costs of inputs used in production for sale without establishing elaborate new records, without altering in any fundamental fashion present accounting procedures, and without destroying any data needed for more traditional statements. We need current costs to measure current operating profit and realizable cost savings; we need historic costs as well as current costs to measure realized cost savings and realized capital gains, which together with current operating profit yield realized profit. The system devised clearly must establish the identity of our realized profit with accounting profit as it is now measured so that direct reports of the latter can still be formulated. The system must also provide data for a balance sheet based on historic costs as well as one based on current values. Finally, once such a framework is formulated in money terms, we must make provision for amending it for changes in the general price level in order to present statements of profit and position in real terms.

Current costs can deviate from historic costs when inputs are purchased on one date and sold, held, or used on a later date. In order to develop the kind of flexible data needed for full statements of profit and position in money terms, we must account for this difference for every expense and revenue item and for every asset and liability item with respect to which such a difference has arisen. Fortunately, many of these items require no adjustment because their current costs coincide with their historic costs. Among these are most revenue items, most out-of-pocket expense items, and those short-term claims and liabilities fixed in monetary terms. The adjustment of many other smaller items is a fairly straightforward proposition, as we demonstrate in Chapter VII. But the adjustment of inventories and the related cost of materials used and the adjustment of fixed assets and the related depreciation expense involve both larger magnitudes and a higher order of complication; these two facts warrant treatment in two separate chapters.

Our immediate concern is with the valuation of inventories and the cost of materials used in manufacturing firms (or of goods sold in wholesaling and retailing). We will treat only materials used in production in our development, but different inventory problems are all analogous one to another, and the procedure devised here for materials can be applied readily to handling other assets. Further, we will not need to consider at any length in this chapter the practical problem of obtaining current prices. With inventories, such prices are readily ascertainable for the most part; the assets are generally marketed continuously, and a telephone call or an arrangement with a seller for a period-end statement would be all that is needed. We will not get off so easily, however, when we come to consider depreciation in the next chapter.

Importance of Inventory Values in Cost of Goods Sold

Consider first the significance of deviations between the current cost value and the historic cost value of inventories. The value of inventory stocks relative to annual sales in manufacturing in the United States is normally around 15 per cent, in wholesale trade around 10 per cent, and in retail trade around 12 per cent.[1] Approximately 40 per cent of manufacturing inventories are in raw materials, so these alone amount to 6 per cent of sales; the rest are in goods in process or finished goods.[2] But annual business profits before taxes in the United States also average around 6 per cent of gross sales and are therefore roughly equal in amount to materials inventories. Thus a 10 per cent increase in the valuation of a final inventory will (because the cost of materials used must be reduced by the amount of the increase) increase profits by 10 per cent. In retail trade the impact is likely to be greater both because inventories are a larger percentage of sales and because profits are usually a smaller percentage. Assuming the inventory percentage is 12 and the profit percentage 3, a 10 per cent increase in the valuation of the final inventory would increase profits by 40 per cent. Clearly, the valuation of inventories can have an important effect on costs and thus on business profits.

That such is the case is evident from study of the information in table 6. In national income data, inventories, as reported by

---

[1] Data are computed from U. S. Department of Commerce, *Business Statistics* (1959), as well as from *National Income Supplements* to the *Survey of Current Business*.

[2] M. Abramovitz, *Inventories and Business Cycles*, p. 156.

TABLE 6

CORPORATE PROFITS AND INVENTORY VALUATION ADJUSTMENTS, 1929–1959
(In millions of dollars, except where indicated)

Year	Reported corporate profits before taxes[a] (1)	Inventory valuation adjustment (2)	Adjusted corporate profits before taxes (3) [= (1) − (2)]	Percentage overstatement of operating profit or understatement of operating loss (4) [= (2) ÷ (3)]
1929	9,396	−472	9,868	−4.8%
1930	3,185	−3,260	6,445	−50.6
1931	−776	−2,414	1,638	−147.4
1932	−2,983	−1,047	−1,936	−54.1
1933	153	2,143	−1,990	107.7
1934	1,656	625	1,031	60.6
1935	2,986	277	2,759	8.2
1936	5,636	738	4,898	15.1
1937	6,113	31	6,082	.5
1938	3,053	−963	4,016	−24.0
1939	6,219	714	5,505	13.0
1940	9,086	200	8,886	2.3
1941	16,751	2,471	14,280	17.3
1942	20,657	1,204	19,453	6.2
1943	24,316	773	23,543	3.3
1944	23,027	287	22,740	1.3
1945	18,749	564	18,185	3.1
1946	22,126	5,263	16,863	31.2
1947	28,836	5,899	22,937	25.7
1948	32,164	2,152	30,012	7.2
1949	25,538	−1,856	27,394	−6.8
1950	39,628	4,965	34,663	14.3
1951	40,938	1,199	39,739	3.0
1952	35,570	−981	36,551	−2.7
1953	37,185	997	36,188	2.8
1954	32,648	318	32,330	.1
1955	43,304	1,736	41,568	4.2
1956	43,732	2,560	41,172	6.2
1957	41,501	1,548	39,953	3.9
1958	37,700	200	37,500	.5
1959	47,000	500	46,500	1.1

SOURCES: For 1929–1945, U. S. Department of Commerce, *National Income Supplement* (1954), Tables 18 and 23; for 1946–1957, *National Income Supplement* (1958), Tables VI–5 and VI–11; for 1958 and 1959, *Survey of Current Business* (July, 1960), Table VII–18, p. 34.

[a] Originating in the United States, except for 1958 and 1959.

business concerns and as used in computing the cost of goods sold in business statements of income, are adjusted to a current cost basis to correct for the overstatement or understatement of profit arising from the costing of inputs at prices prevailing prior to the average for the year for which the calculation is made. Table 6 shows that in some years this adjustment was extremely large. In 1930, for example, operating profits were understated by 50 per cent because of valuing inventories at historic rather than current costs; in 1931 the understatement was 150 per cent, and losses were reported although profits were earned on operations. Losses on operations were not actually suffered until 1932, and these continued into the year 1933 although corporations reported a net profit before taxes in that year.

In the period immediately following the end of the Second World War, with both volume and prices of inventories rising rapidly, the inventory valuation adjustment amounted to over $5 billion in two years. Profits on operations were overstated by 25–30 per cent in 1946 and 1947 as a result of valuing inventories at outdated prices, and indeed such profits did not really increase in 1946 over 1945, as reported, but actually declined.

The outbreak of the Korean War led to an overstatement of 14 per cent. Even during the rather quiet decade of the 1950's, there continued to be an understatement or overstatement (more usually of course the latter) by 2 to 6 per cent because of present inventory costing procedures. When one considers that these are aggregative figures for the whole economy and therefore hide what may be very much larger percentage differences for individual firms whose inventory prices fluctuate more than the average, it can hardly be said that the problem is insignificant. Let us see what can be done about it.

Principles of Inventory Costing

Inventory costing[3] arises as a special problem in the measurement of business income because often inputs are not kept track of individually, and there exist, therefore, various alternative possibilities for the establishment of the cost figure to be attached

[3] This section is a review of FIFO and LIFO inventory costing techniques and may be skipped without serious loss by the informed reader, although the example developed is used later for purposes of comparison.

to assets used in production for sale, or sold directly in wholesaling and retailing operations. In manufacturing, for example, we have the traditional formula, $II + P - FI = MU$; that is, initial physical inventory, plus the units purchased, yields the quantity of materials available for use during the period, and subtracting the final physical inventory on hand at the end of the period yields the quantity of materials actually used in production. But we must put these components into dollar terms. The difficult problem is to decide upon the cost figures to be attached to the beginning and end-of-period inventories.

The FIFO Method

Traditionally, inventory costing procedures have been justified largely on an implied assumption that there should be some relationship between the flow of costs established in the accounts, and the actual physical flow of goods into and out of the firm.[4] This form of "realism" seems to us to have doubtful merit as a basis for setting values to be attached to inventories if it conflicts with "realism" in the determination of business profit. It may be, however, a useful analogy for purposes of exposition.

The most common procedure followed in pricing inventories, generally called the FIFO system, is to select prices as though the goods first in are also first out; i.e., it is assumed that inventory turns over regularly and that the goods on hand at the end of the period are those which were purchased most recently. Inventories are thus valued (on the balance sheet and in the computation of cost of materials used) at or near market prices at the end of the accounting period. This means that the computed cost of materials used is based on prices attached to the *opening* inventory (and thus those prices prevailing toward the end of the previous period) and to purchases during the *earlier* part of the present period (for the more recent purchases are considered to be the goods on hand). In accordance with the principle of conserva-

[4] The Committee on Concepts and Standards Underlying Corporate Financial Statements of the American Accounting Association, for example, spends a good bit of time over this issue, describing the flow of assets assumption as "realistic" when "it reflects the dominant characteristics of the actual flow of goods," and as "artificial" when the assumed "flow of costs . . . is clearly in contrast with actual physical movement." "Inventory Pricing and Changes in Price Levels," *Accounting Review* 29 (April, 1954), p. 188.

tism, the method is frequently employed, especially in manufacturing, on the basis of FIFO cost or market, whichever is lower.[5]

Consider the following illustration. The XYZ Corporation begins the year with 100 units of materials on hand valued at $500. During the year it makes purchases of the following quantities at the prices shown:

February 15	May 1	September 1	November 20
60 at $5.25 ea.	140 at $5.40 ea.	110 at $5.60 ea.	90 at 5.70 ea.

At the end of the year the firm finds that it has 120 units of materials on hand. Using the FIFO method, the final inventory will be valued at the most recent purchase prices, i.e., 90 at $5.70 plus 30 at $5.60, or $681. The cost of materials used would be $500 + $2,200 − $681 = $2,019, and the Cost of Materials Used account would appear as shown below. HC denotes historic FIFO cost, and AP_c, the weighted average purchase price in the current period.

Cost of Materials Used (FIFO Basis)

Initial inventory, HC	500	Final inventory, HC	681
Purchases, AP_c	2200	To Profit and Loss	2019
	2700		2700

The valuation of the initial inventory at $500 was of course determined at the end of the last period in just the same way as the final inventory was valued in this period. Computing the final inventory on the basis of the most recent purchase prices means that the figure derived for the cost of materials used in production is weighted in favor of early purchase prices. In fact, if inventory turnover was less than one, all materials used would be priced

[5] A variant of the FIFO system of inventory valuation is the moving average method. The price of new purchases is averaged in continuously with the price of units on hand. The final inventory, rather than being valued at the price of goods most recently purchased, as under FIFO, is a composite valuation of goods on hand at the beginning of the period and of those purchased during the year. Like FIFO, the moving average method may approximate the flow of goods, with the assumption here that each lot issued for sale is composed of proportionate amounts from all lots currently on hand. And as in FIFO also, the cost of materials used, under the moving average method, is based on prices weighted toward the early part of the period in question or some time previous to this period.

out at purchase prices prevailing in periods before the current one, and the lower the turnover, the older the prices used would be.

The LIFO Method

As long ago as the early 1920's various companies began experimenting with inventory costing techniques which would minimize the effects of changes in inventory prices on reported profits.[6] With authorization of its use for Federal income tax purposes in 1938, the LIFO method, based on the usually artificial assumption that the goods last in (purchased) are the first out (sold, or used in production for sale), became a major alternative to FIFO. According to the amended 1939 regulations which are still in effect, there are five general conditions to be met by any concern which wishes to adopt LIFO in computing its income tax: (1) it must use LIFO valuation in its regular reports, as well as for income tax purposes; (2) once adopted, LIFO must be maintained unless permission is obtained from tax authorities to give it up—permission which may not be granted very readily; (3) inventories must be carried at cost, not the lower of cost or market; (4) the value of inventories must be recomputed on a cost basis (if not already on that basis) at the time of LIFO adoption, each item in the initial inventory being valued at average cost; and (5) increments to inventories during a period may be valued at average cost, at cost of most recent purchases, or at cost of first purchases in order of acquisition.[7]

Let us suppose that the XYZ Corporation in the illustration

---

[6] In 1920 the National Lead Company adopted the *base-stock* method of inventory valuation. The assumption was that the company needed a certain minimum quantity of inventory on hand; it could never realize profits upon these normal stocks and therefore the company should not deceive its stockholders by marking up the value of the inventory. On the company's books the so-called base stock value was maintained at the price prevailing at the time of the initiation of the scheme. A variant of this was the stated-reserve system of Swift and Company, adopted in 1933. All rises in inventory values went to a "stated reserve" as a capital gain and were thus excluded from reported profit. A good account of the early experiments with inventory costing which formed a background for the adoption of LIFO may be found in J. K. Butters, "Management Considerations on Lifo," pp. 308–312. See also, by the same author, *Effects of Taxation: Inventory Accounting and Policies,* Chapter IV.

[7] See D. T. Smith and J. K. Butters, *Taxable and Business Income,* Chapter 4.

above switched to a LIFO basis of inventory costing at the beginning of the year in question. As the initial inventory is already valued at cost, no adjustment of it is necessary but every item in it is assumed to have cost \$5.00, the average cost. In valuing the final inventory, 100 of the 120 units would be valued at beginning-of-the-period prices, and 20 units would be valued, we assume according to the option in (5) above, at the earliest purchase price in the period (\$5.25); the total value of the final inventory would then be \$605. The cost of materials used on a LIFO valuation basis would be \$500 + \$2,200 − \$605 = \$2,095, and the Cost of Materials Used account would appear as follows:

Cost of Materials Used (LIFO Basis)

Initial inventory, LIFO	500	Final inventory, LIFO	605
Purchases, AP_c	2200	To Profit and Loss	2095
	2700		2700

The materials used up in production for sale are costed as though they were actually the materials purchased most recently. When materials prices are rising therefore, the cost of materials used is larger and reported profit smaller than under FIFO. When materials prices are falling, the cost of materials used is generally smaller and reported profit larger than under a "pure" FIFO system, and this difference is still greater when LIFO is compared with FIFO cost or market, whichever is lower.

In spite of the apparent tax advantages of LIFO over FIFO, given the general bias toward long-run inflation in this country and in the world as a whole, it has been estimated that not more than 10 to 12 per cent of all nonfarm inventories in the United States are computed on a LIFO basis. On the other hand, the ratio is higher in manufacturing, and in certain industries (petroleum, meat products, metals, and textiles in particular) LIFO is the predominant inventory valuation method employed.

The reluctance of some businesses to take the plunge into LIFO is undoubtedly based in part on the fact that it is normally a "point of no return," and that there is no recourse to the "cost or market, whichever is lower" variation which is allowed with FIFO. Clearly, firms could suffer in a depression by reporting for tax purposes the relatively higher profits engendered by use of LIFO under these circumstances, even though during depression tax rates may be less and over-all profits lower. The firm's tax position could be made substantially worse if inventory volumes were reduced, as shown more fully below.[8]

There are also other difficulties inherent in the use of LIFO which may offset any tax advantages, such as the fact that there is no recognition of realizable or even realized cost savings on inventories anywhere in the accounts—these holding gains are simply "lost"—and the fact that inventory values on the balance sheet are badly distorted. Surely what is needed is a method of valuing inventories which will yield a "true" statement of profit over the whole phase of the cycle, with proper separation of its components, as well as accurate values for the balance sheet.

The Current Cost Method

Computing Current Costs, Asset Values, and Profit Components

The current cost of materials used can easily be computed directly without resort to the $II + P - FI = CMU$ formula. It is simply the quantity sold multiplied by the weighted average purchase price during the period in question.[9] In our hypothetical

[8] Of course, if FIFO losses are being made and these are large enough, even LIFO profits may be negative and so taxes would be zero in any event.

[9] Theoretically, each time a unit is sold its current cost should be obtained on that date. The sum of these current costs would yield the current cost of materials used. The method given in the text is really an approximation which is completely accurate only if sales and purchases (not of the same goods) take place on the same dates (or continuously), and the ratio of the quantity sold to the quantity purchased on each date is equal to the ratio of the total quantity sold to the total quantity purchased during the period. This is demonstrated below for a firm growing at the constant rate, r.

Let the quantity of sales (S_t) on any date be e^{rt} and the quantity of materials bought (B_t) be ke^{rt}, where k is the constant ratio of purchases to sales. Assume that purchase prices at any time are given by e^{pt} and that p is initially unity, i.e., we select quantity units so as to normalize prices. The cost of materials used on a current cost basis is at any time:

$$C_t = e^{rt} \cdot e^{pt}. \tag{1}$$

Over the accounting period, measured as 0 to n, this aggregates to:

$$C = \int_0^n e^{t(r+p)} = \frac{e^{n(r+p)} - 1}{r + p}. \tag{2}$$

example the average purchase price is \$5.50[10] and the quantity sold is 380. It follows that the current cost of materials used is $380 \cdot \$5.50 = \$2{,}090$. This is the figure for cost of materials used which, along with other costs, must be subtracted from the value of sales to yield current operating profit. (As can be seen, the current cost value of materials used is very close to the LIFO figure arrived at above, \$2,095, and would be identical to the LIFO figure if inventory volume was constant.) It follows immediately and by definition that the amount of realized cost savings is \$71, the excess of the current cost of materials used over the historic (FIFO) cost of materials used, which we have already shown to be \$2,019.[11]

We wish to show that the same result can be achieved by multiplying sales by the weighted average purchase price. The quantity of sales over the full accounting period is:

$$S = \int_0^n e^{rt} = \frac{e^{rn} - 1}{r}. \tag{3}$$

The weighted average purchase price is:

$$\frac{\Sigma(B_t \cdot p_t)}{\Sigma B_t} = \frac{\int_0^n ke^{rt} \cdot e^{pt}}{\int_0^n ke^{rt}} = \left(\frac{r}{r+p}\right) \cdot \frac{e^{n(r+p)} - 1}{e^{rn} - 1}. \tag{4}$$

Multiplying this amount by the quantity of sales, given in equation (3), we have:

$$C = \frac{e^{n(r+p)} - 1}{r + p}, \tag{5}$$

which is seen to be identical to equation (2).

[10] $\$5.50 = \frac{(60) \cdot \$5.25 + (140) \cdot \$5.40 + (110) \cdot \$5.60 + (90) \cdot \$5.70}{400}.$

[11] Since 380 units of our purchased 400 units of materials were sold, we can assume that there were sales equal to 380/400, or 95 per cent of purchases on the dates when purchases were made, in accordance with the assumption of footnote 9. This means that sales were 57 units on February 15, 133 units on May 1, 104.5 units on September 1, and 85.5 units on November 20. Thus, cost savings were realized during the period as follows:

on February 15:	(\$.25)	(57)	=	\$14.25	initial inventory
on May 1:	(\$.40)	(43)	=	17.20	initial inventory
	(\$.15)	(60)	=	9.00	inventory purchased February 15
	(0)	(30)	=	0	inventory purchased May 1
on September 1:	(\$.20)	(104.5)	=	20.90	inventory purchased May 1
on November 20:	(\$.30)	(5.5)	=	1.65	inventory purchased May 1
	(\$.10)	(80)	=	8.00	inventory purchased September 1
				\$71.00	

It remains only to compute realizable cost savings in order to have available all of the additional raw data we require. Two short-cut methods are available. We can assume (for computational purposes only) that the initial inventory is held over the entire period while its current cost changes from that prevailing at the beginning to that prevailing at the end. The realizable cost savings arising on it would be determined as the quantity so held multiplied by the change in current cost over the period. We can also assume (again for computational purposes only) that any excess of final inventory over initial inventory was acquired at the average purchase price and held to the end of the period. The realizable cost savings arising on the increment in inventories would be determined by multiplying the incremental quantity by the excess of current cost at the end of the period over the average purchase price.

Suppose that the purchase price was $5.15 at the beginning of the period and $5.75 at the end of the period. Then we "held" 100 units throughout the period while prices of materials rose from $5.15 to $5.75. Also we increased our inventory volume by 20 units at an average cost price of $5.50, but these 20 units too are valued at $5.75 at the end of the period. As our first method of computing realizable cost savings, we thus have:

Realizable cost savings on 100 units of initial inventory while prices rose from $5.15 to $5.75 = $.60 · (100) =	$60
Realizable cost savings on 20 units of increment to inventory while prices rose from $5.50 to $5.75 = $.25 · (20) =	5
Total realizable cost savings	$65

The other method assumes that the initial inventory is held while its value changes from its current cost at the beginning of the period to the average purchase price and that the final inventory is acquired at the average purchase price and held while its value rises to current cost at the end of the period. The computation for our hypothetical example follows:[12]

[12] Theoretically, of course, we should again take each item, whether in the initial inventory or purchased during the period, and identify its current cost at the end of the period or at the time it or the product in which it is embodied is sold. The sum of the excesses of current costs, so defined, over purchase costs (if the item is purchased during the period) or over current costs at the beginning of the period (if the item is a part of the initial inventory) represents the amount

Realizable cost savings on 100 units of initial inventory while prices rose from \$5.15 to \$5.50 = \$.35 · (100) =	\$35
Realizable cost savings on 120 units of final inventory while prices rose from \$5.50 to \$5.75 = \$.25 · (100) =	30
Total realizable cost savings	\$65

of cost savings that have become realizable over the period. Fortunately, the simple methods in the text are good approximations, ones that are completely accurate when the assumptions in footnote 9 hold.

The final inventory priced at costs current at the end of the period is:

$$F_c = \left(I + \int_0^n ke^{rt} - \int_0^n e^{rt}\right) \cdot e^{pn}, \tag{1}$$

where I is the initial physical inventory, the second term in the parentheses is physical purchases, and the third term is physical sales. The inventory deduction in the Cost of Materials Used account necessary to leave as a balance the current cost of materials used can be defined as the initial inventory at current cost at the beginning of the period plus purchases at current cost (average purchase prices) less the current cost of goods sold:

$$F_d = I + \int_0^n ke^{rt} \cdot e^{pt} - \int_0^n e^{rt} \cdot e^{pt}. \tag{2}$$

The excess of F_c over F_d represents the realizable gains that have accrued during the period, or:

$$F_c - F_d = Ie^{pn} + (k-1)e^{pn} \cdot \frac{(e^{rn}-1)}{r} - I - (k-1) \cdot \frac{(e^{n(r+p)}-1)}{r+p}, \tag{3}$$

which simplifies to the following:

$$F_c - F_d = I(e^{pn}-1) + (k-1)\left[\frac{(e^{rn}-1)e^{pn}}{r} - \frac{(e^{n(r+p)}-1)}{r+p}\right]. \tag{4}$$

This equation can be rearranged to yield both of the computations we have indicated. First, equation (4) can be rewritten as follows:

$$F_c - F_d = I(e^{pn}-1) + \left[(k-1)\frac{(e^{rn}-1)}{r}\right]\left[e^{pn} - \frac{r}{r+p} \cdot \frac{(e^{n(r+p)}-1)}{(e^{rn}-1)}\right]. \tag{5}$$

The first term indicates gains which would arise if the size of the inventory were unchanged over the period (remember that p is initially unity). The first part of the second term is the excess of the final physical inventory over the initial inventory. It is multiplied by the excess of costs current at the end of the period over the weighted average of purchase prices. The rearrangemnt given by equation (5), therefore, corresponds to the first method used in the text.

The rearrangement corresponding to the second method is the following:

$$\begin{aligned} F_c - F_d = {} & I\left[\frac{r}{r+p} \cdot \frac{(e^{n(r+p)}-1}{(e^{rn}-1)} - 1\right] \\ & + \left[I + (k-1)\frac{(e^{rn}-1)}{r}\right]\left[e^{pn} - \frac{r}{r+p} \cdot \frac{(e^{n(r+p)}-1)}{(e^{rn}-1)}\right]. \end{aligned} \tag{6}$$

These data and those on inventory values are summarized below and compared with FIFO costs:

	Current Costs	FIFO Costs
Initial inventory, 100 at $5.15	$ 515	$ 500
Cost of materials used, 380 at $5.50 . .	2090	2019
Realized cost savings	71	. . .
Realizable cost savings	65	. . .
Final inventory, 120 at $5.75	690	681

The remaining problem is to find techniques for incorporating data on current costs into the accounts without destroying the data on historic (FIFO) costs. To that problem we now turn.

Introducing Current Costs into the Accounts

We assume that the usual accounts have been kept by the firm on the historic (FIFO) cost basis and that in addition we have the accounts necessary to handle the adjusted data. As we reach the end of the period, the relevant accounts have in them the following balances before adjustments are made. HC denotes historic (FIFO) cost; AP_c, average purchase prices of this period; and CC_b, current cost at the beginning of the period.

Materials Inventory

Initial inventory at HC	500	

Inventory Valuation Adjustment

Initial balance, CC_b – HC	15	

Purchases

At AP_c	2200	

The first term represents the initial inventory multiplied by the excess of the weighted average purchase price over the price prevailing at the beginning of the period. The second term is the final physical inventory multiplied by the excess of the price current at the end of the period over the weighted average purchase price of the period.

It can be further shown that if prices rose evenly during the period and purchases were evenly spaced, both of the above results for realizable cost savings would be identical to multiplying the average inventory volume (110 in our example) by the rise in price ($.60). The cost saving in this case comes to $66 rather than $65 in our example, because prices are not assumed to have risen evenly with purchases evenly spaced; i.e., our average purchase price is $5.50 rather than $5.45.

Cost of Materials Used	

Realizable Cost Savings	

Unrealized Cost Savings		
	Initial balance	15

Realized Cost Savings	

The initial inventory is recorded at historic (FIFO) cost. The balance in the Inventory Valuation Adjustment account is the amount necessary to adjust the inventory to a current cost basis at the beginning of the period. The balance in the Unrealized Cost Savings account indicates that the valuation adjustment had not been realized at the beginning of the period.

The journal entries we suggest for incorporating current cost data into the accounts without demolition of historic costs are as follows:

		Debit	Credit
(1)	Inventory Valuation Adjustment	65	
	Realizable Cost Savings		65
	To record gains that have become realizable during the period.		
	On initial inventory, 100 · ($5.50 – $5.15) = $35		
	On final inventory, 120 · ($5.75 – $5.50) = 30		
	Total $65		
(2)	Cost of Materials Used	500	
	Materials Inventory		500
	To transfer the initial inventory valued at historic (FIFO) cost.		
(3)	Cost of Materials Used	50	
	Inventory Valuation Adjustment		50
	To adjust the initial inventory to average prices of the period.		
(4)	Cost of Materials Used	2200	
	Purchases		2200
	To transfer purchases at average prices of the period.		

		Dr.	Cr.
(5)	Materials Inventory	681	
	Cost of Materials Used		681
	To enter the final inventory value at FIFO historic cost.		
(6)	Cost of Materials Used	21	
	Inventory Valuation Adjustment		21
	To adjust the final inventory in the Cost of Materials Used account to average prices of the period.		
(7)	Current Operating Profit	2090	
	Cost of Materials Used		2090
	To transfer the cost of materials used at average prices of the period.		
(8)	Realizable Cost Savings	65	
	Unrealized Cost Savings		65
	To transfer realizable cost savings. (The credit would normally go to business profit and thence to unrealized cost savings.)		
(9)	Unrealized Cost Savings	71	
	Realized Cost Savings		71
	To transfer realized cost savings from the unrealized account.		
(10)	Realized Cost Savings	71	
	Realized Profit		71
	To transfer realized cost savings.		

When these adjusting entries have been recorded, the relevant accounts would appear as shown below. CC_e denotes current cost at the end of the period.

Materials Inventory

Initial inventory at HC	500	(2) To CMU	500
(5) Final inventory at HC	681		

Inventory Valuation Adjustment

Initial balance, CC_b – HC	15	(3) To CMU on II	50
(1) II, \$35(AP_c – CC_b); FI, \$30(CC_e – AP_c)	65	(6) To CMU on FI	21
		To balance	9
	80		80
Balance applicable to final inventory	9		

Purchases

At AP_c	2200	(4) To CMU	2200

Cost of Materials Used

(2) Initial inventory at HC	500	(5) Final inventory at HC	681
(3) To adjust II to AP_c ($= AP_c - HC$)	50	(7) To COP	2090
(4) Purchases at AP_c	2200		
(6) To adjust FI to AP_c ($= HC - AP_c$)	21		
	2771		2771

Realizable Cost Savings

(8) To unrealized account	65	(1) Accrued this period	65
[normally via Business Profit]			

Unrealized Cost Savings

(9) Realized cost savings	71	Initial balance	15
To balance	9	(8) Realizable cost savings	65
	80		80
		Unrealized cost savings, end of year	9

Realized Cost Savings

(10) To Realized Profit	71	(9)	71

The first entry records the amount of cost savings that have become realizable during the period and indicates through its debit element that the corresponding valuation adjustment applies to inventories. We shall return to the account credited shortly.

Entry (2) transfers the initial inventory at historic (FIFO) cost to the Cost of Materials Used account, and entry (3) transfers that part of the inventory valuation adjustment necessary to raise the inventory value to average purchase prices (current cost at time of sale) in the Cost of Materials Used account. With entry (4) purchases are transferred in automatically at average purchase prices. The total in the account at this time represents the cost of goods available for sale stated entirely in average purchase prices.

To state the cost of materials used at average purchase prices, we need only take out of the account the final inventory at average purchase prices ($660). This is accomplished by entries (5) and (6), which also provide data to record the final inventory at its historic (FIFO) cost ($681) and to reduce the amount in the Inventory Valuation Adjustment account to that necessary ($9) to raise the final inventory to its current cost at the end of the year ($690) for balance sheet purposes.

The current cost of materials used, $2,090, can now be transferred, entry (7), to a Current Operating Profit account (not shown) where with other current costs it will be subtracted from sales to arrive at the figure indicated by the account title. The cost of materials used that would be transferred to a Profit and Loss account under traditional accounting procedures would be $2,019, so we have at this point apparently understated accounting profit by $71.

Let us return to the credit aspect of entry (1). That amount, $65, represents cost savings that have accrued to the firm during the period through the holding of materials while prices rose. This amount, together with realizable cost savings on other assets, and current operating profit represents Business Profit, the account to which the amount would normally be transferred. For explanatory purposes we have transferred it by entry (8) directly to Unrealized Cost Savings. The new balance in that account at this moment ($80) represents the maximum amount that could be realized in this period. Our computations reveal that only $71 of it was in fact realized, the $15 in the account initially plus $56 that became realizable in this period. (This $71 is also revealed in the Cost of Materials Used account as the sum of the two adjusting entries, $50 + $21.) Entry (9) transfers the $71 to the appropriate account. The balance left in the Unrealized Cost Savings account represents the cost savings yet to be realized when the final inventory is sold; this amount will appear in the equity section of the balance sheet.

The realized cost savings will in turn be transferred to a Realized Profit account (not shown). The Current Operating

Profit account balance will ultimately be transferred here also. As noted above, the amount of current operating profit will be less than traditional accounting profit by $71, the excess of the current cost of materials used ($2,090) over the historic cost of materials used ($2,019). But as the Realized Profit account receives realized cost savings of $71, the total in this account will just equal traditional accounting profit. The traditional statement of profit and loss could easily be prepared from the data in this account.[13]

Comparison of Profit Concepts for a Given Period

Completion of the full set of accounts for this problem must wait until Chapter VII, after we have treated valuation problems

[13] We hold no strong brief for the specific entries and accounts employed in this example so long as the technique used generates data on both realized and realizable cost savings as well as on historic costs. We know of no alternative proposals that lead to this result. C. F. Schlatter developed and advocated a system before World War II which has attracted considerable attention but which takes no account of realizable cost savings (*Advanced Cost Accounting*, Chapter X). Translated into our terminology, his system would determine realized cost savings as the excess of the current cost over the historic cost of materials used. This amount would be debited to the Cost of Materials Used account and credited to Realized Cost Savings. The method yields no data on realizable cost savings, on unrealized cost savings, or on the current cost value of inventories.

Professor W. S. Mackey, Jr., of Rice University, has suggested to us that our entries would be streamlined if a perpetual inventory system were being employed, and indeed this is the inventory system used by most large corporations in the United States. In this case the end-of-period adjustments in our ledger accounts could be simplified to the following:

Inventory

	500	(1)	2019
	2200	To balance	681
	2700		2700
Balance	681		

Inventory Valuation Adjustment

	15	(3)	71
(2)	65	To balance	9
	80		80
Balance	9		

Current Operating Profit

(1)	2019		
(3)	71		

Realizable Cost Savings

(4)	65	(2)	65

Realized Profit

		(5)	71

Unrealized Cost Savings

(5)	71		15
To balance	9	(4)	65
	80		80
		Balance	9

relating to fixed assets and securities. Only then can we bring the entire system together in an integrated fashion. It is important at this point, however, to see clearly the relationship between the three concepts of profit treated in Chapter IV, business profit, realized profit, and accounting profit, as they are affected by inventory costing problems. The three (gross) profit concepts may be compared as shown below. Sales are assumed to be $4,000.

The Accounting Profit Concept

Sales (at current prices)		$4000
Cost of materials used (at historic costs)		2019
Accounting profit		$1981

The Realized Profit Concept

Sales (at current prices)		$4000
Cost of material used (at current prices)		2090
Current operating profit		$1910
Cost of materials used (at current prices)	$2090	
less Cost of materials used (at historic costs)	2019	
Realized cost savings		71
Realized profit		$1981

The Business Profit Concept

Sales (at current prices)	$4000
Cost of materials used (at current prices)	2090
Current operating profit	1910
Realizable cost savings	65
Business profit	$1975

Accounting profit is identical to realized profit in the aggregate, but the latter effectively breaks the aggregate into operating and holding gain components. Further, it should be noted that it is not necessary for realized profit to exceed business profit. In our example, the amount of cost savings which were realized in this period—cost savings which accrued in part during this period but in part during the last period—exceeds the amount of cost savings which are newly accrued in this period. Realized cost savings are based on the difference between current cost at the time of use (and sale) and historic cost at the time of purchase; realizable cost savings are based on the difference between current costs at the end of the period (or at the time of use and sale) and current costs at the beginning of the period (or at the time of acquisition during the period).

We have compared our profit concepts with respect to inventory costing for one year. But the differences and the significance of the differences are brought more clearly into focus when we compare the concepts over several periods.

Comparison of Profit Concepts over Time

For purposes of illustrating the way in which reported profits over time are affected by inventory costing procedures and the consequent derivation of data on the cost of goods sold, we have set forth an example in table 7 based on the assumption that all purchases are treated in the accounts as though made at average prices, or more restrictively that sales and purchases occur together at only one date in each of five periods. This treatment makes the computation easy, but does not affect the generality of the basic principles about inventory costing which we wish to derive from this table.

Initial and final inventory values have been computed on the basis of FIFO and LIFO historic cost, and on the current cost basis sketched above (initial and final inventories each adjusted to average purchase prices) for the computation of current operating profit. The total of realizable cost savings accruing in each period is the sum of the initial inventory times the difference between the average price of the period and the initial price, and the final inventory times the difference between the end-of-period price and the average price; i.e., it is the sum of line A4 in table 7 less line A3, and line C4 less line C3 for each period.

The total of realized cost savings in our simple illustration is the sum of the realizable gains on the initial inventory in this period and the realizable gains on the final inventory of the last period, since accrued cost savings are all realized at the single time of purchase and sale in each period. Thus, realized cost

TABLE 7

CONCEPTS OF MONEY PROFIT COMPARED FOR DIFFERENT INVENTORY COSTING PROCEDURES WITH CHANGING PRICE AND VOLUME

(In thousands, except for prices)

	Period				
	1	2	3	4	5
Sales, less expenses	30 at $21 = $630	24 at $18 = $432	28 at $17 = $476	30 at $18.50 = $555	24 at $18 = $432
A. Initial inventory	10	10	6	8	10
1. FIFO	at $20 = $200	$200	$102	$128	$175
2. LIFO	at $20 = $200	200	120	152	187
3. Current cost, beginning of period	at $20 = $200	200	90	136	200
4. Current cost, adjusted for COP	at $20 = $200	at $17 = 170	at $16 = 96	at $17.50 = 140	at $17 = 170
B. Purchases	30 at $20 = $600	20 at $17 = $340	30 at $16 = $480	32 at $17.50 = $560	20 at $17 = $340
C. Final inventory	10	6	8	10	6
1. FIFO	at $20 = $200	at $17 = $102	at $16 = $128	at $17.50 = $175	at $17 = $102
2. LIFO	at $20 = $200	at $20 = $120	{6 at $20 + 2 at $16 = $152	{6 at $20 + 2 at $16 + 2 at $17.50 = $187	at $20 = $120
3 Current cost, adjust for COP	at $20 = $200	at $17 = $102	at $16 = $128	at $17.50 = $175	at $17 = $102
4. Current cost, end of period	at $20 = $200	at $15 = $ 90	at $17 = $136	at $20 = $200	at $15 = $ 90
Accounting Profit, FIFO	$ 30	−$ 6	$ 22	$ 42	$ 19
Accounting Profit, LIFO	$ 30	$ 12	$ 28	$ 30	$ 25
Current operating profit	$ 30	$ 24	$ 28	$ 30	$ 24
Realized cost savings	0	−30	−6	12	−5
Realized Profit	$ 30	−$ 6	$ 22	$ 42	$ 19
Current operating profit	$ 30	$ 24	$ 28	$ 30	$ 24
Realizable cost savings	0	−42	14	29	−42
Business Profit	$ 30	−$ 18	$ 42	$ 59	−$ 18

saving in period 3, for example, is the realizable gain on the final inventory of period 2 (– $12) and the realizable gain on the initial inventory of period 3 ($6). The total of – $6 is the difference between average price in period 2 and average price in period 3, times the 6 units held between time of purchase in period 2 and time of sale in period 3.

Five principles setting forth the relationships among the profit concepts can now be enumerated, four of which can be verified by direct examination of the illustrative data:

1. All concepts of operating profit are identical if purchase prices are constant (see period 1);
2. Realized profit equals FIFO profit at all times;
3. LIFO operating profit and current operating profit are less than FIFO operating profit when purchase prices are rising and greater than FIFO operating profit when purchase prices are falling;
4. Only the amounts of business profit before taxes, and its components, are always identical for different periods containing the same events (see periods 2 and 5);
5. If increments in inventories are priced under LIFO at early purchase prices, in any period in which physical inventory has increased, LIFO operating profit is slightly less than current operating profit if purchase prices are rising, and slightly greater than current operating profit if purchase prices are falling; if physical inventory has decreased, either may be the larger. If increments are priced in at average purchase prices, the two concepts will be equivalent; if priced in at late purchase prices, LIFO profit will slightly exceed COP.

Principle (1) expresses the fact that if individual prices were constant, as one might expect in a stationary state, present accounting procedures would yield the desired data. Principle (2) is really a matter of the definition of realized profit; we have based realization on first-in, first-out assumptions. Principle (3) derives from the fact that when purchase prices are rising, the FIFO final inventory value exceeds its initial value by more than the other final inventory values exceed their initial values because the whole final inventory is valued at the more recent (higher) prices. As a consequence, the FIFO cost of materials used is lower and operating profit higher than in the cases of the other techniques. Principle (4) is a matter of the definition of business profit. It is in our view the most important principle of the five, and is discussed further below.

Principle (5) is not borne out in our illustration because all purchases are considered to be concentrated at one date. Principle (5) expresses the fact that if physical inventory is increasing while purchase prices are rising, the increase in inventory at the end of the period is valued according to one LIFO option at early purchase prices which will usually be less than the average purchase price. This raises the LIFO cost of materials used above the COP cost of materials used, and lowers LIFO operating profit below current operating profit. For example, in period 3, early purchases might have been made at $15.50 instead of at the average purchase price of $16. The final inventory value on a LIFO basis would then be $1 less (2 units at $.50), and LIFO operating profit would be $1 less than current operating profit. The other LIFO options can be similarly reasoned.

So long as purchase prices are constant, it is immaterial which method is used in computing values for initial and final inventory and the cost of materials used. All methods yield identical results. When these prices are changing, however, differences in reported profits appear. The advantages of business profit and its components in the evaluation of business decisions are illustrated most strikingly by principle (4). A comparison of periods 2 and 5 in table 7 shows that for two periods containing identical events only business profit and its components do not differ. The FIFO and LIFO methods result in much higher reported profit in period 5 although the market value and physical quantities of inventories at the beginning and end of the period, and the quantities and prices of purchases and sales during the period are identical to those in period 2. Because the application of FIFO and LIFO techniques has not recorded all of the events prior to period 5, the FIFO and LIFO initial inventories for period 5 are undervalued. These unrecorded gains of past periods are recorded instead as events of period 5. Only current operating profit and realizable cost savings, the components of business profit, are unaffected because all past events have already been recorded and the events of period 5 are not therefore clouded by events of periods other than the one under consideration.

Summary and a Look Ahead

We have tried to show in this chapter that straightforward end-of-period adjustments can be made in existing accounting records so as to yield both the current cost and historic cost of materials used in production for sale, or of finished goods sold in wholesaling and retailing operations. These adjustments require no information which a firm does not already have, namely, the purchase prices and quantities of its materials inputs during this and the last period. To compute realizable cost savings, one additional piece of information is needed, the purchase price at the end of each period assuming no purchases are made on this data, but this figure surely would be readily ascertainable at no additional cost. The accountant is then in a position to compute the full range of cost information on materials used which is necessary to arrive at statements of business profit and realized profit (and thus also traditional accounting profit), as well as a balance sheet expressed in either current values or historic costs or both.

A more extensive development of the advantages of making these adjustments to the accounts and deriving the full range of data on profits suggested here must be postponed until after we have shown how other types of assets can be adjusted in a manner similar to inventories, and how these adjustments can all be woven together into integrated statements. But it is apparent from the illustrations in this chapter that if "truthful accounting" means "rendering reality accurately," only the inventory method used in the development of business and realized profit can be considered entirely "truthful," for it is the only method which always reports identical figures for any two periods when identical events occur in those two periods. Surely this is the type of information which is needed if past business decisions are to be evaluated properly in order to make better new decisions about the uncertain future.

Although we do not underrate the many smaller obstacles that may exist in the way of practical application of the inventory methods here suggested in a large, complex, multiprocess firm, the framework would appear to be feasible and reasonable. We must now turn to the case of fixed assets, where the practical problems of deriving current costs of use are of a different order, and application of the framework to these inputs therefore perhaps more debatable.

VI *Application to Fixed Assets:*

DETERMINING CURRENT COST DEPRECIATION

The issues involved in valuing fixed assets and determining depreciation charges during periods of changing prices have been discussed more widely in recent years than those relating to inventories and the cost of materials used.[1] Several reasons account for this. First, when the price trend is upward as it has been since 1900, the effects on reported profit of different techniques for computing depreciation expense are more enduring than are the effects of different inventory costing techniques. Second, the depreciation problem is complicated by the fact that, unlike inventories of materials, fixed assets cannot even be assumed to be used up in any one accounting period; periodic

[1] *Depreciation* means here the decline in the value of fixed assets over time, both because of wear and tear, and normal (or expected) obsolescence. In this book we restrict discussion to the depreciation problem; accounting techniques for handling depletion of mineral resources and amortization of intanglible assets can be developed along similar lines.

charges even on the basis of original cost are at best estimates under any circumstances. Finally, the determination of current costs is a much more difficult problem in the case of fixed assets than in the case of inventories. This is so because there may be no established markets for used fixed assets, and technological change may mean the disappearance from markets of new assets exactly like (except for age) those owned by the firm.

Because fixed assets are long-lived and because price effects are more enduring, discussion of the depreciation problem has frequently been bound up with the question of providing for the eventual replacement of fixed assets. While we shall touch upon this issue toward the end of this chapter, we shall take the general position, as we did with inventories, that such matters fall outside our central objective in this book. We are interested in depreciation because of its effect on the measurement of income and on the reporting of balance sheet values. The disposition of funds that result if income covers these charges is a separate managerial decision, one which if it is to be arrived at properly, however, inevitably involves a knowledge of all of the profit data which we are seeking to develop. The decision to replace or not to replace is a decision about the future; it must be based on the most accurate knowledge possible about decisions in the past as well as on additional data relating to the future. That expenses and decisions to replace should not be linked to each other is perhaps more apparent in the case of fixed assets than in the case of inventories of materials, because depreciation charges are made long before replacement occurs and replacement itself seldom means replacement in kind because of technological change which has occurred since the purchase of the asset being replaced.[2]

In this chapter, then, we concentrate upon the problems encountered in depreciation as they relate to the valuation of fixed assets and the determination of income. Depreciation expense is the second principal "out-of-line" cost mentioned at the beginning of Chapter V. In theory, the problems involved are no different from those relating to inventories and treated in that

[2] One of the authors has considered the replacement problem at some length elsewhere. See E. O. Edwards, "Depreciation and the Maintenance of Real Capital" in J. L. Mey (ed.), *Depreciation and Replacement Policy*.

chapter. We must estimate the current cost of using fixed assets in production for sale and the current values of the fixed assets at the beginning and end of the accounting period, in order to determine current operating profit and realizable cost savings, the components of business profit, and to provide data for a balance sheet based on current values; and we must estimate the historic cost of using fixed assets in production for sale and historic cost values at the beginning and end of the period in order to measure realized cost savings and realized capital gains, which together with current operating profit yield realized profit, and a balance sheet based on historic costs. Again we must establish the identity of our realized profit with accounting profit as it is now measured. Finally, we wish to do all this by making only end-of-period adjustments in accounting records; existing procedures generally must be left intact.

Before developing a framework which might yield these objectives, however, let us first consider, as we did in the case of inventories, the importance of the problem we are investigating, the extent to which the costs of using fixed assets may actually get "out of line" when prices change over the course of time.

Importance of Fixed Asset Values in Measurement of Profit

On the basis of Raymond Goldsmith's careful estimates of the excess of current cost over historic cost depreciation for the years 1929 through 1949, we can derive a table, following the model used in the previous chapter for inventories, for the overstatement and understatement of operating profits during these years because of the use of historic rather than current costs in depreciating fixed assets. The data are shown in table 8.

As we would expect, movements in the difference between reported profits and profits adjusted for the current cost of using fixed assets are much less erratic than movements in the difference between reported profits and profits based on adjusting inventory values to current costs. In the case of fixed assets, historic costs are based on prices ranging many years back, rather than on prices prevailing toward the end of the previous year, so that costs tend to get "out of line" only slowly. Also, fixed asset prices generally do not fluctuate as sharply as do inventory prices. The

TABLE 8

CORPORATE PROFITS AND CURRENT COST DEPRECIATION ADJUSTMENTS, 1929–1949
(In millions of dollars, except where indicated)

Year	Reported corporate profits before taxes[a]	Excess of current over historic cost depreciation[b]	Adjusted corporate profits before taxes	Percentage overstatement of operating profit or understatement of operating loss
	(1)	(2)	(3) [= (1) − (2)]	(4) [= (2) ÷ (3)]
1929	9,396	861	8,535	10.1%
1930	3,185	544	2,641	20.6
1931	−776	256	−1,032	20.0
1932	−2,983	−115	−2,868	−3.7
1933	153	−102	255	−40.0
1934	1,656	199	1,457	13.7
1935	2,986	225	2,743	8.2
1936	5,636	235	5,401	4.4
1937	6,113	477	5,636	8.5
1938	3,053	448	2,605	17.2
1939	6,219	452	5,767	7.8
1940	9,086	517	8,569	6.0
1941	16,751	722	16,029	4.5
1942	20,657	954	19,703	4.8
1943	24,316	997	23,319	4.3
1944	23,027	988	22,039	4.5
1945	18,749	1,026	17,723	5.8
1946	22,126	1,530	20,596	7.4
1947	28,836	2,677	26,159	10.2
1948	32,164	3,268	28,896	11.3
1949	25,538	3,018	22,520	13.4

SOURCES: For column (2), R. W. Goldsmith, *A Study of Saving in the United States*, v. I, Table C-41, p. 955; for column (1), U. S. Department of Commerce, *National Income Supplement* (1954), Table 18, p. 184.

[a] Originating in the United States.

[b] Goldsmith's estimates are based on the following technique: (1) estimated annual expenditure on different types of producer durable goods was adjusted to 1929 prices; (2) estimates of depreciation on each of these twelve types of equipment were made on a straight-line basis, using annual expenditures and the average lengths of life given in Treasury tax bulletins; (3) the resultant historic cost depreciation estimates in 1929 prices were then adjusted to a current cost basis through use of separate price indexes of the different categories of fixed assets with 1929 = 100. Similar techniques were employed for nonresidential construction, and the difference between current cost depreciation and historic cost depreciation thus derived. Goldsmith's data go back to 1897.

magnitude of the difference, nevertheless, is substantial, and was particularly large in the immediate postwar period. Furthermore, because there are lags involved, an overstatement of profit tends to persist through smaller recessions such as 1938 and 1949, and through the early stages of a major depression, a phenomenon which we suggest in Chapter VII has considerable implications with respect to problems of business decision-making over the course of the cycle, and indeed perhaps even with respect to the cyclical behavior of the economy as a whole.

While we have not tried to carry Goldsmith's monumental work forward, there is reason to believe that the gap between reported profits and actual operating profits because of depreciation at historic rather than current cost widened rather than narrowed between 1949 and 1954. Fixed asset prices rose rather sharply following the outbreak of war in Korea, as shown in table 9. At the same time, physical accretions to plant and equipment did not keep pace. Thus the age distribution of existing fixed assets was probably not greatly updated, but the replacement costs of those assets in existence before 1950 rose sharply While current cost depreciation probably rose considerably, therefore, historic cost depreciation increased as well, especially in 1951, as shown in table 10, probably in good part because of the accelerated amortization provisions allowed on some new equipment related to our wartime needs. On balance it seems unlikely that use of the special five-year amortization provisions was sufficient to make allowances for depreciation based on original cost keep pace with the allowances which would have been necessary on the basis of current costs of replacement. The excess of current cost over historic cost depreciation probably increased in absolute terms between 1949 and 1954, and perhaps as a percentage of the adjusted profit figure as well [column (4), table 8].

Unfortunately, the situation becomes still more clouded after 1954. The new tax regulations of that year allowed business firms to adopt various types of accelerated depreciation methods in computing allowances for depreciation, methods which could have meant substantial increases in historic cost depreciation (see below). Undoubtedly in response to these new possibilities, corporate depreciation charges at historic cost jumped in 1955. Since that year, however, as can be seen in table 10, increases in depreciation allowances have not been large in percentage terms, not nearly so large, for example, as in the immediate postwar years when accelerated depreciation was not possible.[3] In a guarded

[3] Yet total expenditure on new plant and equipment rose sharply in 1956 and remained high in 1957, after a period of relative stability between 1953 and 1955.

TABLE 9

ESTIMATED PHYSICAL ACCRETIONS AND PRICE RISES, CORPORATE FIXED ASSETS, 1946–1959

	1946	1947	1948	1949	1950	1951	1952	1953	1954	1955	1956	1957	1958	1959
New private, nonresidential construction activity:														
Expenditure on, in billions of 1954 dollars	10.1	10.3	11.4	11.3	12.0	13.3	13.3	14.0	14.3	15.7	16.1	16.5	14.9	15.0
Related price index (1954 = 100)	63.0	76.3	84.6	83.0	87.5	94.3	97.2	99.6	100.0	103.2	109.8	113.5	114.1	117.2
Producers' durable equipment:														
Expenditure on, in billions of 1954 dollars	16.1	21.7	22.8	19.8	21.3	22.0	21.8	22.5	20.8	22.5	25.0	24.6	19.4	21.3
Related price index (1954 = 100)	66.7	76.8	83.1	87.0	89.0	96.8	97.5	99.0	100.0	102.5	109.0	115.7	119.0	121.3

SOURCES: For 1946–1954, U. S. Department of Commerce, *National Income Supplement* (1958), Tables V–4, V–6, VII–14, and VII–15, pp. 191, 192, 228, and 229; for 1955, *Survey of Current Business* (December, 1958), 14–15; for 1956–1959, *Survey of Current Business* (July, 1960), Tables I–5 and VII–7, pp. 10 and 33.

TABLE 10

CORPORATE DEPRECIATION CHARGES AT HISTORIC COST, 1946–1959

	1946	1947	1948	1949	1950	1951	1952	1953	1954	1955	1956	1957	1958	1959
In millions of dollars	4,267	5,280	6,340	7,223	7,904	9,129	10,423	12,029	13,694	15,928	17,488	19,333	20,517	21,800
Percentage increase over previous year		23.7	20.0	13.9	9.4	15.4	14.1	15.4	13.8	16.3	9.8	10.5	6.1	6.2

SOURCES: For 1946–1955, U. S. Department of Commerce, *National Income Supplement* (1958), Table VI–18, p. 216; for 1956–1959, *Survey of Current Business* (July, 1960), Table VI–18, p. 31.

statement, the Office of Business Economics of the Department of Commerce suggests the following interpretation of the effects of changes in tax laws on the recent depreciation pattern of American business:

The profit ratios charted here [corporate profits before taxes relative to total income originating in American corporations, a ratio which normally fluctuates between 20 and 25 per cent] . . . reflect changes in the tax laws, such as the special amortization provisions enacted in 1950 and the legislation of alternative formulae which permitted accelerated depreciation under the Revenue Code of 1954. Profit ratios adjusted to eliminate the effects of these changes might be higher by one or two percentage points for 1957, and would show a somewhat different movement over the past few years.[4]

Until the careful study is made which will bring Goldsmith's estimates up to date, taking account of changes in the tax laws and their effect on historic cost depreciation charges, no one can really know the present magnitude of the aggregate error in reported operating profits of American business due to understatement of the current costs of using fixed assets. Our suggestion is that it must still be substantial.

All of this has to do only with aggregate figures for the economy as a whole. But the impact of a given price change in fixed assets may differ substantially as among different firms. The extent of the difference between current and historic cost depreciation depends upon both the average life of the firm's fixed assets and upon the rate at which the firm is growing or declining (and thus increasing or decreasing its stock of fixed assets).[5] The effect of this historic cost / current cost differential on reported profit, in turn, depends upon the ratio of depreciation charges to reported profits.

---

[4] U. S. Department of Commerce, *National Income Supplement* (1958), p. 15.

[5] The difference between current cost and historic cost depreciation may also be affected by the method of charging depreciation, but we will not expand upon that facet of the problem here. In general, the difference will be larger the less accelerated the method of writing off fixed assets; i.e. the distortion will be greater for straight-line depreciation than for one of the diminishing balance methods discussed in the next section of this chapter. For a detailed proof of this fact, as well as for an elaboration of the effects of differential rates of growth and different asset lives on the current cost / historic cost depreciation differential, see the chapter by E. O. Edwards in J. L. Mey, *op. cit.*

Consider first the effect of rates of growth or decline and of average asset life on the differential between current and historic cost depreciation. Table 11 shows the ratio of current cost depreciation to historic cost depreciation for alternative possible equi-

TABLE 11

RATIO OF CURRENT COST DEPRECIATION TO HISTORIC COST DEPRECIATION

Effect of Alternative Assumptions for Growth and Asset Life, Given Annual 10 Per Cent Increase in Fixed Asset Prices and Use of Straight-Line Method[a]

Average life of assets (years)	Annual rate of growth of firm (per cent) −10	−5	0	+5	+10
10	1.72	1.65	1.59	1.52	1.47
20	3.20	2.73	2.33	1.97	1.72
30	6.36	4.48	3.13	2.36	1.88

[a] The table is based upon the following formula. Let k denote the equilibrium real rate of growth in the firm's assets and p the equilibrium rate of increase in the price of these assets, with $k = p = 1$ at time $t = 0$. Then the historic cost of the annual accretion in the stock of assets at any time t is

$$a_h(t) = e^{t(p+k)}, \tag{1}$$

and the historic cost value of the firm's existing stock of assets at the present time (where n is the life of the fixed asset and therefore $t = n$) is determined by integrating this expression over n years, or

$$A_h = \int_0^n a_h(t)\,dt = \frac{(e^{n(p+k)} - 1)}{p + k}. \tag{2}$$

The current cost of any past acquisition in period t, its cost if purchased new today, is

$$a_c(t) = e^{t(p+k)} \cdot e^{p(n-t)} = e^{pn+kt}, \tag{3}$$

and therefore the current cost value of the firm's stock of assets at the present time is

$$A_c = \int_0^n a_c(t)\,dt = e^{pn} \cdot \left(\frac{e^{kn} - 1}{k}\right). \tag{4}$$

Depreciating on a straight-line basis, we simply divide (2) and (4) by n, the number of years over which each asset can be used. Thus, if D_h and D_c denote annual historic cost depreciation and current cost depreciation, respectively, we have

$$\frac{D_c}{D_h} = \frac{e^{pn} \cdot (e^{kn} - 1)/kn}{(e^{n(p+k)} - 1)/n(p + k)},$$

and simplifying,

$$\frac{D_c}{D_h} = \frac{(p + k)(e^{kn} - 1)}{k\,(e^{kn} - e^{-pn})}. \tag{5}$$

librium rates of growth of the firm and different possible asset lives, on the assumption that depreciation is charged on a straight-line basis and that fixed asset prices are increasing at 10 per cent a year (a not unrealistic figure on the basis of postwar experience for some types of fixed assets, as can be seen from figure 1 in Chapter I). Clearly the difference in the depreciation charge is smaller the more rapid the rate of growth or less rapid the rate of decline in the firm's assets over time, as can be seen by reading across any of the rows in table 11; a growing firm's assets are, on the average, more recently dated than the assets of a declining firm, and their historic cost value is therefore based on newer and higher prices so that there is less difference between historic and current cost depreciation charges. Each of the columns in table 11, on the other hand, illustrates the fact that a firm with short-lived assets suffers less distortion than a firm with long-lived assets; again, since prices are assumed to increase 10 per cent each year, the historic cost value of long-lived assets is, on the average, more outdated than the historic cost value of short-lived assets.

The effect on reported profits of this divergence between current cost and historic cost depreciation depends upon the size of the depreciation charge relative to profits. Thus, if S denotes sales revenue, C all costs other than depreciation expense, D_h historic cost depreciation, D_c current cost depreciation, and P profits, we can establish two measures as follows:

$$P_h = S - C - D_h, \qquad (1)$$

$$P_c = S - C - D_c. \qquad (2)$$

If the ratio D_c/D_h used in table 11 is denoted by d, and the ratio of historic cost depreciation to accounting profit (D_h/P_h) by f, these become:

$$P_h = S - C - fP_h, \qquad (3)$$

$$P_c = S - C - dfP_h. \qquad (4)$$

Subtracting (4) from (3) and simplifying, we obtain

$$(P_h - P_c)/P_h = f(d - 1).^6 \qquad (5)$$

[6] A more correct statement of the distortion in true operating profits would be the following:

$$(P_h - P_c)/P_c = f(d - 1)(P_h/P_c).$$

The amount given by this expression will generally be somewhat larger when prices are rising than that given by (5).

The value of f differs substantially as among different sectors of the economy and as among industries within a sector. A comprehensive survey of the annual reports of 2,600 leading nonfinancial corporations in 1948, for example, showed that in that year depreciation was approximately 15 per cent of reported profits in manufacturing, 30 per cent of reported profits in transportation, and 40 per cent of reported profits in utilities. Within manufacturing this proportion was less than 5 per cent in tobacco products, cotton goods, and woolen goods, but over 25 per cent in dairy products, meat packing, rubber products, and iron and steel.[7] In that same year, Goldsmith's estimates indicate that the ratio d for the economy as a whole was 1.5, although, as stressed above, this ratio will differ for different firms and in different industries and will be higher the longer the average life of the fixed assets held by the firm and the smaller the rate of growth. In general, we would expect d to be large in just those industries for which f is large, namely, in transportation, in utilities, and in some heavy manufacturing. Formula (5) thus suggests that the overstatement in reported operating profit during much of the postwar period, created by increasing prices of fixed assets, may have been negligible for some firms but as high as 40 or 50 per cent for others.

Let us then turn to discussion of the way in which end-of-period adjustments can be made to correct for our second principal out-of-line cost, depreciation expense, providing us with data for our different profit concepts and their components. As we did with inventories, we will start with some basic principles of depreciation accounting, without regard to price changes. The depreciation problem is more complex than the inventory problem, and we must devote more time to it if we are to provide a satisfactory basis for discussion of price corrections. We shall consider first, therefore, some of the many difficult problems involved in estimating depreciation charges when fixed asset prices are constant over time.

---

[7] National City Bank of New York, *Monthly Letter,* April, 1949, and August, 1949. In making computations we have simply doubled their figures on reported profits after taxes given for forty or so subgroups in order to arrive at a rough estimate of reported profits before taxes for these subgroups, and then aggregated the data on these subgroups.

Depreciation of Fixed Assets: Principles and Procedures When Prices Are Fixed

The central difficulties in accounting for depreciation are created by the fact that fixed assets are long-lived, that their services are difficult to identify and quantify, and that the prices of these services are difficult to determine. If asset services could be quantified and the market yielded prices for them, current cost depreciation could be computed directly as the product of services used (elapsed or expired) and the current purchase price of such services. Typically this direct procedure cannot be utilized and the value of asset services must be determined indirectly by (1) estimating asset life, (2) estimating the pattern the asset services will form over time (or production), and (3) applying this pattern to a base, namely, the value assigned to a new asset (installed, less scrap value) to estimate the value of the asset services used (or whose use is forever foregone) in this period.

The first two steps of this procedure are common to computations of both historic cost depreciation and current cost depreciation (though theoretically they are necessary only for historic cost). The two computations diverge mainly in the base to which the asset-service pattern is to be applied, the one utilizing the historic cost of the asset, the other, its current cost. We are therefore digressing somewhat in this section in which we discuss some fundamental problems relating to the first two procedural steps.

Determination of Asset Life

In Chapter II we discussed the factors which determine whether or not an entrepreneur will purchase a producers' durable good, let us say a machine. There we assumed some definite, given lifetime for the machine, at the end of which time it would be worth nothing. Under these assumptions we could say that an entrepreneur would purchase such a machine if the present value of expected future quasi-rents, over the lifetime of the machine or the entrepreneur's horizon, whichever is shorter, exceeded the cost of the machine at the time of purchase. In the language of Chapter II, purchase would be made if subjective value exceeded market value, the difference being subjective goodwill. Quasi-rents are determined by deducting from the proceeds realized from selling the machine's output all costs incurred in producing and selling that output except depreciation on the machine and any interest costs related to the acquisition of the machine.

Similar considerations are bound up in the question of how long the entrepreneur will use the machine, once purchased. The *maximum technical lifetime* of a machine ends when repair is physically impossible. The *maximum economic lifetime* terminates at that point when repair cost exceeds replacement cost. But, of course, normally neither of these points is reached, and we must consider those factors which may cause economic life to be shorter than maximum.

If a machine has zero disposal value throughout its economic lifetime after purchase, and no replacement is contemplated, it will be used as long as the present value of the expected future stream of quasi-rents is positive. A machine of *constant economic efficiency* yields a stream of constant quasi-rents, and its actual economic life under the assumptions of zero disposal value and no replacement is therefore equal to its maximum economic life. A machine of *declining economic efficiency* yields a stream of declining quasi-rents, and its actual economic life is ended when it has reached maximum economic life or when the quasi-rent becomes zero, whichever comes first.

The introduction of a positive disposal value will normally shorten the expected economic life of any machine. With a given, fixed disposal value, it will not pay the entrepreneur to hold the machine beyond the point where its quasi-rent is equal to the interest he can obtain on the disposal value. A machine of, let us say, monotonically declining economic efficiency, therefore will be sold before its quasi-rent becomes zero. But disposal value is also likely to decline over time, and this implies an additional cost of using the machine to the entrepreneur. The machine should be sold if its expected quasi-rent for the coming period is less than the interest on disposal value now plus the expected decline in disposal value over the period.

The economic life of the machine will normally be shortened still further by the possibilities of replacement. Interest on the subjective goodwill of the new machine represents an addition to the possible earnings of the entrepreneur should he dispose of his existing machine, i.e., an additional opportunity cost of continuing to use the old machine. Replacement will be worthwhile when the declining quasi-rent per period on the old machine falls below the sum of (1) interest on the old machine's disposal value, (2) the decline in its disposal value over a period, and (3) interest on the subjective goodwill of the replacement machine.

These, then, in abbreviated form, are the variables which determine the length of an asset's useful economic life, namely, the pattern and magnitude of quasi-rents earned from using the machine, changes in its disposal value over time, the rate of interest, repair costs over time, and expectations entertained about replacement. All these factors should be considered by the entrepreneur in estimating the length of time the asset will be used and therefore the length of time over which he expects to depreciate the asset.

The principles just discussed deal with the determination of asset life in a subjective sense. The accountant may question the use of such asset lives as a basis for the determination of accounting data, which should reveal the actual course of events, and therefore actual asset life when that becomes known. Accounting data then become a basis for verifying the accuracy of expectations about asset life and for revealing errors in those expectations. This is, of course, the function to which we attached so much importance in Chapter II. The accountant has a valid point.

Pushed to its conclusion, this line of reasoning will reveal that asset life for accounting purposes cannot be known in advance but can only be revealed by actual events. It follows that asset life, as a basis for accounting computation, should be open-ended. This feature could be obtained in several ways; for example, by using the diminishing balance method or a straight-line method with a realistic disposal value which could itself be depreciated if asset life extended beyond expectations; but the appropriate approach is intimately related to the pattern of asset use, a matter to which we now turn.[8]

[8] In practice, of course, *useful life* has become that which is specified in Treasury regulations. In the early 1930's, after allowing business firms to establish whatever length of life they wished over which assets were to be depreciated for tax purposes, and even to alter this life almost at will, the Treasury began to regulate this matter carefully, establishing a list of average lives for fixed assets over which depreciation was to be charged for tax purposes. The first such table was

Pattern of Asset Services and Timing of Depreciation Charges

A fixed asset may yield its services as a simple function of time or of use, but it is more likely that a complex function of both would be necessary to identify properly the stream of asset services. We seek a measure for each period of the asset services actually used by the firm or permanently foregone. This measure would indicate the economic resources (fixed asset type) absorbed by the firm in conducting its business during the period. If the firm did not operate at all, for example, but some asset services elapse nevertheless, these resources are an economic cost of not operating and should be reflected in the firm's statement of loss.

If the stream of asset services was strictly a function of use or of time, a unique pattern could be established for the computation of depreciation charges. But usually at least some asset services are postponable and more may be conserved if higher maintenance costs are undertaken. Usually, too, the quantity of product that can be produced with a given asset can be extended with careful use and an appropriate repair and maintenance policy. The pattern of asset services is therefore not uniquely related to the asset but depends as well on the care and maintenance which the individual management feels is optimal.[9] If assets are appropriately classified, however, it is possible that deviations from "normal" use will have little effect on the pattern of asset services.

---

published as a supplement to the 1931 edition of the Treasury's Bulletin "F" while use of the table was made more or less mandatory by Treasury Decision 4422 in 1934, and the supplementary instructions which accompanied this document that signaled a major shift in Government policy toward depreciation. The list of average asset lives was then extended and amended in the Treasury's 1942 revision of Bulletin "F," *Income Tax Depreciation and Obsolescence—Estimated Useful Lives and Depreciation Rates,* revised January, 1942.

If actual asset lives tend to cluster around these averages, the error involved in using them for purposes of income determination could be quite small. The use of reasonable disposal values in conjunction with the estimated asset lives would make them quite workable, but in a sense, of course, unnecessary.

[9] It depends also on the particular use to which the asset is put. A truck used to haul logs in timber country is not likely to yield the same pattern of services as one used to haul produce over superhighways. Physically identical assets having sharply different uses should be placed in separate categories and treated as different assets, for example, logging trucks and produce trucks. How fine a distinction should be drawn is a matter of practicality.

The preceding discussion permits us to make an important theoretical point. If historic cost is to be allocated among the asset's services as time passes, it is necessary to know in advance the total stock of these services. Otherwise there can be no basis for apportionment. Current cost depreciation, on the other hand, requires in theory no such clairvoyance. We need only know the services used or foregone this period and the price this period of those services. A truly open-ended approach to the life of a fixed asset is therefore conceivable. True, the historic cost of these services would still be needed to measure realized cost savings, but current operating profit itself could be uniquely defined, and both the asset services used and the price this period could be compared with expectations.

FIXED INTERNAL RATES OF RETURN AND MARKET VALUES

But as a practical matter the quantification and valuation of asset services used is not a simple matter and we must fall back on estimated patterns as a basis for current cost as well as historic cost depreciation. For those fixed assets which have active second-hand markets the problem is not overly difficult. A pattern of service values can be obtained at any time by comparing the market values of assets of different ages or degrees of use. The differences so obtained, when related to the value of a new asset, yield the proportions of asset value which are normally used up or foregone in the various stages of asset life.[10] Even if second-hand markets operate only sporadically, a pattern can be obtained if it is reasonable to assume that the proportions we seek are fairly constant over time so that price changes affect proportionately the values of assets of different ages.

But even when patterns can be obtained in this way, the patterns appropriate to individual firms may deviate somewhat from the market pattern even though assets have been classified by type of use as well as by physical characteristics. As we have

[10] The question may arise as to whether this procedure yields current cost data or opportunity cost data. If installation (and transportation) costs are added to market values and these costs are independent of asset age, the differences obtained are not affected. The proportions derived would be smaller when computed against the current cost of the new asset but the service values which emerge would be the same. It is, of course, the current cost data which should be carried on the balance sheet until final disposal of the asset.

noted before, care and maintenance policies may differ, though market pressures should force all toward the optimal policy. To develop this and related points, we must delve a bit more deeply into the determination of relative market values and the asset-service pattern apparent in them.

Let us put aside supply considerations to examine the subjective valuations assigned by individual firms to assets of the same kind. What we want here are not subjective values as discussed in Chapter II but rather those hypothetical market values which would permit the firm to earn at a fixed internal rate of return if expectations are realized.[11] The internal rate is defined in such a way that by the end of the machine's life, the total depreciation plus scrap value is just equal to the original cost (and under our present assumptions of no price changes also the current cost) of the machine. Given the original cost, C, the estimated pattern of future quasi-rents $a, b, c, \ldots,$ and the estimated scrap value at the end of the machine's useful life, s, we solve for r, the internal rate of return, in the equation: [12]

$$C = \frac{a}{(1+r)} + \frac{b}{(1+r)^2} + \frac{c}{(1+r)^3} + \cdots + \frac{s}{(1+r)^n}.$$

This gives us the internal rate of return over the life of the asset which can be used to divide each quasi-rent into depreciation and income elements: The internal rate is applied to the book value of the machine each period (having deducted past depreciation allowances) in order to determine income of that period, and this income figure is then subtracted from the quasi-rent of the period to determine the depreciation charge, a residual.

Consider, for example, a three-year machine of constant efficiency, i.e., yielding a constant stream of quasi-rents, which costs $3,300, is expected to yield a quasi-rent of $1,484 in each of the three years of its life, and which is expected to have a scrap value of $300 at the end of its three-year life. Solving the equation above for r, given these values, we see that the internal rate of return is 20 per cent, and we can then establish our depreciation

[11] See, for example, G. A. D. Preinreich, "Annual Survey of Economic Theory: The Theory of Depreciation;" W. A. Paton, *Advanced Accounting*, p. 282; R. C. Jones, *Effects of Price Level Changes on Business Income, Capital, and Taxes*, especially 111–113.

[12] See Appendix A of Chapter II, equation (3).

pattern in accordance with the constant internal rate method as shown below.

	Period 1	2	3	Total
1. Book value of machine, beginning of period	$3,300	$2,476	$1,487	. . .
2. Expected quasi-rent	$1,487	$1,487	$1,487	$4,452
3. *less* Income from machine (20% of book value)	660	495	297	1,452
4. Depreciation charge	$ 824	$ 989	$1,187	$3,000
5. Scrap value				300
6. Original cost				$3,300

The logic of the fixed internal rate method of computing depreciation charges is that, at least under certain ideal conditions associated with long-run static equilibrium, the method should yield a book value for fixed assets which is equal to their market value at every point in their history. If transportation and installation charges are ignored, if the machine has a single use, and if all single enterprise firms who employ the machine are equally efficient, then the current cost of acquiring a one-year-old machine should be $2,476, and the current cost of acquiring a two-year-old machine should be $1,487. Arbitrage between the new machine and the used machine markets would tend to bring market values into conformity with the computed book values.

Suppose now that the maintenance policy implicit in this example is optimal but that another firm using the same machine mistakenly spends less on maintenance, increasing its quasi-rent by $13 but reducing the disposal value of its machine to $64. Because the policy is below optimum this firm earns a rate of return of only 18 per cent and its depreciation charges should appear as computed below. Its machine would bring less in the market after use than the machine optimally maintained.[13] In effect the firm conserves fewer machine services each period (and therefore uses or foregoes more) than the optimal firms.

[13] A firm's mistake might be over-maintenance rather than under-maintenance, in which case its depreciation charges would be less rather than greater than optimum.

	Period 1	2	3	Total
1. Book value of machine, beginning of period	$3,300	$2,394	$1,325	. . .
2. Expected quasi-rent	$1,500	$1,500	$1,500	$4,500
3. *less* Income from machine (18% of book value)	594	431	239	1,264
4. Depreciation charge	$ 906	$1,069	$1,261	$3,236
5. Scrap value				64
6. Original cost				$3,300

Market forces should cause the firm to adopt an optimal maintenance policy, but until this happens the depreciation pattern for this firm is given by the market values of its own asset but not by general market value relationships. If the individual deviations from the market value pattern are great, patterns may have to be determined by appraisal subject to occasional recheck. But if market forces are at all effective, reliance on the more objective market pattern will yield little error.

It might be thought that the internal rate method could be used to determine directly the depreciation pattern applicable to each firm and this position could be defended in principle if differences among firms were restricted to variances in maintenance policies. Unfortunately such is not the case. Assume, for example, that a firm uses the optimal replacement policy but is inefficient in its use of complementary factors of production. The market value of the firm's machine should not differ from the values assigned to machines of other firms, but the internal rate method would yield a different pattern. Assume that a firm wastes complementary material so that its quasi-rent falls to $1,236 per period. As it maintains its machine optimally, however, scrap value remains at $300. This firm earns 10 per cent on its investment. Its computed depreciation charges would be as shown below.

The depreciation pattern depicted differs considerably from that of the efficient firms (and from market value relationships if we assume that most firms are efficient), yet this firm is using the

	Period 1	Period 2	Period 3	Total
1. Book value of machine, beginning of period	$3,300	$2,394	$1,396	. . .
2. Expected quasi-rent	$1,236	$1,236	$1,236	$3,708
3. *less* Income from machine (10% of book value)	330	238	140	708
4. Depreciation charge	$ 906	$ 998	$1,096	$3,000
5. Scrap value				300
6. Original cost				$3,300

same machine services having the same market value as those used by its efficient competitors. If the firm depreciated according to the market pattern, a declining rate of return would be revealed which should induce the firm to employ only new assets (a paradoxical result). A comparison with other firms would reveal inefficiency and should lead to corrective measures.

It is market values, then, that measure the value of resources used in the firm and it is the relationships among them that reveal the depreciation pattern to be applied to either the historic cost or current cost base. The estimation of such a pattern may require recourse to various approximations in the absence of second-hand markets. The internal rate approximation suffers not only from the defect discussed above but also from the fact that, when applied by management, it is highly subjective in nature. A dishonest management could select an arbitrarily low rate of return in an effort to postpone tax payments, for example, and proof of fraud would be difficult to find.

In the absence of market relationships, reliance may have to be placed on occasional appraisals. These would be used to obtain a depreciation pattern, not to obtain current values though they would undoubtedly be involved in the estimation. Thus appraisals would not have to be periodic. Estimates of tax authorities or of independent auditors might be used. If the internal rate method is used, the actual rate of return earned by the firm in recent years could be employed if there is reason to feel that this is applicable to assets currently being depreciated. Perhaps the average rate earned by the industry would yield a better approximation. In exceptional circumstances, and upon adequate evidence, individual deviations from generalized patterns might be allowed.

CONSTANT, INCREASING, AND DECREASING EFFICIENCY

The nature of generalized patterns of asset service values can be briefly explored here on a theoretical plane assuming that firms of equal efficiency employ identical assets in the same use so that internal rate depreciation equals market depreciation. The constant efficiency asset such as that considered above, a phenomenon which is surely rare but which might apply to railroad tracks for example, should be subject to increasing depreciation charges over its lifetime according to the fixed internal rate method.

Most assets, however, are probably of the declining efficiency type; quasi-rents decrease over time not only because of wear and tear and consequent increases in repair costs but also because obsolescence may injure a firm's relative position in a market. If quasi-rents fall only moderately over the life of the asset, the straight-line method of determining depreciation charges may be the appropriate pattern, as in the example below.

	Period 1	Period 2	Period 3	Total
1. Book value of machine, beginning of period	$3,300	$2,300	$1,300	. . .
2. Expected quasi-rent	$1,660	$1,460	$1,260	$3,380
3. *less* Income from machine (20% of book value)	660	460	260	1,380
4. Depreciation charge	$1,000	$1,000	$1,000	$3,000
5. Scrap value				300
6. Original cost				$3,300

This assumption about the efficiency path of (all) fixed assets was effectively written into Treasury regulations on depreciation procedures in 1934. For while a corporation was free under the regulations to propose to the Treasury any depreciation pattern it wished, if the pattern deviated from straight-line depreciation, "the burden of sustaining the deductions [rested] squarely upon the taxpayers."[14] There can be little doubt but that the "burden" proved to be heavy, and that between 1934 and 1954 most of the depreciation charges by American business firms, for tax purposes as well as for final statements, were based on the straight-line method using the Treasury list of average lives of fixed assets.[15]

In 1954 Congress altered the Treasury's rather rigid policy of adherence to straight-line depreciation by giving business firms the option to choose any pattern for recovering historic cost they wished, so long as the cumulative charge did not exceed that which would be provided by the "double-rate declining balance method," wherein twice the straight-line rate is applied to the book value of the asset each year (rather than to original cost). This method provides for more rapid acceleration of depreciation charges than any of the other standard methods involving decreasing charges over the life of the machine. The most common method of accelerating depreciation charges, used widely in England and countries of the British Commonwealth over many years, and in this country, for example, by the petroleum industry for depreciation of pipe lines carrying oil, is the diminishing balance method; a fixed percentage rate is applied to the book value of the asset at the beginning of each period, which just exhausts depreciable cost over the life of the asset. The formula which yields this result is the following:

$$R = 1 - \sqrt[n]{\frac{s}{C}},$$

where s again denotes scrap value, C denotes original cost, and n denotes the number of periods over which depreciation is to be taken. An alternative method of accelerating depreciation charges, commonly discussed and used more and more since the 1954 change in tax regulations, is the sum-of-the-year digits method, wherein the depreciation charge each year is a declining percentage of original cost (rather than a fixed percentage of declining book value). If n again denotes service life, and d the number of periods remaining to be depreciated (including the

---

[14] L. H. Kimmel, *op. cit.*, p. 20.

[15] See, for example, E. L. Grant and P. T. Norton, Jr., *Depreciation*, pp. 89–91.

present one), the percentage rate to be applied each year is computed as follows:

$$R = \frac{2d}{n\,(1+n)}.$$

The following illustration shows the extent to which quasi-rents must be assumed to fall over time to justify the simple declining balance method, which generally accelerates depreciation charges more than the sum-of-the-year digits method, but less than the double declining balance method.

	Period 1	Period 2	Period 3	Total
1. Book value of machine, beginning of period	$3,300	$1,485	$668	. . .
2. Expected quasi-rent	$2,475	$1,114	$502	$4,091
3. *less* Income from machine (20% of book value)	660	297	134	1,091
4. Depreciation charge (55% of book value)	$1,815	$ 817	$368	$3,000
5. Scrap value				300
6. Original cost				$3,300

Too great a concern with market patterns for individual assets is possible. A firm usually operates with many assets. If the firm has reached a point of stable size, if its stock of fixed assets has an even-age distribution, and if there are no price changes, the total depreciation charge for the firm is independent of the individual asset pattern. An accelerated method will yield the same total as the straight-line method, or as an increasing charge method. In the case of an accelerated technique, for example, high charges on new assets will be compensated by low charges on old assets yielding a total charge equal to that obtained with the straight-line, or any other, technique. The pattern of asset use is immaterial in this case.

When growth is admitted to the picture, however, the individual asset-service pattern again assumes importance. A growing firm will employ relatively newer assets than will the stationary firm (it is by definition adding more new assets each year than it is losing in old assets). An accelerated technique will now yield larger total charges than the straight-line method because the (many) newer assets are depreciated more heavily than the (fewer) older assets.

This effect has been used to justify the acceleration of depreciation charges whether the acceleration is warranted by the service pattern of the asset or not. It is argued that the effect will be to stimulate growth, and compensate for price increases if these occur. The first consideration may be a perfectly sound one, but it has nothing whatsoever to do with income determination and can be accomplished without affecting income measurement, which we feel plays an important role in decision-making. But what then of the second consideration?

ACCELERATION TO COMPENSATE FOR PRICE CHANGES

If we employ some form of declining balance depreciation rather than a straight-line rate, if the asset is actually of the moderately declining efficiency type, and if the asset is rising in price, the accelerated depreciation method does increase the total depreciation charge. The historic costs of the newer assets, which are depreciated most heavily, will exceed the historic costs of the older assets. Total depreciation using the accelerated technique will exceed total depreciation by any less accelerated method, whether the firm is growing or not. Growth, of course, will increase the accelerated charge relatively more than the less accelerated charge, making the discrepancy even greater. If the price of this type of fixed asset rises steadily, the increased charges are in the right direction to state costs in terms of current costs year after year, but only happenstance could make the arbitrary charge equal to current cost depreciation. It is almost a certainty that the arbitrary charge will either overstate or understate the current cost amount, and the overstatement, if it occurs, may exceed the understatement yielded under these circumstances by the straight-line method.[16]

[16] For detailed examples and more extensive discussion of the effects of acceleration for growing, stable, and declining firms, see E. O. Edwards, "Depreciation and the Maintenance of Real Capital," in J. L. Mey, *op. cit.*, and the references contained therein.

The use of accelerated depreciation methods as a means of attacking the problems engendered by changing prices of fixed assets, however, has another important limitation, one which we feel completely destroys the possibilities of utilizing such a technique as a substitute for current cost data. Even if by some odd stroke of fate or through some remarkably expert forecasting, accelerated charges did closely approximate the current cost of using fixed assets, nowhere in the firm's records would there be recognized the cost savings generated by holding and using assets which had risen in price. We would have something exactly analogous to the use of LIFO inventory valuation as a substitute for full current cost pricing of materials used. Operating profit might be stated accurately, although it is difficult to imagine that it would work out in just this way; but even then there would be no recognition of realizable cost savings accrued, nor of the realization of cost savings as the assets were used. And clearly balance sheet values, as in the case of LIFO, would be badly distorted.

We are driven to the same conclusion that we reached in the case of inventory valuation procedures. We need a method of valuing fixed assets and allowing for depreciation which will permit us to develop a full statement of total profit, with proper separation of its components, as well as provide accurate values for the balance sheet. We return, then, to the central depreciation problem: Whatever the appropriate depreciation pattern, against what base should it be applied and by what technique?

Adjusting for Price Changes: The Current Cost Method

A current cost method of handling fixed assets and depreciation expense can be devised along lines analogous to the procedure developed in Chapter V for the handling of inventories and the cost of materials used. Again we use only end-of-period adjustments in the accounts, and again we keep track of both historic costs and current costs separately, providing full information on each in our final statements. We need both types of data, of course, to compute realized profit. But that consideration aside, it is perhaps particularly important in the case of fixed assets to furnish data on historic as well as current costs, for the element of estimate in the latter may be considerably more significant than in the case of inventories.

Computing Current Costs

The accountant who assumes the task of estimating a future pattern of market values and / or a future stream of quasi-rents on a fixed asset, in order to determine a general pattern for the timing of depreciation charges over the asset's useful life, and who then accepts a procedure which at best is an arbitrary approximation of an assumed relationship between depreciation charges and quasi-rents, or of the change in market value over time, may shudder at the prospect of determining current values for fixed assets, even when historic costs are to be retained in the accounts. Visions are called forth of the era between 1918 and 1934, when corporations frequently wrote up or wrote down the value of fixed assets on the balance sheet by some arbitrary amount and altered depreciation charges accordingly. Often the revaluations made then seemed to have more to do with influencing the value of the company's securities on the stock exchange or with controlling dividend payments than with efforts to take account of changing prices in order to obtain a meaningful statement of profit.[17] The business climate, as well as the information available for making objective judgments on current values, has changed since the 1920's, however; and now, unlike the period prior to 1934, historic costs are not to be abandoned in accounting records according to our system. How, then, can the current values of fixed assets best be determined?

Some types of fixed assets are marketed continuously as new products and are subject to little technical change. The current purchase price of such assets new, at the end of a period, may be obtained in the same way as the current purchase price of raw

---

[17] For an excellent treatise on business accounting practices in this respect between 1919 and 1934, see S. Fabricant, *Capital Consumption and Adjustment,* especially Chapters 4 and 12. Revaluations were especially common during the boom and subsequent depression of 1921–1922, but Fabricant shows that in his sample of 272 large corporations for the period 1925–1934, there were 345 revisions, or on the average each corporation did it nearly 1.3 times. Very few, if any, corporations practiced revisions annually, but a great many revalued at infrequent intervals. *Ibid.,* p. 215.

materials, by a telephone call or by arrangement for a year-end statement from the selling company. And assuming the accuracy of the depreciation method used, the current cost of a used fixed asset can then be derived by taking depreciation on the new (current cost value) base. But obviously this simple procedure will not be possible for assets built to individual specification, or for assets subject to marked technological change. A specially designed warehouse building, or assembly line layout, clearly has no readily obtainable new purchase price which can be used as a base for current cost depreciation. Nor can a construction firm which still uses a steam-powered steam shovel ascertain the exact cost of a new one if such equipment is no longer manufactured. The cost of a new electric or diesel-powered shovel might serve as a reasonable approximation of what a new steam shovel would cost today, or it might not; if the quality changes are significant (as we would expect them to be in this case), it will be misleading to use the price of the new, improved substitute product as a basis for determining the current cost of using the old one.[18]

Where no market exists for new fixed assets of the type used by the firm, two means of measuring current costs are available: (1) appraisal, and (2) the use of price index numbers for like fixed assets to adjust the original cost base to the level which would now have to be paid to purchase the asset in question. For some major asset items which are a complex and specialized

[18] It must be remembered that it is not the current cost of equivalent services provided by the fixed asset over some time period which we wish to measure, but the current cost of using the particular fixed asset which the entrepreneur chose to adopt and is still using. It is that particular decision that the entrepreneur wishes to evaluate on the basis of accounting data. It may well be that he then may wish to compare these data with opportunity cost data relating to selling and / or replacing the fixed asset, but in order to make this decision about the future, he must have information about the actual present and past. This position on fixed asset depreciation conforms to the approach to profit measurement developed in Chapters II and III. The position that accounting data on depreciation be based on replacement-cost-of-service was once espoused by Bain. See, for example, J. S. Bain, "The Profit Rate as a Measure of Monopoly Power," p. 280. Any profit rate based on such opportunity costs, however, could in our opinion provide an extremely misleading impression of actual monopoly power. In his more recent work, Bain seems to have given up any concept of current costs at all (for further discussion, see footnote 15 at the end of the section on rates of return in Chapter VIII, below).

bundle of different types of materials, a factory plant for example, periodic appraisal by independent experts every five years or so might be in order, with the adjustment of current cost values during the interim years made on the basis of changes in a general construction cost price index, or some special composite of price index numbers worked out by the appraisers. For most assets which do not have a current market purchase value, however, it should be feasible to estimate current values on the basis of one or another of various price indexes compiled by either the Department of Labor or the Department of Commerce. The Bureau of Labor Statistics compiles an index of wholesale prices which is at present based on the prices of over 1,800 separate items, but more useful for our purposes are the Bureau's composite indexes for various groups and subgroups of fixed assets, in particular, machinery and motive products (with separate indexes for agricultural machinery, construction machinery, electrical machinery, metalworking machinery, and general purpose machinery), and metals and metal products (with a separate index for heating equipment). These indexes are published monthly, usually with a lag of only one month but sometimes of two months, i.e., the maximum delay is for December figures to be reported in the February issue of the *Monthly Labor Review*. The Department of Commerce publishes various indexes of construction costs, including their own composite index, with the same degree of lag. Further, in order to express the main components of gross national product in real terms, the Department of Commerce develops a more general index (price deflator series) for the two major types of producer fixed assets: producers' durable equipment and new construction. And these are available for each quarter in the middle month of the next quarter.

The use of indexes such as those above to adjust known historic costs in order to estimate current costs of purchase implies the necessity of individual judgment, of course. So, too, does the estimation of an asset life and the establishment of a pattern for depreciation charges over the life of the asset. But we believe that (1) the derivation of current cost values for fixed assets can be accomplished on a consistent and objective basis with the information now available; (2) the quality of the information and the speed of reporting should improve if there is more extensive use of the data; (3) such estimates would be necessary only for some of the fixed assets held by the firm, i.e., only for those assets not currently marketed; (4) historic costs would be retained in the accounts; and (5), as shown in figure 1 of Chapter I and in the first section of this chapter, adjustment on the basis of such indexes would make a substantial difference in the information available to managers and outsiders on operating gains and holding gains—for the decade 1947–1949 to 1957–1959, prices in general rose by only 15–18 per cent, but construction costs increased by 40 per cent, and the price of machinery rose by 50–70 per cent.[19]

All of these considerations taken together, we suggest, justify and indeed demand the accumulation of current cost data on fixed assets. How then are we to use such data in deriving profit figures and balance sheet values?

Profit Components and Balance Sheet Values

For the sake of simplicity of explanation, let us assume that our hypothetical XYZ Corporation treated in Chapter V has a composite of fixed assets which can be treated as having a 20-year life and which is depreciated on a straight-line basis. We could consider this to be a group of machines purchased at different times and depreciated on a group basis, or simply as a single machine or group of machines all purchased at the same time. We shall choose the latter assumption to avoid making the illustration unduly cumbersome; the principles involved are identical, and what can be applied to depreciation on an item method can be applied to depreciation by the group method. Finally, we will assume that no machines are bought or sold during the period; in Chapter VII we treat the case of a capital gain realized through the sale of securities, and the sale of machinery would be handled in analogous fashion.

The original cost of the machinery, purchased at the begin-

[19] If an asset is truly outmoded, the accountant might have to rely on present costs (a concept developed early in Chapter III) as a substitute for current costs. For such assets, whose long-run use is clearly not even possible, present costs as a balance sheet valuation (properly labeled, of course) might even be more meaningful, as indicated later in Chapter III.

ning of 1951, was \$2,000. It is a type of machinery which is not traded regularly on second-hand markets of any kind so that we choose to measure current cost value on the basis of changes in the index number of prices on machinery of a comparable type; this index, according to the Bureau of Labor Statistics, stood at 120 at the beginning of 1951 (1947–1949 = 100) and at 180 at the end of 1959 (the approximate change in the price index for metalworking machinery over this period, as can be seen from figure 1). By the end of 1960 we assume that the index has increased to 204. Thus the current cost value of new machinery of this type at the beginning of 1960 is estimated to be \$3,000 [\$2,000 + (60/120) · \$2,000], while at the end of the year the current cost value is estimated to be \$3,400 [\$2,000 + (84/120) · \$2,000].

As in the case of inventories, the current cost of using this machinery during 1960 can be computed directly as $\frac{1}{20}$ of the average current cost value during the year. Here there is no averaging problem such as we met with inventories, and we simply multiply $\frac{1}{20}$ times \$3,200 to obtain a current cost of use of \$160. This is the figure for depreciation which must be subtracted from sales to yield current operating profit. And the excess of current cost depreciation over the historic cost depreciation of \$100, i.e., \$60, is the total cost saving realized during the year by having purchased an asset at a price lower than that prevailing at the time asset services were used.

Realizable cost savings accruing during the year can be computed most simply by assuming that $\frac{11}{20}$ of the original stock of machinery, the proportion available for use at the beginning of the period after nine years of life have expired, is held for half of the year while the price of new machinery rose by \$200; and that only $\frac{10}{20}$ of our original stock of machinery is held over the second half of the year while new prices again rose by \$200. This is analogous to the second inventory method treated in the section on current costs in Chapter V; the initial stock of machinery is assumed to be held over the first half of the year, and the final stock of machinery is assumed to be held over the second half of the year. Total realizable cost savings which accrue during the year are computed according to this method as follows:[20]

Realizable cost savings on the initial stock of machinery while the price of new machinery rose from

$$\$3{,}000 \text{ to } \$3{,}200: \qquad \frac{11}{20} \cdot (\$3{,}200 - \$3{,}000) = \$110$$

Realizable cost savings on the final stock of machinery while the price of new machinery rose from

$$\$3{,}200 \text{ to } \$3{,}400: \qquad \frac{10}{20} \cdot (\$3{,}400 - \$3{,}200) = 100$$

Total realizable cost savings $210

Now the realizable cost savings which accrue in any period must be amortized over the life of the asset on the assumption that it is to be held to the end of its service life. In other words, these gains are realized as the asset is used, and if it is used (depreciated) on a straight-line basis, then the gains will be amortized on a straight-line basis. The depreciation of our asset and its effect upon balance sheet values from the beginning of 1960 to the end of its service life in December 1970, on the basis of events during 1960 and before, are depicted in table 12.

There is $550 initially in the Unrealized Cost Savings account (later to be called Unrealized Surplus account) because machinery which originally cost $2,000 has a current purchase price at the beginning of 1960 of $3,000 and $\frac{11}{20}$ of its life remains $\left(\frac{11}{20} \cdot \$1{,}000 = \$550\right)$. These cost savings are amortized at the rate of $50 a year over the 11 years of service life remaining. This

[20] Alternatively, we arrive at the same figure by reasoning that, had we held the 11/20 of our original stock of machinery throughout the period, we would have accrued a realizable cost saving of $220 [($3,400 – $3,000) · 11/20]. But in fact we used up 1/20 of the stock at the average price of $3,200 during the year and so did not accrue cost savings on this portion of our initial stock to the extent that the price at the end of the year exceeded this average price, i.e., from $220 we must deduct 1/20 ($3,400 – $3,200) = $10, leaving the same net realizable cost savings actually accrued of $210. This method of computing the realizable cost savings on machinery is analogous to the first inventory method described in Chapter V.

TABLE 12

THE DEPRECIATION PATTERN FOR THE FIXED ASSETS OF THE XYZ CORPORATION

	1960 Beginning-of-year		1960		1960 End-of-year		1961–1970[a]	
			Events newly realizable	Events realized			Realized each year	Ten-year total
Original cost	$2,000				$2,000			
Historic cost depreciation	900			$100	1,000		$100	$1,000
Depreciated historic cost value		$1,100				$1,000		
Cost savings								
a) initial unrealized		550	...	50		500	50	500
b) accruing on initial stock		...	$110	10		100	10	100
c) accruing on final stock		...	100	...		100	10	100
Current cost value, beginning of 1960		$1,650						
plus Total realizable cost savings accruing during 1960			$210					
less Current cost depreciation for 1960				$160				
equals Current cost value, end of 1960						$1,700		
less 10-year current cost depreciation								$1,700
equals Current cost value, end of 1970								0

[a] On the assumption that there are no further changes in the price of fixed assets.

total of \$550 is also the amount which must be added to the depreciated historic cost value of the asset at the beginning of 1960 to obtain its current cost value, which is $\frac{11}{20} \cdot \$3{,}000$, or \$1,650.

During 1960 new realizable cost savings accrue amounting to \$210 as already shown. The portion accruing on the *initial stock* of assets must be amortized over 11 years, so that \$10 of this \$110 is realized in 1960, the other \$100 being carried over as unrealized cost savings, to be amortized at \$10 a year for each of the 10 years of life remaining after 1960. The portion of realizable cost savings accruing on the *final stock* of assets, amounting to \$100, is amortized only over the 10 years 1961 to 1970 at \$10 a year. The current cost depreciation figure, which was arrived at above by taking $\frac{1}{20}$ of the average current cost value during the year of \$3,200, is seen to be also the sum of historic cost depreciation plus cost savings realized through use of the asset. This follows of course from the definition of realized cost savings: The asset services used up had a current value of \$160 but cost the firm only \$100, so the difference is the amount of cost savings realized through use.

Finally, table 12 shows how the current cost value of the fixed asset changes over time when prices change. To the initial current value at the beginning of 1960 of \$1,650 are added all the realizable cost savings which accrue because of the rise in price of the asset. From this valuation adjustment we must deduct the decrease in value because of use over the period (depreciation at current cost) to obtain the current cost value of the asset which remains at the end of the period. If there are no further price changes after 1960, this current cost value of \$1,700 (the amount of historic cost depreciation remaining plus the unrealized cost savings which have accrued in the past and are still to be realized) will be used up over the remaining 10 years of the asset's life at \$170 a year.

Before turning to the end-of-period adjustments which must actually be made in the accounts to arrive at these results, one point deserves special emphasis although it is peripheral to the main theme of this book. If price changes occur during the life of a fixed asset, the cumulative amount of the depreciation charges on a current cost basis will not normally equal the replacement cost of the machinery at the end of service life. If prices rise during the lifetime of the machinery, the cumulative depreciation charge will always be less than the replacement cost.[21] For the cumulative charge to equal the actual cost of replacement, depreciation would have to be charged on a replacement cost base throughout its life; ultimate replacement cost must be exactly anticipated.

There is no reason, however, why the cumulative charge should equal replacement cost. Any assumption of such a relationship appears to be related to the old fallacy that depreciation automatically provides funds for replacement. A correct statement of income may aid management in the making of replacement decisions, but this would seem to be the only direct interdependency which should exist between the determining of depreciation charges and the replacement of fixed assets. Replacement is clearly not automatic, and will often be made by purchasing an asset which differs substantially from the existing one. During the life of the asset, management has had access to funds, as a result of deducting current cost depreciation, which are in excess of the funds which would have been acquired on the basis of historic cost depreciation if prices are rising. Such earnings may be more than or less than sufficient for purposes of replacement, depending upon the exact pattern of price changes and the skill of management in using the earnings during the interim period. Continuous investment of income-covered depreciation funds in like assets, for example, will insure that the firm can always maintain its stock of machines.[22]

---

[21] In our example, suppose that the rise in price of new machinery before the beginning of 1960 all occurred on the day after the machinery was purchased. Current cost depreciation would be at the rate of $150 a year for 20 years, and if there had been no further price changes, this would just cumulate to the replacement cost of $3,000. But with any subsequent price rises during the life of the asset, this will not be true. If prices rise only during the year 1960 and are unchanged thereafter, cumulative current cost depreciation at the end of the asset's life in our example would amount to $3,210 ($150 · 9 + $160 · 1 + $170 · 10), which would be $190 short of the replacement cost of $3,400 at the end of 1970.

[22] See the excellent article on this matter by W. P. Trumbull, "Price-Level Depreciation and Replacement Cost."

But any attempt to link depreciation charges directly to replacement needs automatically negates efforts to obtain a realistic and useful measure of business income. There are other ways in which business firms and/or Government can seek to influence replacement and growth, ways which will not have the detrimental effect of misallocating resources in the economy in the manner that distortion of incomes misallocates resources, as we try to illustrate in the next chapter.

Introducing Current Costs into the Accounts

At the end of 1960 before any adjustments are made for the depreciation of fixed assets, the relevant ledger accounts of the XYZ Corporation were as follows (again HC denotes historic cost and CC_b denotes current cost at the beginning of the period):

Fixed Assets (Machinery) at Historic Cost

Initial balance at HC	2000		

Allowance for Depreciation at Historic Cost

		Initial balance at HC	900

Fixed Asset Valuation Adjustment

Initial balance, $CC_b - HC$	550		

Depreciation

Realizable Cost Savings

Unrealized Cost Savings

		Initial balance	550

Realized Cost Savings

The initial entries in these accounts should be clear from the discussion of the information in table 12.

The journal entries we suggest as end-of-period adjustments in order to keep track both of current costs and of historic costs on fixed assets are as follows:

(1) Fixed Asset Valuation Adjustment	210	
Realizable Cost Savings		210
To record the increase in the value of fixed assets and the related cost savings accruing:		
(a) on the initial stock of assets to year-average $\left[\frac{11}{20} \cdot (\$3{,}200 - \$3{,}000) = \$110\right]$ and		
(b) on the final stock from year-average to year-end $\left[\frac{10}{20} \cdot (\$3{,}400 - \$3{,}200) = \$100\right]$.		
(2) Depreciation	100	
Allowance for Depreciation		100
To record depreciation at historic cost $\left[\frac{1}{20} \cdot \$2{,}000 = \$100\right]$.		
(3) Depreciation	60	
Fixed Asset Valuation Adjustment		60
To adjust depreciation to current cost by depreciating the excess of current cost over historic cost at average prices of the year $\left[\frac{1}{20} \cdot (\$3{,}200 - \$2{,}000) = \$60\right]$.		
(4) Current Operating Profit	160	
Depreciation		160
To transfer current cost depreciation to Current Operating Profit.		
(5) Realizable Cost Savings	210	
Unrealized Cost Savings		210
To transfer realizable cost savings. (The credit would normally go to Business Profit and thence to Unrealized Surplus as shown more fully in Chapter VII.)		
(6) Unrealized Cost Savings	60	
Realized Cost Savings		60
To transfer the amount of cost savings which are realized during the period.		
(7) Realized Cost Savings	60	
Realized Profit		60
To transfer realized cost savings.		

When these adjusting entries have been recorded and the accounts closed, the relevant ledger accounts would appear as follows (CC_e denotes current cost at the end of the period, and AP_c denotes average current price during the period):

Fixed Assets (Machinery) at Historic Cost

Initial balance at HC	2000	To balance	2000
Balance at HC	2000		

Allowance for Depreciation at Historic Cost

To balance	1000	Initial balance at HC	900
		(2) Expense this period, HC	100
	1000		1000
		Balance at HC	1000

Depreciation

(2) Expense at HC	100	(4) To COP	160
(3) Adjusted to CC	60		
	160		160

Fixed Asset Valuation Adjustment

Initial balance, $CC_b - HC$	550	(3) To dajust HC depreciation	60
(1) On initial stock, $AP_c - CC_b$	110	To balance	700
(1) On final stock, $CC_e - AP_c$	100		
	760		760
Balance, $CC_e - HC$	700		

Realizable Cost Savings

(5) To Unrealized CS	210	(1) On fixed assets	210

Unrealized Cost Savings

(6) Realized during period	60	Initial balance, $CC_b - HC$	550
To balance	700	(5) Realizable during period	210
	760		760
		Unrealized Cost Savings, end of year, $CC_e - HC$	700

Realized Cost Savings

(7) To Realized Profit	60	(6) Realized during period	60

We have, then, everything that we need. The current cost value of the fixed assets at the end of the period is the amount in the Fixed Asset (Machinery) account ($2,000) less the balance in the Allowance for Depreciation account ($1,000) plus the balance in the Fixed Asset Valuation Adjustment account ($700), or $1,700. The current cost of using the assets during the period ($160) is given in the Depreciation account which is closed to Current Operating Profit and thus deducted from sales revenues at current prices. But the excess of current cost depreciation over historic cost depreciation is recorded in the Realized Cost Savings account, which is closed to Realized Profit. This amount, then, is added to Current Operating Profit to obtain Realized Profit, i.e., we do not simply lose track of this holding gain but rather record it separately for what it is. Finally, the balance in the Unrealized Cost Savings account, which consists of the initial balance plus gains which have become realizable during the period less gains which have been realized during the period yields the amount which is to be amortized over the remaining 10 years of life of the asset on a straight-line basis, i.e., at $70 a year.

Comparison of Profit Concepts

We can compare briefly the three concepts of (gross) profit as they relate to the using up of fixed assets, as we did for the case of the using up of raw materials in Chapter V. Again sales are assumed to be $4,000, and we have then the following:

The Accounting Profit Concept

Sales (at current prices)	$4000	
less Depreciation expense (at historic cost)	100	
Accounting profit		$3900

The Realized Profit Concept

Sales (at current prices)	$4000	
less Depreciation expense (at current cost)	160	
Current operating profit		$3840
Realized cost savings		60
(Excess of current over historic cost depreciation)		
Realized profit		$3900

The Business Profit Concept

Sales (at current prices)	$4000	
less Depreciation expense (at current cost)	160	
Current operating profit		$3840
Realizable cost savings		210
Business profit		$4050

It would be tedious to extend the discussion of the differences among these profit concepts at this stage; all that was said about the differences with respect to inventories and the cost of using raw materials applies to the case of fixed assets and depreciation expense as well. We shall proceed with the other adjustments necessary for full statements of profit and of position and then comment upon the significance and utility of the flexible current cost–historic cost approach as a whole.

VII *Concepts of Money Profit:*

THE FUNDAMENTAL ROLE OF INDIVIDUAL PRICE CHANGES

With the computations of the cost of materials used and depreciation expense completed and the related asset valuations established, the principal steps necessary for the presentation of fundamental statements in terms of current costs have been taken. For many remaining revenue and expense items, current cost and historic cost coincide and only minor adjustments of regularly collected data are required. With the recognition of some other realizable cost savings and the adjustment of the related asset valuations, the basic statements can be prepared and the end-of-period adjustment process, which would develop the required data in the formal accounts, demonstrated. The usefulness of the flexible data which are the end result can then be more carefully appraised.

Treatment of Money Claims

The current cost adjustments for assets other than those discussed in the preceding two chapters, and for liabilities, follow the principles already established. These assets and liabilities are mainly money claims of one kind or another. We shall distinguish and discuss briefly three kinds of claims of this type, namely, cash (with which we shall group other short-term money claims such as accounts and notes receivable and payable), stocks, and bonds. Current values for these items are usually readily obtainable and any aversion to current costs cannot be rationalized on the grounds that price data are subjective in nature.

Cash and Other Short-Term Claims

Cash requires no adjustment for current cost statements. It is by definition stated in current money values. Price level movements, introduced in Chapter VIII, will occasion adjustment, but none is needed for present purposes. In effect, the current value of cash is equal to its historic cost and no departure is possible.

Accounts receivable and payable, unlike cash, have no ready marketability, but they are so short-term in nature that it seems reasonable to classify them with cash as having a current value which is fixed in money terms.

Notes receivable (including short-term government securities) and notes payable are more readily marketable (at least current values can be easily assigned to them, given the current market rate of interest), but the gains and losses made on such short-term securities are usually too small to warrant adjustment to current values. Generally speaking, these can be safely classed with cash as having current values which are fixed in money terms. If the values of short-term assets and/or liabilities do fluctuate seriously, the adjustment procedure spelled out below for bonds could also be applied to notes.[1]

---

[1] An adjustment to current value should not be confused with an interest adjustment following from the fact that accounts and notes, unlike cash, represent dated values. An account or note receivable of $100 due in 60 days is presently worth more than a note receivable of $100 due in one year, given the interest rate. The reduction in the excess of the amount receivable over its present value as the maturity date is approached can be regarded as accrued interest receivable (a new receivable) rather than an increase in the value of the original receivable. In any event keeping track of this interest adjustment does not imply keeping track of current values. The latter depend on the current rate of interest.

Take as an example a 6 per cent, $100, 60-day discounted note, which would

Securities Promising No Fixed Return

If a company invests funds in common stocks as a speculation, it is clearly buying an asset whose current value can fluctuate and whose return is subject to the periodic decisions of the boards of directors of the issuing companies.[2] Such securities will usually give rise to positive or negative realizable cost savings as time passes and, when sold, will yield realized capital gains. It is probably immaterial whether such securities are valued at opportunity costs (current market price less commissions) or at current costs (current market price plus commissions) because the difference (commissions) is so small. Indeed, if commissions are treated as a current expense when incurred, the two become identical to market price. The important question is how to handle the changes in market price which occur.

Let us assume that at the beginning of a period a firm holds a group of such securities having a historic cost of $200,000 and a current cost of $272,000. The relevant accounts would appear as follows:

Securities

At cost	200,000		

Security Valuation Adjustment

Balance	72,000		

Unrealized Cost Savings

		Balance	72,000

We shall assume the following events during the period:

1. Securities rise in value to $274,000 at mid-year.
2. Securities costing $18,000 are sold at mid-year for $30,000.

---

have a present value of $99. This present value would gradually increase over 60 days to $100, yielding a pattern of discounted historic costs. If the market rate of interest on such notes was also 6 per cent throughout this period, current values and historic costs would coincide. But if the current interest rate rose to 7 per cent during the 60-day period the current value of the note at that time would be less than its historic cost. It is the spread between current and historic cost which concerns us.

[2] Purchasing power bonds would also fall in this group. Although board discretion is restricted, the money amount paid is currently determined. Deflation for price level changes should reveal the constant real amount promised.

3. The remaining securities, with a current value of $244,000 at mid-year, rise in value to $248,000 by year end.

The sale would be recorded at time of sale under established practice as follows:

(1960) Cash	30,000	
Securities		18,000
Realized Capital Gains		12,000
To record the sale of securities and the associated gain.		

At the end of the period adjustments to current cost would be made as follows:

(1) Security Valuation Adjustment	6,000	
Realizable Cost Savings		6,000
To record increases in the value of securities held during the year and the related cost savings accruing. The amount includes the rise in value from $272,000 to $274,000 on the initial stock and the rise in value from $244,000 to $248,000 on securties held after sale.		
(2) Realizable Cost Savings	6,000	
Unrealized Cost Savings		6,000
To transfer realizable cost savings. (The credit would normally reach this account via the Business Profit account.)		
(3) Unrealized Cost Savings	12,000	
Security Valuation Adjustment		12,000
To relieve both accounts of amounts realized during the period.		

The relevant accounts would appear as follows:

Securities

Balance	200,000	1960	18,000
		To balance	182,000
	200,000		200,000
Balance	182,000		

Security Valuation Adjustment

Balance	72,000	(3) Amount realized	12,000
(1)	6,000	To balance	66,000
	78,000		78,000
Balance	66,000		

Realized Capital Gains

To Realized Profit	12,000	1960	12,000

Realizable Cost Savings

(2) To the unrealized account	6,000	(1)	6,000
[normally via Business Profit]			

Unrealized Cost Savings

(3) Amount realized	12,000	Balance	72,000
To balance	66,000	(2)	6,000
	78,000		78,000
		Balance	66,000

This series of entries is mainly self-explanatory. Entry (3) differs from its counterpart in earlier chapters (see, for example, Entry (9) in Chapter V) because the credit to Realized Capital Gains has in this case been made during the normal course of events whereas the record of realized cost savings needed in those chapters had not been regularly recorded.

The only other explanatory note needed regards the omission of any adjustment to dividend income on the securities owned. As the amount involved is declared currently, it can scarcely require adjustment to put it in terms of current values. The situation is less simple, however, in the case of fixed income securities which are discussed in the next section.

Fixed Return Securities

Bonds receivable and payable can fluctuate in value, but an additional complication enters the picture because the periodic receipts or payments are contractual; i.e., they are not currently declared.[3] The procedure for handling bond investments on a current cost basis is similar to the treatment accorded bonds payable when the appropriate changes in sign are recognized. We shall set forth the procedure for bonds payable only.

Assume that a firm sold $600,000 worth of 4 per cent, five-year bonds at par three and one half years before the beginning of the current period (interest is assumed to be paid semiannually). The market value of these bonds has remained at par over the three-and-a-half-year period, but during the current period this value falls as the market rate of interest gradually rises to 5 per cent by year end. The market value at year end, after the coupon payment, would be $597,073. We assume that the regular coupon payments have been made and recorded during the year. The following entries record current cost data:

(1) Bonds Payable Valuation Adjustment		2927	
Realizable Cost Savings			2927
To record the decrease in the market value of bonds payable (over the period) and the related realizable cost savings.			
Market value, beginning of period	$600,000		
Market value, end of period	597,073		
Decrease	2,927		
(2) Interest Expense		3000	
Realizable Cost Savings			3000
To adjust interest expense to reflect the current cost of capital borrowed and to record realizable cost savings (which are also realized). The amount is computed as follows:			
Interest at average annual rate, 4½% of $600,000 =	$27,000		
Contractual interest at 4% of $600,000	24,000		
Excess of current over contracted cost	3,000		
(3) Realizable Cost Savings		5927	
Unrealized Cost Savings			5927
To transfer realizable cost savings (normally via Business Profit).			

[3] Rental income and expense are often contractual also and theoretically should require adjustment similar to that spelled out for bonds below.

(4) Unrealized Cost Savings	3000	
Realized Cost Savings		3000
To record realized cost savings as explained in Entry (2).		

The adjusted accounts would appear as follows:

Bonds Payable

		Balance	600000

Bonds Payable Valuation Adjustment

(1)	2927		

Realized Cost Savings

To Realized Profit	3000	(4)	3000

Realizable Cost Savings

(3) To Unrealized Cost Savings (via Business Profit)	5927	(1) On future interest	2927
		(2) On current interest	3000
	5927		5927

Unrealized Cost Savings

(4) Realized Cost Savings	3000	(3)	5927
To balance	2927		
	5927		5927
		Balance	2927

Interest Expense

1960	24000	To COP	27000
(2)	3000		
	27000		27000

The adjustment to bonds payable indicates (1) that only \$597,073 could now be borrowed on the existing terms and maturity date and (2) that bonds could now be retired for \$597,073. The first is a current cost interpretation, the second, an opportunity cost view. In either case the \$2,927 indicates a realizable cost saving because the liability is now less than that originally contracted for. Even if early bond redemption is expressly forbidden, the current cost view is valid. It indicates to management, owners, and outsiders that $2,927 was saved by borrowing at more favorable terms than now exist and that currently only $597,073 could be borrowed whereas $600,000 is in fact the amount procured by the firm. The $2,927 is the change in the excess over the period of the present value (computed at the market rate of interest) of future current cost interest payments over future contractual interest payments. In our example, it is simply ($27,000 – $24,000)/1.025, the final interest payment being only six months away. The adjustment to interest expense restates that item at current cost, the amount that the firm would currently have to pay in order to use $600,000 for this year on current market terms. The realized cost saving of $3,000 reflects the good judgment of management in borrowing at lower contractual rates than now exist. It is a holding gain, not an operating one; the current cost of capital, of the resources currently used, is $27,000 while its contractual or historic cost is $24,000.[4]

The adjusting entries for the following period in which the bonds mature would appear as follows:[5]

---

[4] The following technique parallels more closely the procedure followed in adjusting other items to current cost but accords less well with standard bond treatment:

		Dr.	Cr.
(1)	Bonds Payable Valuation Adjustment	5927	
	Realizable Cost Savings		5927
	To record realizable cost savings accruing during the period.		
(2)	Interest Expense	3000	
	Bonds Payable Valuation Adjustment		3000
	To adjust interest to a current cost basis and to write off the valuation adjustment applicable to current interest.		

Entries (3) and (4) as in text.

This procedure is used in the integrated example developed in the next section.

[5] Following the procedure in the preceding footnote, entries (1) and (2) below would appear as follows:

		Dr.	Cr.
(1)	Bonds Payable Valuation Adjustment	73	
	Realizable Cost Savings		73
	To record cost savings accruing this period.		
(2)	Interest Expense	3000	
	Bonds Payable Valuation Adjustment		3000
	To adjust interest to current cost.		

(1) Realizable Cost Savings		2927	
Bonds Payable Valuation Adjustment			2927
To record the increase in the value of bonds payable and the related adjustment of realizable cost savings just prior to redemption.			
(2) Interest Expense		3000	
Realizable Cost Savings			3000
To adjust interest expense to reflect the current cost of capital borrowed and to record as realizable the cost savings realized this period.			
2½% of $600,000	$15,000		
2% of $600,000	12,000		
Realized cost savings	3,000		
(3) Realizable Cost Savings		73	
Unrealized Cost Savings			73
To transfer realizable cost savings (normally via Business Profit).			
(4) Unrealized Cost Savings		3000	
Realized Cost Savings			3000
To record realized cost savings as explained in Entry (2).			

The net increase in Realizable Cost Savings during the year is the increase from $2,927, the present value of future interest savings at the beginning of the period, to $3,000, the interest saving in fact realized at time of bond redemption. The adjusting entries together with those made in the normal course of events close out all accounts related to Bonds Payable.

The principal individual adjustments necessary to procure current cost data have now been described. We can proceed to gather these adjustments together, to demonstrate that these data can be developed in the accounts through end-of-period adjustments alone without loss of historic cost data, and to illustrate the kind of statements that can be used to present the flexible data which result.

End-of-Period Adjustment Process

To present a complete picture of the adjustment process suggested here, we shall go through it for the hypothetical XYZ

Corporation for the year 1960. We assume that the corporation has been keeping track of current as well as historic cost data over past periods, and had at the end of 1959 the following assets, liabilities and equities (in thousands of dollars):

	Historic Cost	Current Cost
Assets		
Cash and receivables	$ 600	$ 600
Securities	200	272
Inventories	500	515
Fixed assets, depreciated	1100	1650
Total assets	$2400	$3037
Liabilities		
Current	$ 500	$ 500
Fixed	600	600
Total liabilities	$1100	$1100
Equities		
Capital stock	$ 600	$ 600
Realized surplus	700	700
Unrealized surplus savings		637
Total equities	$1300	$1937

Initial balances have been taken from the examples used in Chapters V and VI for inventories and fixed assets (the amounts multiplied by 1,000), and from the first section of this chapter for securities and bonds payable. The appropriate accounts have been set up and the initial balances, recorded and so labeled. To conserve space, current liabilities have been amalgamated with cash and receivables to form an account entitled Net Money Claims.

It is assumed that traditional accounting practices have been followed during the year 1960 and the net amounts involved have been posted in the accounts, each such posting being labeled "1960." At this point the adjustment stage is reached. The adjustments to be made are taken from examples already cited on securities, inventories, fixed assets, and bonds payable. The first twelve entries relate to these individual adjustments and are restated for convenience. Entries (13) through (24) accumulate data on the various concepts of profit and will be further explained after the entries have been stated and posted as follows:

Adjusting Entries, XYZ Corporation
1960

(1)	Security Valuation Adjustment	6	
	Realizable Cost Savings		6
	To record increases in the value of securities held during the year and the related cost savings accruing. The amount includes the rise in value from \$272 to \$274 on the initial stock and the rise in value from \$244 to \$248 on securities held after sale.		
(2)	Inventory Valuation Adjustment	65	
	Realizable Cost Savings		65
	To record increases in the value of inventories held during the year and related cost savings accruing. The amount was computed as follows: On initial inventory, 100 (\$5.50 – \$5.15) = \$35 On final inventory, 120 (\$5.75 – \$5.50) = 30 Total \$65		
(3)	Fixed Asset Valuation Adjustment	210	
	Realizable Cost Savings		210
	To record increases in the value of fixed assets held during the year and the related cost savings accruing. The amount was computed as follows: On initial stock, $\frac{11}{20}$ (\$3200 – \$3000) = \$110 On final stock, $\frac{10}{20}$ (\$3400 – \$3200) = 100 Total \$210		
(4)	Bonds Payable Valuation Adjustment	6	
	Realized Cost Savings		6
	To record the decrease in the value of bonds payable and of current interest payments and the cost savings accruing this period on current and future interest payments. Market value of bonds at beginning of period \$600 Market value at end of period 597 Net change in B.P. Valuation Adjustment \$ 3		

Interest expense at current cost, 4½% of $600	= $27	
Interest at contractual cost, 4% of $600	= 24	
Realized cost savings on interest		3
Realizable cost savings on bonds and current interest		$ 6

		Debit	Credit
(5)	Cost of Materials Used	500	
	Materials Inventory		500
	To transfer the initial inventory value at historic (FIFO) cost.		
(6)	Cost of Materials Used	50	
	Inventory Valuation Adjustment		50
	To adjust the initial inventory to average prices of the year. [100 ($5.50 – $5.00) = $50.]		
(7)	Cost of Materials Used	2200	
	Purchases		2200
	To transfer purchases at average prices of the year.		
(8)	Materials Inventory	681	
	Cost of Materials Used		681
	To enter the final inventory at historic (FIFO) cost.		
(9)	Cost of Materials Used	21	
	Inventory Valuation Adjustment		21
	To adjust the final inventory figure removed from the Cost of Materials Used account to average prices of the year. [120 ($5.50) – $681 = –$21.]		
(10)	Depreciation	100	
	Allowance for Depreciation		100
	To record depreciation at historic cost. $\left[\frac{1}{20} \cdot \$2000 = \$100.\right]$		
(11)	Depreciation	60	
	Fixed Asset Valuation Adjustment		60
	To adjust depreciation to current cost, i.e., to depreciate the excess of current cost over historic cost at average prices of the year. $\left[\frac{1}{20} \cdot (\$3200 - \$2000 = \$60.\right]$		

(12)	Interest Expense	3	
	Bonds Payable Valuation Adjustment		3
	To adjust interest to current cost and to write off the valuation adjustment applicable to it. [(4½% − 4%) $600 = $3.]		
(13)	Sales	4000	
	Current Operating Profit		4000
	To transfer sales.		
(14)	Current Operating Profit	3813	
	Cost of Materials Used		2090
	Wages and Miscellaneous		1536
	Depreciation		160
	Interest		27
	To transfer current costs related to sales.		
(15)	Current Operating Profit	187	
	Business Profit		187
	To transfer one element of business profit.		
(16)	Realizable Cost Savings	287	
	Business Profit		287
	To complete data on business profit.		
(17)	Business Profit	187	
	Realized Profit		187
	To transfer current operating profit.		
(18)	Business Profit	287	
	Unrealized Surplus		287
	To transfer realizable cost savings.		
(19)	Unrealized Surplus	134	
	Realized Cost Savings		134
	To transfer cost savings realized this year, namely, the excess of current over historic costs.		
	On cost of materials used, $2090 − $2019 = $71		
	On depreciation, $160 − $100 = 60		
	On interest, $27 − $24 = 3		
	Total 134		
(20)	Unrealized Surplus	12	
	Security Valuation Adjustment		12
	To cancel cost savings realized as capital gains. (The realized capital gains were recorded at time of sale.)		

		Dr.	Cr.
(21)	Realized Cost Savings	134	
	Realized Capital Gains	12	
	Realized Profit		146
	To transfer to realized profit.		
(22)	Realized Profit	333	
	Disposition of Realized Profit		333
	To transfer to a disposition account.		
(23)	Disposition of Realized Profit	333	
	Tax Liability		170
	Dividends Payable		74
	Realized Surplus		89
	To dispose of realized profit. Taxes include those on Accounting Operating Profit (52% of \$321 = \$167) and those on Realized Capital Gains (25% of \$12 = \$3).		
(24)	Tax Liability	170	
	Dividends Payable	74	
	Net Money Claims		244
	To record payment.		

The ledger accounts would then be as follows:

Sales

(13) To COP	4000	1960	4000

Purchases

1960	2200	(7) To Cost of Materials	2200

Cost of Materials Used

(5) Initial inventory, at cost	500	(8) Final inventory, at cost	681
(6) Adjustment of I.I. to average prices	50	(14) To COP	2090
(7) Purchases	2200		
(9) Adjust F.I. to average prices	21		
	2771		2771

Wages and Miscellaneous

1960	1536	(14) To COP	1536

Depreciation

(10) On historic cost	100	(14) To COP	160
(11) To adjust to current cost	60		
	160		160

Interest Expense

1960	24	(14) To COP	27
(12) To adjust to current cost	3		
	27		27

Current Operating Profit

(14) Cost of materials	2090	(13) Sales	4000
(14) Wages, etc.	1536		
(14) Depreciation	160		
(14) Interest	27		
(15) To Business Profit	187		
	4000		4000

Realizable Cost Savings

(16) To Business Profit	287	(1) On securities	6
		(2) On inventories	65
		(3) On fixed assets	210
		(4) On bonds payable	6
	287		287

Realized Cost Savings

(21) To Realized Profit	134	(19) On cost of materials	71
		(19) On depreciation	60
		(19) On interest	3
	134		134

Realized Capital Gains

(21) To Realized Profit	12	1960	12

Business Profit

(17) To Realized Profit	187	(15) COP	187
(18) To Unrealized Cost Surplus	287	(16) Realizable Cost Savings	287
	474		474

Realized Profit

(22) To the Disposition account	333	(17) COP	187
		(21) Realized Cost Savings	134
		(21) Realized Capital Gains	12
	333		333

Disposition of Realized Profit

(23) Taxes (Income, $167; Gains, $3)	170	(22) Realized Profit	333
(23) Dividends	74		
(23) Realized Surplus	89		
	333		333

Net Money Claims
(Cash and Receivables less Current Liabilities)

Initial balance	100	1960 Wages, etc.	1536
1960 Sales	4000	1960 Interest	24
1960 Securities sold	30	1960 Purchases	2200
		(24) Taxes and dividend payments	244
		To balance	126
	4130		4130
Balance	126		

Securities

Initial balance	200	1960 Sale	18
		To balance	182
	200		200
Balance	182		

Security Valuation Adjustment

Initial balance	72	(20) On securities sold	12
(1) Increases during the year	6	To balance	66
	78		78
Balance	66		

Materials Inventories

Initial balance, 100 @ $5.00	500	(5) To Cost of Materials	500
(8) Final inventory, 120 @ $5.675	681		

Inventory Valuation Adjustment

Initial balance, 100 ($5.15 – $5.00)	15	(6) To Cost of Materials (on I.I.)	50
(2) Increases during the year	65	(9) To Cost of Materials (on F.I.)	21
		To balance	9
	80		80
Balance	9		

Fixed Assets

Initial balance	2000		

Allowance for Depreciation

To balance	1000	Initial balance	900
		(10) At historic cost	100
	1000		1000
		Balance	1000

Fixed Asset Valuation Adjustment

Initial balance $\left(\frac{11}{20} \cdot \$1000\right)$	550	(11) Realized during the year	60
		To balance	700
(3) Increases during the year	210		
	760		760
Balance $\left(\frac{10}{20} \cdot \$1400\right)$	700		

Tax Liability

(24) Payments	170	(23) On Realized Profit	167
		(23) On Realized Capital Gains	3
	170		170

Dividends Payable

(24) Paid	74	(23) Declared	74

Bonds Payable

		Initial balance	600

Bonds Payable Valuation Adjustment

(4) Decreases during the year	6	(12) Realized during the year	3
		To balance	3
	6		6
Balance	3		

Capital Stock

		Initial balance	600

Realized Surplus

To balance	789	Initial balance	700
		(23) Retained realized profit	89
	789		789
		Balance	789

Unrealized Surplus

(19) Realized Cost Savings	134	Initial balance	637
(20) Realized Capital Gains	12	(18) Realizable Cost Savings	287
To balance	778		
	924		924
		Balance	778

Entries (13) and (14) determine current operating profit, and entries (15) and (16) determine business profit. Entry (17) transfers current operating profit from Business Profit to Realized

Profit. Entry (18) transfers the balance of business profit to Unrealized Surplus. This amount together with the initial balance in the account represents the maximum cost savings that could be realized this period, either through direct sale and so be realized capital gains, or through use and so be realized cost savings. (We shift at this point from using the term "unrealized cost savings," which has been useful, for purposes of exposition, in relating realizable, realized, and unrealized cost savings, to the broader term "unrealized surplus," which is consistent as a counterpart in the balance sheet to "realized surplus.") Entries (19) and (20) transfer the actually realized amounts to the appropriate accounts leaving as a balance the amount unrealized on December 31, 1960. Entry (21) brings these realized amounts into Realized Profit. Entries (22) and (23) dispose of realized profit. Entry (24) is a straightforward payment entry which might have been made in large part during the year if dividends and taxes were paid earlier.

Data have now been developed for current operating profit, business profit, realized profit, and, as the latter equals accounting profit, for traditional accounting profit as well. Further, all assets and liabilities are stated on a current cost basis as of December 31, 1960, through the media of valuation adjustment accounts so that no historic cost data have been destroyed. We are in a position to draw up comprehensive statements for the firm.

The Fundamental Statements

The statements we propose are designed to divulge the maximum information on the various concepts of profit and on the two types of balance sheet valuation. The profit and loss statement illustrated in statement 1 is divided into three sections. The first section contains a statement of current operating profit.[6] The second section on cost savings and capital gains has two parts, one leading to realized profit, the other to business profit. The third section depicts the disposition of both kinds of profit and reconciles the two through the increment in unrealized surplus.

---

[6] This section could, of course, be divided into two parts, one for manufacturing operations and one for financial operations.

STATEMENT 1

STATEMENT OF PROFIT AND LOSS
XYZ CORPORATION
for the year 1960
(In thousands of dollars)

Sales		$4000	
Cost of materials used	$2090		
Wages and miscellaneous	1536		
Depreciation	160		
Interest	27		
		3813	
Current Operating Profit			$187

Current Operating Profit		$187	*Current Operating Profit*		$187
Realized Cost Savings			*Realizable Cost Savings*		
On cost of materials	$71		On inventories	$65	
On depreciation	60		On fixed assets	210	
On interest	3		On securities	6	
		134	On bonds payable	6	
Realized Capital Gains					287
On securities sold		12			
Realized Profit		$333	*Business Profit*		$474

The Disposition of Profit

Federal income taxes	$170
Dividends	74
Realized surplus	89
Realized Profit	$333
Unrealized surplus	141*
Business Profit	$474

* On which the contingent tax liability is approximately $73.

The realized profit section of the statement can be quickly converted into a traditional statement of profit by subtracting from the indicated expense items in the current operating profit section those cost savings realized during the period. Thus statement 2 has been obtained from statement 1 by adding realized cost savings on cost of materials, $71; on depreciation, $60; and on interest expense, $3; to operating profit by reducing the amounts listed as expenses. Realized capital gains are separately reported in both statements and the total of accounting profit is just equal to realized profit. But the realized profit concept requires the identification of realized cost savings while accounting profit does not. Thus accounting operating profit includes cost savings currently realized whether they accrued this period or not. Evaluating operating activities accurately would be a difficult matter on the basis of such data.

STATEMENT 2

STATEMENT OF ACCOUNTING PROFIT
XYZ CORPORATION
for the year 1960
(In thousands of dollars)

Sales		$4000	
Cost of materials used	$2019		
Wages and miscellaneous	1536		
Depreciation	100		
Interest	24		
		3679	
Operating profit			$321
Capital gains			12
Accounting profit			$333
Disposition:			
Federal income taxes		$170	
Dividends		74	
Earned surplus		89	
			$333

Business profit in statement 1 not only states operating profit on a current basis but reports as cost savings only those increments which came into existence this period. No events of past periods are permitted to affect the reported profit whether they result from operating or holding activities. How much better off the firm really is is clearly revealed, but the breakdown also discloses how heavily dependent the firm has been on favorable price movements as opposed to successful operating activities.

Statement 3 is a comparative balance sheet containing data on both historic and current costs. The excess of current over historic cost is explicitly shown as a valuation adjustment for every item except fixed liabilities, where the amount can readily be determined. It follows that the excess of net assets at current cost over net assets at historic cost at any moment is the net amount of all valuation adjustments. This sum represents increases in value which are as yet unrealized and is reported in the equity section as unrealized surplus. The net increment in equities and in net assets over the year is the retained realized amount of $89 on the historic cost basis and the retained realizable amount of $230 (realized of $89 plus unrealized of $141) on the current cost basis. These amounts can be verified in statement 1.

Usefulness of Current Cost Data

The advantages of current cost data to the management and owners of a business firm can be realized in good part if the firm chooses to develop such data only for its own internal use. The full value of such data cannot be realized even by management, however, and certainly not by outsiders, unless most firms both develop and report data on a current cost basis. After all, outside users of accounting data lean heavily on intercompany comparisons, and uniform reporting is extremely helpful in this respect. But the full impact of current cost data should extend beyond decision-making and evaluation. To the extent that decisions are improved and competition tends to spread the benefits, the economy as a whole should function better through an improved allocation and use of resources both within and among firms, and through greater output and less cyclical instability. Finally the availability of current cost data may not only reveal tax discrepancies but may also be a step toward more equitable taxation.

STATEMENT 3

Comparative Balance Sheet of the XYZ Corporation
HISTORIC COSTS AND CURRENT COSTS

(In thousands of dollars)

	December 31, 1959				December 31, 1960				Increase or decrease* in net assets or equities			
	Historic cost		Current cost		Historic cost		Current cost		Historic cost		Current cost	
Assets												
Cash and receivables		$ 600		$ 600		$ 576		$ 576		$ 24*		$ 24*
Securities, at cost		200	$ 200			182	$ 182			18*	$ 18*	
Valuation adjustment			72				66				6*	
at current cost				272				248				24*
Inventories, at cost (FIFO)		500	$ 500			681	$ 681			181	$ 181	
Valuation adjustment			15				9				6*	
at current cost				515				690				175
Fixed assets, at cost	$2000				$2000				$ ...			
less Allow. for depreciation	900				1000				100*			
at depreciated cost		1100	$1100			1000	$1000			$ 100*	$ 100*	
Valuation adjustment			550				700				150	
at current cost				1650				1700				50
Total Assets		$2400		$3037		$2439		$3214		$ 39		$ 177
Liabilities												
Current	$ 500		$ 500		$ 450		$ 450		$ 50		$ 50	
Fixed	600		600		600		597		...		3	
Total Liabilities		1100		1100		1050		1047		50		53
Net Assets		$1300		$1937		$1389		$2167		$ 89		$ 230
Equities												
Capital stock, at par		$ 600		$ 600		$ 600		$ 600		$ ...		$ ...
Realized surplus		700		700		789		789		89		89
Unrealized surplus				637[a]				778[a]				141[a]
Total Equities		$1300		$1937		$1389		$2167		$ 89		$ 230

[a] On which the contingent tax liability was approximately $331 on Dec. 31, 1959, and $404 on Dec. 31, 1960, the increase being $73.

Decision-Making and Evaluation

The usefulness of current cost data for the making of business decisions depends upon the correction of two of the three major defects of accounting profit, namely, the neglect of realizable cost savings and the confusion of realized cost savings with operating profit. The third defect, the omission of price level changes, is discussed in Chapter VIII.

The omission of realizable cost savings from accounting data as presently constructed carries three important implications for the evaluation of business decisions, all of which are corrected by current cost data. Those assets or portions of assets which are neither sold nor used during the period are carried at the same value at the end of the period as that assigned to them at the beginning of the period regardless of what has happened to the values of such assets during the period. If such assets have gone up in value, this gain is not recorded in the accounts and as a result all of the gains accruing to the firm during the period are not recorded. In effect, present accounting data are predicated on the assumption that holding activities do not represent a purposeful means by which management can enhance the market position of the firm. To the extent that the firm attempts to make gains in this fashion, traditional accounting data fail to inform management, owners, and outsiders as to the progress the firm has made during the current period.

A second consequence of not counting gains when they arise is that when such gains are in fact realized, the gains earned over the entire time span during which the assets were held by the firm are attributed entirely to the period in which the gains are realized. And because the gains so recorded are net gains, there is no way to determine in what period holding activities were successful and in what periods they were unsuccessful.

Imagine, for example, the firm which has purchased marketable securities for $100,000 for speculative reasons. Suppose that these securities have a market value at the end of the next five consecutive years as follows: $150,000, $200,000, $250,000, $250,000, and $200,000. If the securities are sold at the end of the fifth year, the accountant would record a realized gain of $100,000. This gain would be attributed to the current period in the reports of the firm despite the fact that the gain has been earned over a five-year period. While the reported evidence is skimpy, one might be inclined to say that the management is currently more successful than it has been in the past. As a matter of fact, however, the firm was fairly successful in its holding activities during the first three of the five years, broke even in the fourth year, and actually suffered a loss during the fifth year. On the basis of this information, other things being equal, it might not be unfair to suggest that managerial efficiency is decreasing in this firm so far as its holding activities are concerned. Certainly the accretion of market value which the management has succeeded in obtaining differs substantially from the gains reported in the accounts.

The third consequence of the failure to report capital gains and losses as they occur is the badly distorted balance sheet values which result. This distortion makes comparisons among business firms, whether by the management of one of them or by outsiders, extremely hazardous. Because historic costs are reported in balance sheets instead of current values, the relative positions of business firms are impossible to ascertain. It is true, of course, that many accountants would argue that it is not their function to account for current values. But if current data are relevant to management, owners, and outsiders, whose function is it to accumulate such data if accountants refuse the responsibility?

But it is the second major defect of accepted accounting procedures which is in our view the most damaging of all. Those holding gains and losses which are realized through the use of asset services in production are not identified as cost savings but instead are included in what is called operating profit.

An asset is in an important sense nothing but a stock of asset services which may gradually be used in production over a long period of time. In an economy characterized by change it is very likely that the value of these asset services at the time they are committed to the production process will be substantially different from their original cost. Yet in following the historic cost precept, accountants must deduct from the output so produced and sold the historic cost of the contributing asset services. If the value of these asset services has risen over time, the operating profit reported by the accountant is misleadingly high.

The excess of the value of the asset services at the time of their use over their historic cost cannot be attributed to the operating activities of the business firm by any stretch of the imagination. This excess is attributable to the firm's holding activities; the firm has held the asset services while their value has increased. By committing these asset services to production and by selling the resulting product, the firm merely realizes this gain.

But to call the gain (more accurately the cost saving achieved by buying when prices were low) an operating profit is simply not an accurate representation of the facts. The confusion may even tempt management into unsound decisions and is almost certain to perform this disservice for outsiders. Consider the following situation. A wise management enters an industry at a time when the necessary assets can be purchased at exceedingly favorable prices. As time passes, other firms enter the industry purchasing their assets at substantially higher prices. If all firms now in the industry are equally efficient in their operating activities, the first firm will record a substantially larger "operating profit" than the other firms in the industry. After all, the depreciation charges of the first firm are substantially lower in terms of historic cost than are those for the newer firms in the industry. But this excess does not result from the wisdom with which the management operates its assets; it is the result of the wisdom which the management displayed at the time it purchased the assets and in its many subsequent (perhaps passive) decisions to hold the asset.

Suppose for example that the firm's managerial efficiency had deteriorated over time to the point where its reported operating profit was identical to that of the other firms in the industry. The inefficiency of the firm's operating activities would now be disguised by the gains realized through its holding activities. It would take a rather sophisticated analysis to disclose the inefficiency, and if management has deteriorated over time, the operating inefficiency is not likely to be discovered immediately. As the firm's assets wear out, replacement decisions must be made. If the apparent success of the firm is projected into the future, these replacement decisions may be made rather casually. Once replacements have been made at the higher prices paid by its competitors, the inefficiency of the firm, which may by now be deep-seated after a long but hidden history, will finally be revealed in the firm's accounting reports. In fact, if asset prices have risen substantially since the firm first entered the industry, it may now be reporting sizable losses while its efficient competitors continue to earn profits. The managerial house-cleaning which should have taken place years ago may finally be accomplished.

Meanwhile what has been happening to the stockholders? If the operating efficiency of the first firm was maintained over time, its reported profits should show a rising trend as the price of the product rises sufficiently to induce new firms to enter the industry with the higher priced assets. The firm will also be reporting higher profits than its competitors. As the basic tools of the security purchaser (and frequently the security analyst has little more with which to work) are profit trends and profit comparisons, it would not be surprising if the stock of the first firm were bid up substantially above the stock of its competitors. In fact, the excess is likely to be greater the longer the upward trend in the firm's profits has continued and the longer it has reported a profit in excess of the profits of its competitors. Yet (paradoxically perhaps) as replacement approaches, these apparently favorable factors have a steadily shorter life. When the first reports are published following replacement, the stockholders must face reality for the first time in many years.

The high security prices of the firm will of course enable it to raise capital at a very favorable price. As a consequence the firm may be able to expand and may be induced to do so to such an extent that its size exceeds the optimum. If so, replacement will reveal that the operating profits of this firm are less than those of its competitors. The economy has been duped into misallocating its resources.

But the allocation of resources may be even more severely distorted if the firm's operating efficiency has decreased over time. If this decrease is not too great, the firm may still show a rising profit trend and may still report profits in excess of its newer competitors. The possibility that the capital market will divert funds from efficient to inefficient firms is heightened. Even if the firm's inefficiency has reached the point where the reported profits of the firm are equal to those of its competitors, it can still attract capital at the same rate as can others in the industry. Only after what may be a considerable period of time will the error in resource allocation become apparent.

If business profit figures had been reported for the firm in our hypothetical example and similar figures had been reported for its competitors, the difficulties we have noted could have been avoided. The business profit concept requires that operating profit be carefully distinguished from gains resulting from holding activities. Any decrease in operating efficiency of a firm, therefore, would be reflected in its reported current operating profits. Not only would management have thought carefully before replacing assets at high prices which were currently yielding only a small or negative operating profit, but outsiders too would have been warned not to allocate capital in the direction of the inefficient firm. Appropriate corrective steps could have been taken at a much earlier moment than if the firm relied solely on traditional accounting data.

Traditional accounting operating profit cannot be expected to yield identical data for two different periods whose current events are identical. Current operating profit does fulfill this criterion; it depends for its determination on the events which are current in the period under consideration. The figures derived when historically oriented profit concepts are used depend only partly on current events; their measurement is influenced heavily by events of preceding periods, namely, historic costs. Yet it seems reasonable to expect that if a firm operates during two periods with the same endowment of assets, contributes the same factors to the same production and sale processes, finds the prices of its factors to be the same, and sells the same output at the same prices, the firm should report the same profit. The fact that present accounting procedures will not meet this criterion we regard as a strong argument in favor of the kind of accounting modification we propose.

A higher current operating profit will generally mean a higher operating efficiency for the firm. It need not imply, however, an increase in social efficiency. The firm's current operating profit may rise because it has solidified a monopoly or monopsony position, because it has crushed competitors with predatory practices, or because it has used misleading advertising effectively. All of these may indicate efficiency so far as stockholders are concerned; they can scarcely be said to do so for the economy as a whole. But then this function is not performed by existing accounting data either. Indeed, the current operating profit concept would remove some of the difficulties now involved in inferring welfare effects from private profit computations.

Stability and Cyclical Effects of Current Operating Profit and Holding Gains

By combining data on the current cost of goods sold and on current cost depreciation presented in Chapters V and VI, it is possible to construct estimates of current operating profit for the economy as a whole for the period 1929 to 1949. These estimates are presented in table 13 in a manner compatible with the framework we are suggesting in this book. Realized cost savings are holding gains based on the use of inputs, which have risen in price while held by the firm, in production for sale. They comprise the difference between the current cost of inputs at time of use and the historic cost of these inputs at time of purchase. The inventory valuation adjustment in national income accounts and Goldsmith's estimates of the excess of current cost over historic cost depreciation provide us with an estimate of the realized cost savings on the two principal assets which are based on outdated prices in accounting records. Reported accounting profit less these realized cost savings yields an estimate of current operating profit.

Table 13 shows vividly first of all how reported accounting profit, which combines operating and holding gains and losses in one component termed "profit or loss on operations," grossly exaggerates both the magnitude and timing of fluctuations in true operating profits. In 1931, corporations in the aggregate were still making profits on their operating activities; it was their holding activities which produced the realized losses in reported statements. Losses on operations were overstated by more than 60 per cent in 1932. On the other hand, the depth of the depression in 1933 saw corporations realize their largest losses on operations in the modern era, although reported profits were positive in that year. There thus tended to be a substantial lag in current operating profit behind realized (accounting) profit as we moved into the depression. The same type of lag appears in 1946, when

TABLE 13

ESTIMATED CURRENT OPERATING PROFIT AND REALIZED COST SAVINGS OF AMERICAN CORPORATIONS, 1929–1949
(In millions of dollars)

	1929	1930	1931	1932	1933	1934	1935	1936	1937	1938	1939
1. Current Operating Profit	9,007	5,901	1,382	−1,821	−1,888	832	2,534	4,663	5,605	3,568	5,053
2. Realized Cost Savings											
a) on inventories	−472	−3,260	−2,414	−1,047	2,143	625	227	738	31	−963	714
b) on fixed assets	861	544	256	−115	−102	199	225	235	477	448	452
Total	389	−2,716	−2,158	−1,162	2,041	824	452	973	508	−515	1,166
3. Realized Profit (equals reported Accounting Profit)	9,396	3,185	−776	−2,983	153	1,656	2,986	5,636	6,113	3,053	6,219
4. Tax liability	1,369	842	498	385	521	744	951	1,409	1,502	1,029	1,441
5. Dividends	5,724	5,464	4,125	2,609	2,078	2,579	2,803	4,556	4,674	2,970	3,651
6. Undistributed profits	2,303	−3,121	−5,399	−5,977	−2,446	−1,667	−768	−329	−63	−946	1,1

	1940	1941	1942	1943	1944	1945	1946	1947	1948	1949
1. Current Operating Profit	8,369	13,558	18,499	22,546	21,752	17,159	15,333	20,260	26,744	24,376
2. Realized Cost Savings										
a) on inventories	200	2,471	1,204	773	287	564	5,263	5,899	2,152	−1,856
b) on fixed assets	517	722	954	997	988	1,026	1,530	2,677	3,268	3,018
Total	717	3,193	2,158	1,770	1,275	1,590	6,793	8,576	5,420	1,162
3. Realized Profit (equals reported Accounting Profit)	9,086	16,751	20,657	24,316	23,027	18,749	22,126	28,836	32,164	25,538
4. Tax liability	2,834	7,610	11,415	14,074	12,949	10,689	9,111	11,283	12,483	10,375
5. Dividends	3,894	4,349	4,182	4,347	4,570	4,616	5,655	6,300	6,989	7,168
6. Undistributed profits	2,358	4,792	5,060	5,895	5,508	3,444	7,360	11,253	12,692	7,995

SOURCES AND NOTES: Realized Profit [line (3)] is corporate profits before taxes as given in the U. S. Department of Commerce, *National Income Supplement* (1958). Realized Cost Savings on inventories is the inventory valuation adjustment for corporations, given in the same source. Realized Cost Savings on fixed assets is Goldsmith's careful estimate of the excess of current cost over historic cost depreciation, described in the notes to Table 8. Current Operating Profit is the residual of line (3) less the total for line (2). Lines (4), (5), and (6) are given in the *National Income Supplement* (1958).

current operating profit actually continued the decline begun in 1943, but the rise in prices and volume of inventories and the price increases in fixed assets led to substantial cost savings realized through use, and thus a substantial rise in reported profits.

The way in which holding gains exaggerate the magnitude of fluctuations in operating gains is depicted in figure 8. Note in particular the much larger percentage fall in reported profits as compared with current operating profit in the recession years of 1938 and 1949. In the latter year, reported profits were not only off substantially from the peak year of 1948 but indeed were lower than profits in 1947 as well. Actually, however, true operating profit was off only slightly from 1948 and was substantially above the operating profit of 1947.

To the extent that operating activities are fundamental to business activities, the stability of current operating profit relative to accounting (operating) profit would be likely to have a stabilizing effect on business decisions and on the economy as a whole. But if business decisions of this sort are based on movements in holding gains, cyclical movements are likely to be exaggerated.

The inherent instability of accounting (operating) profit is attributable to the effect price changes have on realized cost savings, on the excess of the current cost over the historic cost of services used. Realizable cost savings, an element in business profit, should be even more sensitive to current price changes because the effect of these on all assets and liabilities of the firm, whether used or not, is measured. To the extent that holding activities govern a firm's decisions, therefore, negative realizable cost savings may signal a postponement of purchases if they generate expectations of even lower prices in the future. Instability would be increased by such behavior, but the decisions of the individual firm would nonetheless be based on more appropriate information than presently.[7]

In summary, current cost data should lead to greater economic stability to the extent that operating activities are basic to a firm's decisions but possibly to greater instability if holding

[7] If other factors lead business firms generally to buy on the downswing, holding activities would tend to stabilize prices.

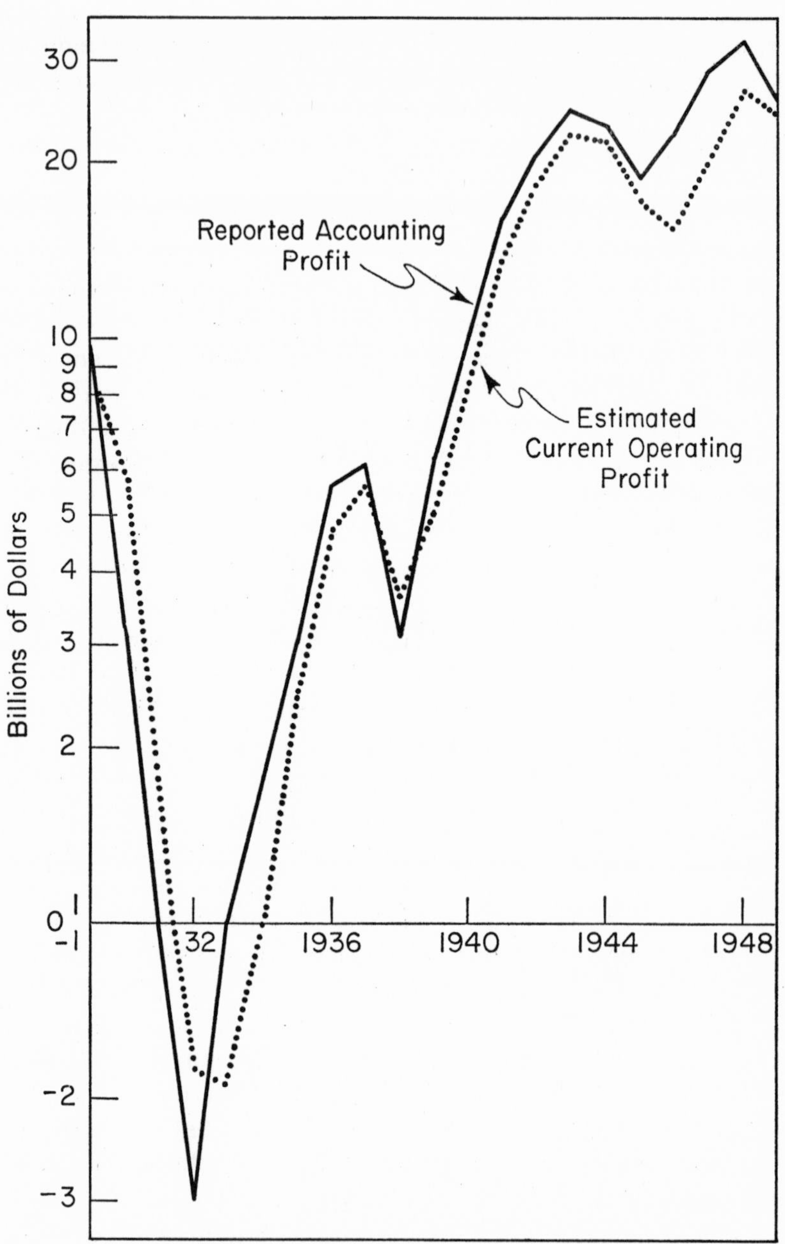

Figure 8. Estimated current operating profit and reported accounting profit of American corporations, 1929–1949.

activities are paramount. Heavier tax rates on capital gains and cost savings and lower ones on current operating profit might shift the balance more strongly toward stability.

Tax Effects of Current Cost Data

The current cost data developed so far are in money terms and a full consideration of tax effects must be postponed until price level changes have been introduced. But the widespread reporting of current cost data in money terms alone could have a major impact on tax matters. When individual prices are rising attention would be directed to the fact that the corporate income tax is levied on accounting operating profit, which includes realized cost savings, while the capital gains tax is levied against realized capital gains alone. There is, however, no essential difference between realized cost savings and realized capital gains, the former being realized through sale of final product, the latter through direct sale. On the other hand, as we have tried to show, realized cost savings differ sharply from profits on operations.

The reporting of current cost data would focus considerable light on this misclassification of realized cost savings, and the pressure to reclassify such gains for tax purposes should be not only strong, but proper as well. If capital gains are to be taxed at a relatively favorable rate, realized cost savings should receive the same treatment. Perhaps both should be taxed at the same rate as operating profit, or perhaps at a higher rate, but any differential which is regarded as desirable should clearly apply to both.

In the case of the XYZ Corporation the reclassification of realized cost savings would have the following effect:

	Current Cost Treatment		Existing Tax Treatment	
	Base	Tax	Base	Tax
Income tax, at 52%	$187	$ 97	$321	$167
Gains tax, at 25%	146	37	12	3
Total taxes		$134		$170

Total taxes would be reduced by 21 per cent. This effect is contingent on current costs exceeding historic costs; taxes would be higher when based on current cost data if current costs were less than historic costs.

Finally, if the current cost system of keeping accounts were adopted, it would seem reasonable to note in reports the contingent tax liability associated with unrealized surplus. Such notes have been appended to our proposed profit and loss statement and balance sheet on the assumption that they will eventually be taxed as realized cost savings under existing law, i.e., at 52 per cent. If this kind of gain were taxed at the capital gains rate upon realization, the contingent tax liability noted would be substantially smaller.

It can be observed in conclusion that the effects of current cost data as they have been briefly described here are completely independent of any adjustment for price level changes. The further modification of accounting data for changes in the purchasing power of the dollar will improve the data, will make certain effects more pronounced, and will introduce some new effects; but the major advantages of recognizing in accounts that our economy is a vibrant and dynamic one depend, in our judgment, on taking full account of individual price changes.

VIII *Concepts of Real Profit:*

THE SUBSIDIARY ROLE OF PRICE LEVEL CHANGES

While we have seen that, for most decision-making purposes, money data (properly constructed, of course) are sufficient unto themselves, it does not follow that data in real terms are insignificant and therefore not worth collection. In matters of choice, managerial decision-makers wish "to do the best they can," and maximization of money profits will generally imply the maximization of real profits as well. But the measurement of money profit alone does not provide information on exactly how well the decision-maker has done. Whether he has successfully maximized or not, we would still like to know just how much profit he has earned and how much he has realized. Measures of real profit are needed principally for this purpose, to provide information on the real position of the firm and on the real increment, if any, in that position.[1]

[1] A secondary contribution of such measures is to make clear the real tax rate that is being paid by the firm, and perhaps as a result to lay the groundwork for a shift in the tax base from one measured in money terms to one measured in real terms.

The determination of *real business profit* is cumbersome, but the principles involved are not difficult to understand, and the development of data for real realized profit introduces little further that is complicated. We start with the assumption that money data have been developed and arranged according to the procedures suggested in Chapter VII. The figure for current operating profit presented there ($187) was determined by subtracting costs (current in average-of-1960 dollars) from sales (also current in average-of-1960 dollars). Current operating profit is therefore already stated in average-of-1960 dollars and requires no adjustment for price level changes; it is all real; none of it is fictional profit.

Realizable and realized gains, on the other hand, must be separated into real and fictional elements and only the real elements included in the statement of real profit. If this is done in average-of-period dollars to conform to COP as already reported, the problem remains to reconcile our real profit statement with the balance sheet which would normally be reported in end-of-period dollars. A choice is open to us: we can adjust every real item on the profit statement to end-of-period dollars by increasing the amounts in average-of-period dollars by the percentage change in the price level from the average to the end of the period; or we can apply this adjustment only to the final undistributed profit figures which become real increments in equity accounts on the balance sheet. The first method has the advantage that every item on the profit statement would be stated in dollars of the same vintage as those used for the balance sheet. A necessary cost of this procedure, however, would be the loss of direct comparability with profit statements on the historic cost and the current money cost bases. We shall yield to practicality on this matter and suggest end-of-period adjustments which yield a profit statement in average-of-period dollars. The profit statement in end-of-period dollars will, however, be illustrated.

We shall proceed in this chapter to develop statements in real terms, to compare our formulations with those of the "price level school" of accountants, to show how data for our statements can be collected (again on the basis of year-end adjustments alone) in the appropriate equity accounts, and to assess briefly the usefulness of such data.

The procedural steps to be taken in developing the data can be summarized as follows:

A. For data on real business profit and its related balance sheet:

1. Compute fictional realizable cost savings;
2. Subtract these from realizable cost savings in money terms to determine real realizable cost savings;
3. Formulate the statement of real business profit;
4. Allocate fictional realizable cost savings among equity accounts;
5. Formulate the balance sheet in real terms.

B. For data on real realized profit and its related balance sheet:

1. Compute fictional realized cost savings and realized capital gains;
2. Subtract these from realized cost savings and capital gains in money terms to determine real realized cost savings and real realized capital gains;
3. Formulate the statement of real realized profit;
4. Restate assets in terms of historic cost adjusted for price level changes since acquisition;
5. Formulate the balance sheet on the basis of real historic cost.

Steps B-4 and B-5 we consider to be redundant but they will serve us as an explanatory device in comparing our statements with those suggested by price level proponents.

Computation of Basic Data

We shall first compute in terms of our illustrative data Steps A-1 (fictional realizable cost savings), B-1 (fictional realized cost savings and capital gains), and A-2 and B-2 (the real counterparts) as indicated above. We will then have all of the necessary raw data with which to prepare statements in real terms in average-of-period dollars.

Fictional Realizable Cost Savings

To determine those realizable cost savings that are fictional in nature, it is only necessary to know the movements during the

SCHEDULE 1

COMPUTATION OF FICTIONAL REALIZABLE COST SAVINGS
(In thousands of dollars)

	End dollars (index = 102)		Average dollars (index = 100)
Net Money Claims			
On initial balance, $\frac{4}{98} \cdot 100$	4.08		
On increments, $\frac{2}{100} \cdot (126 - 100)$	.52		
Total applicable to net money claims		4.60	4.51
Securities			
On initial balance, $\frac{4}{98} \cdot 272$	11.10		
On increments, $\frac{2}{100} \cdot (248 - 272)$	−.48		
Total applicable to securities		10.62	10.41
Inventories			
On initial balance, $\frac{4}{98} \cdot 515$	21.02		
On increments, $\frac{2}{100}$ (690 − 515)	3.50		
Total applicable to inventories		24.52	24.04
Fixed Assets			
On initial balance, $\frac{4}{98} \cdot 1650$	67.35		
On increments, $\frac{2}{100}$ (1700 − 1650)	1.00		
Total applicable to fixed assets		68.35	67.01
Bonds Payable			
On initial balance, $\frac{4}{98} \cdot 600$	−24.49		
On increments, $\frac{2}{100}$ (597 − 600)	.06		
Total applicable to bonds payable		−24.43	−23.95
Total Fictional Realizable Cost Savings		83.66	82.02

current period in the price level index[2] in addition to the data in money terms contained in the statements presented in Chapter VII. We shall assume the index was 98 at the beginning of the period, 100 at the average-of-the-period, and 102 at the end of the period.

Schedule 1 shows the computation of fictional realizable cost savings (on the basis of the assumed movements in the price level) both in average-of-period and end-of-period dollars. The computations have first been made in end-of-period dollars and then converted to average-of-period dollars by multiplying the end-of-period figures by $\frac{100}{102}$, the average index divided by the ending index. In making the computations it has been assumed that increments to assets have occurred at an even pace throughout the year. On the average, therefore, these increments took place at the average price level for the period.

The inventory computation is reasoned as follows: To keep pace with the price level movement alone, the initial inventory worth $515 at current cost would have to increase in money terms by $21.02, i.e., [(102 – 98)/98] · $515, in order to have the same general purchasing power invested in inventories at the end of the period as was invested at the beginning of the period. The increment in the current cost value of inventories of $170 ($690 – $515) which occurred during the year should have grown by $3.50, i.e., [(102 – 100)/100] · $170, by the end of the year for this incremental investment to have the same general purchasing power then as it had at (average) time of acquisition. Of the total realizable cost savings accruing to the firm over the year through the holding of inventories the sum of these two amounts, $24.52, was necessary just to maintain purchasing power. Therefore, this amount of the apparent gain was purely fictional. This amount stated in average-of-period dollars is $24.04.

The fictional elements in realizable cost savings accruing to the firm on its holding of fixed assets and securities are computed

---

[2] Which index to use is a question that has often been discussed. We shall subscribe to Perry Mason's judgment that "the Consumers' Price Index of the U. S. Bureau of Labor Statistics is probably the best for this purpose." (*Price-Level Changes and Financial Statements: Basic Concepts and Methods,* previously cited, p. 12.)

in similar fashion using as raw data the current costs of these assets at the beginning and end of the period as reported on the comparative balance sheet in Chapter VII.

The net money claims computation may require additional explanation. We have taken all short-term assets and liabilities that are fixed in money terms, i.e., whose current cost is assumed constant, and netted them. The amount of net money claims at the beginning of the period ($100) is the sum of cash and receivables ($600) less the sum of current liabilities ($500). There is, of course, a zero money gain from holding these net money claims simply because their current costs are constant. Yet there is a fictional gain from holding them, it being the amount by which their current cost value should have increased to maintain parity with the price level. The fictional gain will be balanced entirely by a real loss. The zero money gain is broken into exactly offsetting fictional and real elements.

In our example the initial amount of $100 in net money claims should have grown by $4.08, i.e., $[(102 - 98)/98] \cdot \$100$, for it to represent an asset of the same stature in real terms at the end of the period as it represented at the beginning of the period. Because this fictional increase relates to assets, it is a fictional gain for the firm. It has as a counterpart a real loss of $4.08, indicating that the real value of the firm's asset has failed to increase by that amount. The increase in net money claims which occurred over the period is assumed to have occurred on the average when the price level index was 100. If the value of the increase ($26) had moved in proportion to the price level, the increase would be worth $.52, i.e., $[(102 - 100)/100] \cdot \$26$, more by the end of the period. The amount of $.52 is also a fictional gain which, when added to our fictional gain on the initial balance, makes the total fictional gain on the holding of net money claims $4.60 in end-of-period dollars, or $4.51 in average-of-period dollars.

If bonds outstanding were fixed in current value over the period, their treatment would parallel that accorded net money claims except that, being a liability item, a fictional loss (matched by a real gain) would accompany the holding of the initial balance and another fictional loss would arise on any increment in that balance. The fictional losses represent the amounts by which the initial balance (and any increment) should have increased to keep pace with the increase in the price level. The fact that the increase in value of the liability did not occur means the firm has benefited from a real gain.

This parallel treatment must be modified generally and in our example because the current value of bonds payable need not be fixed. When the current values vary from face values, fictional losses should be computed on the current values, not on the face values. In the bonds payable case, for example, the fictional loss on the initial balance is \$24.49, the amount by which the current value of the initial balance (equals face value) should have increased over the period in order to remain constant in terms of purchasing power. As no debt was issued or retired during the period, there can be no change in the face value of the debt. But the market value of the existing debt declined by \$3 in our example, a decrease presumed to take place gradually over the period. The decrease should have amounted to \$3.06, i.e., $(102/100) \cdot \$3$, by the end of the period to keep pace with the price level. The increase of \$.06 is a fictional gain. The fact that the change of \$.06 did not occur means that the firm has incurred a real loss of that amount. A decrease in debt is quite comparable to an increase in an asset.

The total amount of fictional realizable cost savings accruing to the firm over the period and stated in average-of-period dollars is \$82.02. These are the money gains which should have been made on holding activities just to keep the firm even in purchasing power terms. By subtracting the separate amounts which sum to this total from the money gains reported on the profit and loss statement in Chapter VII (zero, for net money claims) we obtain that portion of the money realizable cost savings which is real. We have all the data needed to draw up a statement of real business profit. Before doing so, however, let us compute data for real realized profit.

Fictional Realized Cost Savings and Capital Gains

Fictional realized cost savings (or capital gains) are computed in schedule 2. We assume that all fictional realizable losses on net money claims are realized.[3] Thus the amount in schedule 2 for this item is taken directly from schedule 1.

SCHEDULE 2

COMPUTATION OF FICTIONAL REALIZED GAINS

(In thousands of dollars)

	Average dollars	End dollars
Net Money Claims		
As in schedule 1	4.51	4.60
Securities		
(Index was 90 at purchase [for 18] of securities sold.)		
$\frac{100-90}{90} \cdot 18$	2.00	2.04
Inventories		
(Index was 97 when initial inventory was purchased, and 101 when final inventory was purchased.)		
Initial inventory, average dollars, $\frac{100}{97} \cdot 500 = 515.47$		
Purchases, average dollars, $\frac{100}{100} \cdot 2200 = 2200.00$		
2715.47		
Final inventory, average dollars, $\frac{100}{101} \cdot 681 = 674.26$		
Cost of materials used, average dollars.... 2041.21		
FIFO cost of materials used 2019.00		
Fictional realized cost savings	22.21	22.65
Fixed Assets		
(Index was 80 at purchase [for 100] of services used.)		
$\frac{100-80}{80} \cdot 100$	25.00	25.50
Total Fictional Realized Gains	53.72	54.79

For the other assets we need information on the price level index at the time the services used (or the assets sold) this period were actually purchased. We assume that this index was 90 at the time when the securities which are sold this period were purchased for $18, and 80 on the average when the fixed assets whose services are used during this period were purchased (the

[3] We shall not delve into the rather esoteric question of whether or not fictional gains (and the related real losses) from holding cash are not realized before the cash has been used, i.e., drawn down.

historic cost of these input services being the $100 depreciation charge). As the index was 100 when these inputs were sold or used toward mid-period, the historic cost of these inputs stated in units of constant purchasing power measured in average-of-year dollars was $20, i.e., (100/90) · $18, and $125, i.e., (100/80) · $100, respectively. To recover the same purchasing power as that originally invested in the assets, $20 and $125, respectively, must be realized on them. These amounts exceed unadjusted historic costs by $2 and $25, respectively, amounts which are, then, fictional realized gains, or the amounts of money gains that should be made on them just to maintain parity with the price level.

The same approach could be applied to the cost of materials used. The output into which the materials used have been converted was sold on the average when the price level was 100, the average for the period. We could compute the average lag between purchase, and use and sale, and multiply the historic (FIFO) cost of materials used by the percentage change in the price level index from the average purchase date to the average sale date.[4]

We have chosen instead to use the more traditional formula for obtaining the cost of materials used. We determine that the price level index was 97 on the average date on which the initial inventory was purchased.[5] We determine also that the index was 101 on the average date on which the final inventory was purchased.[6] We adjust both inventories from historic (FIFO) cost on dates acquired to average-of-period dollars. The initial in-

---

[4] In our example the lag might be computed as follows: The average purchase per day, 1⅑ units, is given by dividing purchases of 400 units by 360 days. We assume the first goods purchased are the first sold. At the rate of 1⅑ units per day the initial inventory of 100 units was acquired over 90 days. The additional 280 units sold would have been acquired on the average over an additional 252 days. The total amount sold was therefore acquired over 342 days commencing 90 days into the last period. The average date of acquisition was 171 days along this span, or 81 days into the current period, or 99 days on the average before sale. If the index then was 98.912, the result given in schedule 3 would be obtained directly.

[5] Employing the reasoning in the preceding footnote, this date would be 45 days prior to the end of the preceding period.

[6] At 1⅑ units per day, the final inventory of 120 units was accumulated over 108 days; the inventory is treated as though it were all purchased 54 days before the end of the period.

ventory at the adjusted figure plus purchases (already in average-of-period dollars) less the final inventory at the adjusted figure yields the cost of materials used in dollars of constant purchasing power. This is the amount that should be recovered if the firm is to suffer no real losses on its holding of materials. The excess of this figure over historic (FIFO) cost represents fictional realized cost savings.[7]

The omission of fictional realized cost savings on interest expense and on bonds payable requires some explanation. There are none on interest expense. The payment for the current services of borrowed capital is made currently and not in advance as is the case with cost of materials used and fixed asset services (depreciation). The amount paid is already stated in average-of-period dollars and requires no adjustment.

Whether fictional gains and losses on bonds payable should be treated as realized or not is a more controversial question. We exclude such gains from the realized category until the bonds are redeemed or exchanged, at which time a current market value is realized on the particular issue retired. This treatment accords with our treatment of assets: Fictional gains and losses are considered to be realized on securities sold, on cost of materials used, and on fixed asset services used (depreciation); they are not considered to be realized on assets still held.[8]

If it is preferred to treat fictional gains and losses on bonds payable as realized even though redemption has not occurred and in contrast to the treatment of assets, the section shown below should be included in schedule 2. In keeping with the usual treatment of fictional realized gains, no knowledge of current values is assumed. The difference between the amount realized here and the fictional losses reported as realizable in

[7] Both methods discussed are approximations. Complete accuracy would require an item-by-item analysis of materials used, a technique which would hardly be worth while.

[8] An apparent exception is net money claims. We accept the argument here that such assets and liabilities turn over so fast that the amount of fictional gains unrealized on the items in the final balances is negligible. (See R. C. Jones, *Effects of Price Level Changes on Business Income, Capital, and Taxes,* previously cited, p. 20.)

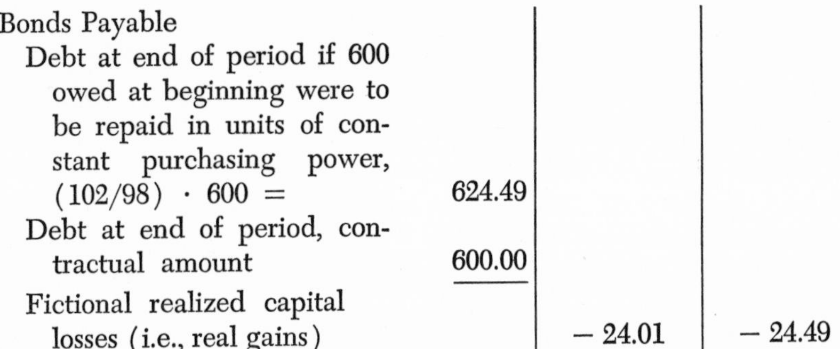

Bonds Payable			
Debt at end of period if 600 owed at beginning were to be repaid in units of constant purchasing power, (102/98) · 600 =	624.49		
Debt at end of period, contractual amount	600.00		
Fictional realized capital losses (i.e., real gains)		– 24.01	– 24.49

schedule 1 is accounted for entirely by fictional realizable gains on the change in market value over the period.[9]

The figures on fictional realized gains obtained in schedule 2 are in average-of-period dollars. They are restated in end-of-period dollars $\left(\text{by multiplying by } \frac{102}{100}\right)$ for use in computing data for statements in end-of-period dollars.

Computation of Real Gains

Schedule 3 summarizes the data on fictional realizable and realized cost savings (and capital gains) and uses them to illustrate the computation of their real counterparts. The schedule has two sections, the upper one containing data in average-of-period dollars, the lower one, data in end-of-period dollars. The realizable and realized amounts in money terms at average-of-period dollars, columns (1) and (2), upper section, are taken from the profit and loss statement in Chapter VII. Columns (3) and (4) contain the data on fictional realizable and realized gains, respectively, which were just explained. Columns (5) and (6) contain real realizable and realized gains, respectively, after the appropriate (indicated) subtractions have been performed. It is these amounts which will be used to formulate the statement of real profit.

Three things merit notice. The fictional increase in net money

[9] We hope it is clear that arguments, such as this one, over realization have no effect on realizable amounts, regardless of the outcome. Because we want real realized profit as a total to equal real accounting profit, we have tended to accept prevailing arguments on matters of realization in defining our concept of realized profit.

claims which would have maintained them at the same amount in terms of real purchasing power did not occur. The firm incurs a real loss of $4.51 because it can now buy less with its claims than it could when they were acquired. Secondly, the negative real realizable gains on securities indicate that the price level increased more rapidly during the period than did the current cost of securities. Realizable money gains were insufficient in this

SCHEDULE 3

Computation of Real Cost Savings and Capital Gains

(In thousands of dollars)

	Money amounts		Fictional amounts		Real amounts	
	Realizable (1)	Realized (2)	Realizable (3)	Realized (4)	Realizable (5) = (1) − (3)	Realized (6) = (2) − (4)
In Average Dollars						
On net money claims	...	...	4.51	4.51	−4.51	−4.51
On securities	6.00	12.00	10.41	2.00	−4.41	10.00
On inventories	65.00	71.00	24.04	22.21	40.96	48.79
On fixed assets	210.00	60.00	67.01	25.00	142.99	35.00
On bonds payable	6.00	3.00	−23.95	...	29.95	3.00
Totals	287.00	146.00	82.02	53.72	204.98	92.28
In End-of-Period Dollars						
On net money claims	...	...	4.60	4.60	−4.60	−4.60
On securities	6.12	12.24	10.62	2.04	−4.50	10.20
On inventories	66.30	72.42	24.52	22.65	41.78	49.77
On fixed assets	214.20	61.20	68.35	25.50	145.85	35.70
On bonds payable	6.12	3.06	−24.43	...	30.55	3.06
Totals	292.74	148.92	83.66	54.79	209.08	94.13

case to cover even the fictional gains needed to keep pace with the price level. A more rapid increase in the price level could cause the same thing to happen with respect to realizable gains on other assets. Finally, the real realizable amount on bonds payable is composed of two parts: the money gain of $6 arising on interest expense and the change in market value of the bonds, and the fictional loss of $23.95 which, because it did not occur, implies a real gain of equal amount.

The amounts in the lower section of the schedule are simply

the amounts in the upper section multiplied by $\frac{102}{100}$ to place them in end-of-period dollars. The figures in columns (5) and (6) can be used to construct a statement of real profit in end-of-period dollars.

THE FUNDAMENTAL STATEMENTS

Real Profit Statement

The statement of real profit in average-of-period dollars follows immediately from the data constructed, and is presented in terms of the data for our example in supplementary statement 1. Because the statement is formulated in average dollars, the section on current operating profit is identical to that presented in Chapter VII. The right-hand middle section adds to current operating profit the real realizable cost savings that accrued to the firm during the period under consideration. These amounts are taken from schedule 3. The total of these gains plus current operating profit thus obtained represents real business profit in average dollars of the period in question. The amount indicates in average dollars by how much the firm's real purchasing power has grown over the period before profit distribution. The left-hand second section adds real realized cost savings and capital gains to current operating profit to yield real realized profit in average-of-period dollars.

The section on disposition of real profit requires more explanation. The tax and dividend items are straightforward and correspond to amounts in the statement in money terms presented in Chapter VII. The amount carried to real realized surplus is the residual of real realized profit after tax and dividend payments. It is stated in average dollars and must be adjusted to end-of-period dollars on the balance sheet. While the amount includes cost savings and capital gains realized this period, it should be borne in mind that the savings and gains in question may have accrued to the firm in prior periods as well as in the present period.

The excess of real business profit over real realized profit represents the net increase in real unrealized surplus (unrealized cost savings and unrealized capital gains) and will be added to

SUPPLEMENTARY STATEMENT 1

COMPREHENSIVE STATEMENT OF REAL PROFIT AND LOSS
XYZ CORPORATION

for the year 1960
(In thousands of average-of-1960 dollars)

Sales		$4000.00	
Cost of materials used	$2090.00		
Wages and miscellaneous	1536.00		
Depreciation	160.00		
Interest	27.00		
		3813.00	
Current Operating Profit			$187.00

Current Operating Profit		$187.00
Real Realized Cost Savings		
On cost of materials	$48.79	
On depreciation	35.00	
On interest	3.00	
		86.79
Real Realized Capital Gains		
On net money claims	$– 4.51	
On securities sold	10.00	
		5.49
Real Realized Profit		$279.28

Current Operating Profit		$187.00
Real Realizable Cost Savings		
On net money claims	$– 4.51	
On securities	– 4.41	
On inventories	40.96	
On fixed assets	142.99	
On bonds payable	29.95	
		204.98
Real Business Profit		$391.98

The Disposition of Real Profit

Federal income taxes	$170.00
Dividends	74.00
Real realized surplus	35.28
Real Realized Profit	$279.28
Real unrealized surplus	112.70
Real Business Profit	$391.98

that equity account. As stated, the increase is in average dollars and must be adjusted on the balance sheet to end-of-period dollars. The increment in the account is the amount of real realizable cost savings accruing this period less the amount of cost savings realized this period though the latter may include amounts accruing in earlier periods.

Real Comparative Balance Sheet

The balance sheet is already stated in end-of-period dollars for the most part. The asset and liability sections are identical to those reported in money terms in Chapter VII. These items, being already stated in current cost values, in terms of end-of-period dollars, require no adjustment. It follows that total equities are unchanged also. The components of the equity portion of the balance sheet, however, will be considerably modified. The appropriately adjusted statement for our example appears as supplementary statement 2.

Consider first the initial balances in the various equity accounts. The amounts opposite the parent Capital Stock and Realized Surplus accounts, $600 and $700, respectively, are those which appeared under Equities in the traditional historic cost balance sheet given in Chapter VII. Similarly, these two figures plus the amount opposite Unrealized Surplus ($637) comprised the equity portion of the balance sheet in current cost values in Chapter VII. Both the items Realized and Unrealized Surplus, when expressed in money terms in this way, however, include some real and some fictional gains which have occurred over the life of the company. Assuming that the general trend in the price level has been upward, we must subtract the fictional gain elements in these equity items in order to state realized surplus and unrealized surplus in real terms. If we had done this each year, we would have a collection of real values, all in dollars of different vintage, values which would then have to be adjusted to 1959 year-end dollars in order to express all balance sheet items in dollars of the same vintage. We assume that the adjustments shown in the first column of supplementary statement 2 under Equities are the amounts which will provide us with the correct initial information for making new adjustments at the end of the current period. Discussion of these new

SUPPLEMENTARY STATEMENT 2

COMPARATIVE BALANCE SHEET OF THE XYZ COPORATION: CURRENT COSTS ADJUSTED FOR CHANGES IN THE GENERAL PRICE LEVEL

	December 31, 1959				December 31, 1960		Increase or decrease* in net assets or liabilities	
	Thousands of Dec. 1959 $		Thousands of Dec. 1960 $		Thousands of Dec. 1960 $			
Assets								
Cash and receivables		600.00		624.49		576.00		48.49*
Securities, at cost	200.00		200.00		182.00		18.00*	
Valuation adjustment	72.00	272.00	83.10	283.10	66.00	248.00	17.10*	35.10*
Inventories, at cost	500.00		500.00		681.00		181.00	
Valuation adjustment	15.00	515.00	36.02	536.02	9.00	690.00	27.02*	153.98
Fixed assets, depreciated cost	1,100.00		1,100.00		1,000.00		100.00*	
Valuation adjustment	550.00	1,650.00	617.35	1,717.35	700.00	1,700.00	82.65	17.35*
TOTAL ASSETS		3,037.00		3,160.96		3,214.00		53.04
less Liabilities								
Current	500.00		520.41		450.00		70.41	
Fixed	600.00		600.00		600.00		...	
Valuation adjustment (Bonds payable)	...		24.49		−3.00		27.49	
TOTAL LIABILITIES		1,100.00		1,144.90		1,047.00		97.90
Net Assets		1,937.00		2,016.06		2,167.00		150.94
Equities								
Capital Stock, mixed dollars	600.00		600.00		600.00		...	
Price level adjustment	160.00		191.02		191.02		...	
Capital stock, current dollars		760.00		791.02		791.02		...
Realized Surplus, as reported	700.00		700.00		789.00		89.00	
Less: fictional element	80.00		80.00		133.72		53.72*	
Real realized surplus, mixed dollars	620.00		620.00		655.28		35.28	
Price level adjustment	140.43		171.47		172.18		.71	
Real realized surplus, current dollars		760.43		791.47		827.46		35.99
Unrealized Surplus	637.00		637.00		778.00		141.00	
Less: fictional elements	310.43		310.43		338.73		28.30*	
Real unrealized surplus, mixed dollars	326.57		326.57		439.27		112.70	
Price level adjustment	90.00		107.00		109.25		2.25	
Real unrealized surplus, current dollars		416.57		433.57		548.52		114.95
Total Equities		1,937.00		2,016.06		2,167.00		150.94

adjustments will make clear what we may assume has been done cumulatively over the past history of the XYZ Corporation.

At the heart of the adjustments necessary at the end of 1960 to formulate a comparative balance sheet corrected for changes in the general price level, a comparative balance sheet which will be consistent with the statement of real profit or loss already devised in supplementary statement 1, there lies a fundamental relationship which is simply an extension of the traditional accounting check between the change in equity values shown on the comparative balance sheet and the net business profit for the year shown on the profit and loss statement.[10] The nature of this relationship for the events of 1960 may be depicted schematically as shown below (where in the usual manner A, L, and E denote assets, liabilities, and equities, respectively, and the subscript c denotes current cost value).

	(1) Money Gain		2 Fictional Gain		(3) Real Gain
Increment to realized surplus	$ 89.00	−	$53.72 (realized)	=	$ 35.28
Increment to unrealized surplus	141.00	−	28.30 (unrealized)	=	112.70
$\Delta A_c - \Delta L_c = \Delta E_c$ = net business profit	$230.00	=	$82.02 (realizable) (price level adjustments to equity accounts)	+	$147.98

In column (1) are the money gains which provided the necessary check between the comparative balance sheet in current cost values and the statement of money business profit, derived in Chapter VII. For our supplementary balance sheet, adjusted for changes in the general price level, we must state our equity items in real terms, and therefore we must subtract the proportion of the money gains which are purely fictional in order to obtain the real increments to realized surplus and to unrealized surplus. These real increments are shown in the first two rows of column

[10] See the discussion, for example, in Chapter IV in the section on developing business profit.

(3) and are the same amounts as those shown on supplementary statement 1, the statement of real profit and loss. They are shown on the comparative balance sheet illustrated in supplementary statement 2 as increments to real realized surplus and real unrealized surplus.

Now if we add the three columns vertically, we obtain the total of money and real gains earned and distributed in columns (1) and (3), respectively, and the total of fictional realizable cost savings in column (2). The necessary identity between realizable gains on the one hand, and realized gains and the change in unrealized gains on the other, has been described before. Realizable gains over any period must either be realized during that period or be added to unrealized gains on hand at the end of the period; or put another way, realized gains over any period must either have accrued during the period and so be realizable gains of the period, or reduce unrealized gains which have accrued over past periods.

It is this identity which provides us with our crucial relationship governing adjustments to equity accounts in the balance sheet, namely, the total of realized and unrealized fictional gains which are subtracted from the money increments to realized and unrealized surplus in order to arrive at the real increments are exactly equal to the net sum of all the price level adjustments to equity accounts made at the end of the period. The real gains of $147.98 which adjust the Real Realized and Unrealized Surplus accounts on the balance sheet differ from the net change in assets less liabilities at current cost values by the amount of the fictionable realizable gains. But fictional realizable gains are by definition the amount of money gains necessary to keep pace with the price level, i.e. those necessary to maintain purchasing power. We have computed them on all assets and liabilities, but as these net to total equities it should not be surprising that these fictional gains are just sufficient, if earned, to maintain the purchasing power of the owners' equity, i.e. to equal the adjustments in the equity items to take account of changes in the general price level. Until this amount is earned, there can be no real increment in that equity.

Schedule 4 illustrates the allocation of the fictional realizable

SCHEDULE 4

DISTRIBUTION OF FICTIONAL REALIZABLE COST SAVINGS AMONG EQUITY ACCOUNTS

(THOUSANDS OF DOLLARS)

Total to be distributed (see schedule 1)				$82.02
To Capital Stock				
On initial balance, $\frac{4}{98} \cdot \$760$			$31.02	
To Real Realized Surplus				
On initial balance, $\frac{4}{98} \cdot \$760.43$		$31.04		
On increment (retained real realized profit)				
On COP, $\frac{2}{100} \cdot \$187.00$	$3.74			
On real realized gains, $\frac{2}{100} \cdot \$92.28$	1.85			
Less: on disbursements, $\frac{2}{100} \cdot \$244.00$	−4.88			
= On retained real realized profit, $\frac{2}{100} \cdot \$35.28$		.71		
Total to Realized Surplus			31.75	
To Real Unrealized Surplus				
On initial balance, $\frac{4}{98} \cdot \$416.57$		$17.00		
On increment				
On real realizable cost savings, $\frac{2}{100} \cdot \$204.98$	$4.10			
Less: on real amount realized, $\frac{2}{100} \cdot \$92.28$	−1.85			
= On the real unrealized increment, $\frac{2}{100} \cdot \$112.70$		2.25		
Total to Real Unrealized Surplus			19.25	
TOTAL				$82.02

cost savings amounting to $82.02 among the various equity accounts.[11] The initial net balances applicable to the three main

[11] As we want to restate equity accounts in end-of-period dollars it would appear reasonable at first glance to allocate the fictional amount as it appears in end-of-period dollars, $83.66. But the fictional gains themselves are in average-of-period dollars, $82.02, and to state them in end-of-period dollars we must use $1.64 ($\frac{2}{100} \cdot \$82.02$) to do so. This leaves $82.02 to be allocated to other equity accounts. (The fictional realizable cost savings account will, of course, have a zero balance when all allocations have been completed.)

kinds of equity, capital stock ($760.00), realized surplus ($760.43), and unrealized surplus ($416.57), are all stated in end-of-1959 dollars when the price index was 98. Their equivalents in end-of-1960 dollars (index = 102) can be obtained by adding [(102 − 98)/98 · initial balance] to the initial balances. It can be seen that most of the fictional realizable cost savings are used in this fashion.

The real increments to the equity categories of realized and unrealized surplus accounts amounting to $35.28 and $112.70, respectively, which are taken directly from the disposition of real profits section of supplementary statement 1, are stated in average-of-year dollars, and must be restated in end-of-period dollars by adding (102 − 100)/100, or 2 per cent, to each. These additional allocations just exhaust fictional realizable cost savings as we showed they must.

In supplementary statement 2 we have used the allocations of fictional gains to initial balances to restate the December 31, 1959 equity items in terms of December, 1960 dollars. The total so allocated, $79.06, is, of course, just equal to the net amount added to net assets in restating those in December, 1960 dollars. By adjusting the December 31, 1959 balance sheet in this way a direct comparison can be made with the balance sheet constructed for December 31, 1960 because both are stated in dollars of the same vintage.

The balance sheet for the close of 1960 reveals in the parent accounts for capital stock and realized surplus, as before, the amounts as they would appear on the historic cost balance sheet. The excess of the price level adjustment to realized surplus for December 31, 1960, over the amount for December 31, 1959, in December, 1960 dollars is the price level adjustment applicable to the real increment in realized surplus of $35.28 and restates it in end-of-period dollars, $35.99. The increase in the price level adjustment for unrealized surplus can be similarly explained.

It follows, of course, that for realized surplus the net amount, namely, real realized surplus in current dollars, is stated in end-of-period dollars. The items leading to this figure (except for the price level adjustment itself) are stated in average-of-period dollars in order to maintain comparability with traditional statements. Similar remarks apply to the unrealized surplus section.

Statements Wholly in End-of-Period Dollars

Supplementary statement 3 reports real profit in end-of-period dollars. It is obtained by multiplying every amount in supplementary statement 1 by $\frac{102}{100}$, the ratio of the end-of-period index to the average-of-period index. The increments to real realized surplus and to real unrealized surplus are now stated in end-of-period dollars and can be directly related to the net changes shown for these items on the balance sheet.

Complete comparability between this statement and the balance sheet would require, however, a restatement of the balance sheet items used to compute real realized surplus and real unrealized surplus. The increment to the parent money realized surplus account, for example, should now be shown as \$90.78, instead of \$89, an increase of $\frac{2}{100}$ to state it in end-of-period dollars. The change in the fictional element would be \$54.79 instead of \$53.72 for the same reason. As a result the real change in realized surplus in end-of-period dollars would be a residual (\$90.78 – \$54.79 = \$35.99) requiring no additional price level adjustment. An equity section constructed in this way might appear as in supplementary statement 4. Net total amounts in the three equity accounts are the same as in supplementary statement 2. Comparability with historic cost statements and the statements in money terms advanced in Chapter VII is now destroyed, however, because some price level adjustments have been hidden with the items adjusted.

We have no objection to the construction of profit statements in end-of-period dollars. Indeed, there is much to be said for presentation in dollars that accord generally with the balance sheet. We do feel strongly, however, that the accounts in which the adjusted data are gathered should be consistent with the profit statement prepared in average-of-period dollars to avoid destruction of historic cost data or the unnecessary duplication of all revenue and expense accounts.

The Accounts and the Accounting Technique

The system we suggest for developing adjusted data utilizes end-of-period adjustments alone, made in accounts which we

SUPPLEMENTARY STATEMENT 3

Comprehensive Statement of Real Profit and Loss
XYZ Corporation
for the year 1960
(In thousands of December 31, 1960 dollars)

Sales		$4080.00	
Cost of materials used	$2131.80		
Wages and miscellaneous	1566.72		
Depreciation	163.20		
Interest	27.54		
		3889.26	
Current Operating Profit			$190.74

Current Operating Profit		$190.74
Real Realized Cost Savings		
On cost of materials	$49.77	
On depreciation	35.70	
On interest	3.06	
		88.53
Real Realized Capital Gains		
On net money claims	$– 4.60	
On securities sold	10.20	
		5.60
Real Realized Profit		$284.87

Current Operating Profit		$190.74
Real Realizable Cost Savings		
On net money claims	$– 4.60	
On securities	–4.50	
On inventories	41.78	
On fixed assets	145.85	
On bonds payable	30.55	
		209.08
Real Business Profit		$399.82

The Disposition of Real Profit

Federal income taxes	$173.40
Dividends	75.48
Real Realized Profit	$284.87
Real realized surplus	35.99
Real unrealized surplus	114.95
Real Business Profit	$399.82

SUPPLEMENTARY STATEMENT 4

Comparative Balance Sheet of the XYZ Corporation (Equity Section): current costs adjusted for changes in the general price level (end-of-period dollars)

	December 31, 1959				December 31, 1960		Increase or decrease* in net assets or liabilities	
	Thousands of Dec. 1959 $		Thousands of Dec. 1960 $		Thousands of Dec. 1960 $			
Net Assets		1,937.00		2,016.06		2,167.00		150.94
Equities								
Capital Stock, mixed dollars	600.00		600.00		600.00		...	
Price level adjustment	160.00		191.02		191.02		...	
Capital stock, current dollars		760.00		791.02		791.02		...
Realized Surplus	712.00[a]		712.00		802.78		90.78	
Less: fictional elements	84.00[a]		84.00		138.79		54.79*	
Real realized surplus, mixed dollars	628.00		628.00		663.99		35.99	
Price level adjustment	132.43[a]		163.47		163.47		...	
Real realized surplus, current dollars		760.43		791.47		827.46		35.99
Unrealized Surplus	647.00[a]		647.00		790.82		143.82	
Less: fictional elements	315.43[a]		315.43		344.30		28.87*	
Real unrealized surplus, mixed dollars	331.57		331.57		446.52		114.95	
Price level adjustment	85.00[a]		102.00		102.00		...	
Real unrealized surplus, current dollars		416.57		433.57		548.52		114.95
Total Equities		1,937.00		2,016.06		2,167.00		150.94

[a] These differ from supplementary statement 2 because it is assumed that all past statements were prepared in the same way as this one. We no longer report realized surplus, for example, as it would appear on the historic cost statement because each retained amount carries some hidden price level adjustment.

assume would be carried in a separate subsidiary ledger. The number of accounts we utilize is eighteen, of which six are simply duplications of general ledger accounts (a few additional accounts would be needed for firms having more than one kind of stock outstanding). Of the eighteen accounts, eight are used to develop balance sheet data and will generally have continuing balances, and ten are used to develop real profit data. The accounts used in developing the data for our hypothetical example are illustrated. Original balances and entries duplicated from general ledger accounts are unnumbered. The numbered entries we shall explain.

We start with the Realizable Cost Savings account duplicated from the general ledger. Entry (1) utilizes data from Schedule 3 to separate the balance in this account into fictional and real elements, identifying in the fictional and real accounts the major groups of assets and liabilities to which particular amounts apply. Entry (2) transfers total real realizable cost savings to Real Business Profit, an account which already contains current operating profit as a duplicate general ledger account posting. The basic data for a statement of real business profit are now available.

Entry (3) transfers the COP element of real business profit to the Real Realized Profit account. Entry (4) transfers real realizable cost savings to the Real Unrealized Surplus–Mixed Dollars account. This amount together with the original balance in the account represents the maximum cost savings which could be realized as cost savings or capital gains in this period. Entries (5) and (6) transfer the amounts actually realized on major groups of assets and liabilities to Real Realized Cost Savings and Real Realized Capital Gains, respectively. The remaining balance in the account will appear on the balance sheet. Entries (7) and (8) transfer real realized cost savings and real realized capital gains to Real Realized Profit. The principal data are now collected in that account for the preparation of a statement of real realized profit.

Entry (9) transfers real realized profit to a Disposition account. Entries (10) and (11) record tax and dividend dispositions, and entry (12) transfers the real increment in realized surplus at average-of-period dollars to the Real Realized Surplus–Mixed

SUBSIDIARY LEDGER ACCOUNTS FOR PRICE LEVEL ADJUSTMENTS

Realizable Cost Savings

Debit		Credit	
(1) Real and fictional elements	287.00	On securities	6.00
		On inventories	65.00
		On fixed assets	210.00
		On bonds payable	6.00
	287.00		287.00

Fictional Realizable Cost Savings

Debit		Credit	
(1) On bonds payable	23.95	(1) On net money claims	4.51
(13) To Cap. Stk.-PLA $\left[\frac{4}{98} \cdot 760\right]$	31.02	(1) On securities	10.41
(14) To Real Realized Surplus-PLA $\left[\frac{4}{98} \cdot 760.43\right]$	31.04	(1) On inventories	24.04
(15) To Real Realized Surplus-PLA $\left[\frac{2}{100} \cdot 35.28\right]$	.71	(1) On fixed assets	67.01
(16) To Real Unrealized Surplus-PLA $\left[\frac{4}{98} \cdot 416.57\right]$	17.00		
(17) To Real Unrealized Surplus-PLA $\left[\frac{2}{100} \cdot 112.70\right]$	2.25		
	105.97		105.97

Real Realizable Cost Savings

Debit		Credit	
(1) On net money claims	4.51	(1) On inventories	40.96
(1) On securities	4.41	(1) On fixed assets	142.99
(2) To Real Business Profit	204.98	(1) On bonds payable	29.95
	213.90		213.90

Real Business Profit

Debit		Credit	
(3) To Real Realized Profit	187.00	COP (from general ledger)	187.00
(4) To Real Unrealized Surplus–Mixed Dollars	204.98	(2) Real realizable cost savings	204.98
	391.98		391.98

Real Realized Cost Savings

Debit		Credit	
(7) To Real Realized Profit	86.79	(5) On cost of materials	48.79
		(5) On depreciation	35.00
		(5) On interest	3.00
	86.79		86.79

Real Realized Capital Gains

Debit		Credit	
(6) On net money claims	4.51	(6) On securities sold	10.00
(8) To Real Realized Profit	5.49		
	10.00		10.00

Real Realized Profit

Debit		Credit	
(9) To Disposition account	279.28	(3) COP	187.00
		(7) Real realized cost savings	86.79
		(8) Real realized capital gains	5.49
	279.28		279.28

Disposition of Real Realized Profit

Debit		Credit	
(10) Taxes, on realized profit (167), on C.G.(3)	170.00	(9) Real realized profit	279.28
(11) Dividends	74.00		
(12) To Real Realized Surplus–Mixed Dollars	35.28		
	279.28		279.28

Tax Liability

Paid (from general ledger)	170.00	(10) Taxes, on realized 167, on cap. gains, 3.	170.00

Dividends Payable

Paid (from general ledger)	74.00	(11)	74.00

Capital Stock (Repeated from G.L.)

		From general ledger	600.00

Capital Stock–Price Level Adjustment

To balance	191.02	Balance	160.00
		(13)	31.02
	191.02		191.02
		Balance	191.02

Realized Surplus (Repeated from G.L.)

To balance	789.00	Balance	700.00
		Retained realized profit	89.00
	789.00		789.00
		Balance	789.00

Real Realized Surplus–Mixed Dollars

To balance	655.28	Balance	620.00
		(12)	35.28
	655.28		655.28
		Balance	655.28

Real Realized Surplus–Price Level Adjustment

To balance	172.18	Balance	140.43
		(14)	31.04
		(15)	.71
	172.18		172.18
		Balance	172.18

Unrealized Surplus (Summarized from G.L.)

To balance	778.00	Balance	637.00
		Increment	141.00
	778.00		778.00
		Balance	778.00

Real Unrealized Surplus–Mixed Dollars

(5) To Real Realized Cost Savings	86.79	Balance	326.57
(6) To Real Realized Capital Gains	5.49	(4) Real realizable cost savings	204.98
To balance	439.27		
	531.55		531.55
		Balance	439.27

Real Unrealized Surplus–Price Level Adjustment

To balance	109.25	Balance	90.00
		(16)	17.00
		(17)	2.25
	109.25		109.25
		Balance	109.25

Dollars account. The real increment in real unrealized surplus was left in the appropriate account after entries (4), (5), and (6). We have now accumulated all necessary data for a statement of real profit and its disposition.

To complete the adjustment process, we have only to allocate fictional realizable cost savings to the appropriate price level adjustment equity accounts. Entries (13) through (17) achieve this effect using data from schedule 4. All of the data for the balance sheet are now available and the adjustment process has been completed for another year.

A Comparison with Price-Level-Adjusted Historic Cost Data

Perhaps some perspective can be gained with the accounting technique behind us by reviewing our fundamental statements and comparing them with statements based on historic costs, but adjusted for changes in the price level. Such statements, which take no account whatsoever of current cost values, have nevertheless received considerable attention in recent years.[12] The comparison can be brief because of its striking similiarity to that

[12] See, for example, the fine but brief theoretical study by Perry Mason (*op. cit.*) and the excellent work of Ralph C. Jones in *Price Level Changes and Financial Statements: Case Studies of Four Companies* and *Effects of Price Level Changes on Business Income, Capital, and Taxes,* previously cited.

drawn in Chapter VII between realized and accounting profit.

The branch of supplementary statement 1 which leads to real business profit informs us that the firm now controls net assets which in terms of real purchasing power have increased by the indicated amount (before tax and dividend payments) over the period in question. Real accounting profit, the statement in which historic costs have simply been adjusted for price level changes, can make no pretense of divulging such information because the current cost values of the firm's net assets are not accounted for at all.

Of the increment in real purchasing power, which we have designated real business profit, a portion is as yet unrealized. The balance of it is realized and includes current operating profit, real realized cost savings, and real realized capital gains. These together represent real realized profit, a figure which is identical to real accounting profit. Thus real accounting profit, like real realized profit, eliminates those real cost savings which have yet to be realized but which are nevertheless an important part of the firm's current position.

Unfortunately real accounting profit does not distinguish between COP and real realized cost savings but treats both as operating profit. Supplementary statement 5 presents this view of profit. Instead of stating real realized cost savings on the cost of materials used ($48.79), on depreciation ($35), and on interest ($3) separately, these amounts are allowed to swell operating profit. This is accomplished by deducting the cost of materials used, depreciation and interest expense in the operating section of the statement at price-level-adjusted historic costs ($2041.21, $125, and $24, respectively, [see schedule 2]) instead of at current costs ($2090, $160, and $27, respectively). This error destroys entirely the significance of operating profit. The balance of the statement is similar to that for real realized profit including, it should be noted, the amount carried to real realized surplus.

The balance sheet which would be completely consistent with a statement of real realized profit alone would also be consistent with real accounting profit. It will be recalled that in each period real business profit exceeds (algebraically, of course) real realized profit by the increment in real unrealized surplus. If only real realized profit were accounted for over time, therefore, the

SUPPLEMENTARY STATEMENT 5
STATEMENT OF REAL ACCOUNTING PROFIT
XYZ CORPORATION
for the year 1960
(In thousands of average-of-1960 dollars)

Sales		$4000.00	
Cost of materials used	$2041.21		
Wages and miscellaneous	1536.00		
Depreciation	125.00		
Interest	24.00		
		3726.21	
Real Accounting Operating Profit			$273.79
Real Realized Capital Gains			
On net money claims		$−4.51	
On securities sold		10.00	
			5.49
Real Accounting Profit			$279.28
Disposition:			
Federal income taxes		$ 170.00	
Dividends		74.00	
Real earned surplus		35.28	
			$279.28

equity section of the balance sheet in supplementary statement 2 would contain no record of unrealized surplus. That part of the equity section would disappear leaving only the sections on capital stock and realized surplus.

To compensate, there must be an equivalent reduction in net assets. This is accomplished by restating all assets in terms of price-level-adjusted historic costs eliminating thereby the excess of current cost over price-level-adjusted historic cost on each asset and liability item. Such a balance sheet is presented in supplementary statement 6. Frankly, we see little use for such a statement if a statement in current cost values, such as supplementary statement 2, is available. Certainly no pretense of current position can be attributed to the statement.[13]

[13] The statement of real accounting profit and its related balance sheet are consistent with the methods advanced by Mason (*op. cit.*), but the terminology is ours.

SUPPLEMENTARY STATEMENT 6

Comparative Balance Sheet of the XYZ Corporation: historic costs adjusted for changes in the general price level

	December 31, 1959				December 31, 1960		Increase or decrease* in net assets or liabilities	
	Thousands of Dec. 1959 $		Thousands of Dec. 1960 $		Thousands of Dec. 1960 $			
Assets								
Cash and receivables		600.00		624.49		576.00		48.49*
Securities, at cost	200.00		200.00		182.00		18.00*	
Price level adjustment	17.78		26.67		24.27		2.40*	
Adjusted historic cost		217.78		226.67		206.27		20.40*
Inventories, at cost	500.00		500.00		681.00		181.00	
Price level adjustment	5.15		25.77		6.74		19.03*	
Adjusted historic cost		505.15		525.77		687.74		161.97
Fixed assets, depreciated cost	1,100.00		1,100.00		1,000.00		100.00*	
Price level adjustment	247.50		302.50		275.00		27.50*	
Adjusted historic cost		1,347.50		1,402.50		1,275.00		127.50*
Total Assets		2,670.43		2,779.43		2,745.01		34.42*
less Liabilities								
Current	500.00		520.41		450.00		70.41	
Fixed	600.00		600.00		600.00		...	
Price level adjustment on bonds payable	50.00		76.53		76.53		...	
Total Liabilities		1,150.00		1,196.94		1,126.53		70.41
Net Assets		1,520.43		1,582.49		1,618.48		35.99
Equities								
Capital stock, mixed dollars	600.00		600.00		600.00		...	
Price level adjustment	160.00		191.02		191.02		...	
Capital stock, current dollars		760.00		791.02		791.02		...
Earned surplus, as reported	700.00		700.00		789.00		89.00	
Less: fictional element	80.00		80.00		133.72		53.72*	
Real earned surplus, mixed dollars	620.00		620.00		655.28		35.28	
Price level adjustment	140.43		171.47		172.18		.71	
Real earned surplus, current dollars		760.43		791.47		827.46		35.99
Total Equities		1,520.43		1,582.49		1,618.48		35.99

Usefulness of Real Data

The real profit concepts are useful for certain decision-making and decision evaluation purposes, but their principal function is as a means of establishing real rates of return and real tax rates.

Relevance for Decision-Making and Evaluation

The efficiency of money profits (business profit variety) as a means of decision evaluation rests essentially on two facts: The maximization of business profit over a given period will, if successful, maximize real profit as well; and in cases where data on real profits are an important input in the decision-making process, current operating profit is already in real terms.

Internal management decisions in particular can be made and evaluated quite effectively without recourse to real data so long as the money data utilized are of the business profit construction. This concept measures the increase in the money value of the firm over a particular period starting from the firm's real position at the beginning of the period. The profit of the present period, so measured, is not clouded with events of past periods, and so we can be sure that a course of action which maximizes money profit over the period (or which leads to that short-run profit which is the appropriate link in long-run profit maximization) will also maximize real profit. The same deflators would apply to alternative courses of action as apply to the one adopted.[14]

As an extension of this same point, if fund retention is determined on the basis of profitable alternatives, the identification of real profit should not alter the amount paid in dividends even if real capital is impaired by the payment. To the extent that management substitutes growth in real capital for profitability as a goal, the new information might well affect decisions but the economist would be hard pressed to rationalize the new decision, whether to owners, investors, or the economy as a whole. The information that real capital is or is not being maintained is perhaps good to have, but it is not relevant to profit-maximizing

---

[14] This theorem is not applicable, however, if profit is measured in any way which permits past profits or losses to be counted currently. Accounting profit, realized profit, real accounting profit, and real realized profit all suffer from this defect although the current operating profit elements of the second and fourth do not.

decisions. When, then, may data on real profits be useful for decision-making purposes?

First, in attempting to maximize profit, the probable impact of alternative movements in the general price level will often be considered. Such movements may have a bearing upon management's access to funds, upon demand considerations, and so forth. It follows that the separation of money gains into real and fictional elements could aid in the analysis of these types of expectations.

Secondly, data on real profits may be useful for comparisons, over time and among firms, comparisons which are an important ingredient of decision-making processes within a business firm and of still greater relevance to outsiders. Most comparisons, however, involve simply operating profits, and current operating profit in money terms is also the real amount in average-of-period dollars. If data on holding gains are needed, however, they should be sorted into real and fictional elements. The following situations, for example, are typical comparison problems for which data on past real profits might prove useful:

1. The comparison among firms at a moment in time, whether by outsiders, owners, or management. Current operating profits can be compared directly because they are already in real terms. Data on cost savings and capital gains should be reduced to real terms before being joined to current operating profit for purposes of comparing the general profitability of different firms. As the data compared apply to the same time interval, the data are already stated in dollars of the same vintage and no further deflation is necessary.

2. The comparison over time of the profits of a single firm. For this, real data adjusted to a common dollar should be used. If the common dollar deflation is not carried out, real gains recorded when the price level is high will be given exaggerated status. If the price level has been rising over time, the upward trend in raw COP figures, for example, will exaggerate the true trend.

3. The comparison among firms of trends over time. Here real data are needed but these need not be adjusted to common dollars. Even if the price level has moved upward so that the trend for each firm is exaggerated, the relative strength of trends will be unaffected by common dollar deflation.

The reader can judge for himself how frequently current operating profits alone would suffice the analyst and how often data on real cost savings would be required.

Measurement of Real Rates of Return

A true demonstration of the effect of different methods of profit measurement on rates of return would require a careful computation of various profit concepts for a selected sample of companies under a variety of conditions. Such an exploration is beyond the scope of this study. We shall therefore compute various rates of return for the hypothetical XYZ Corporation and use these data as a point of departure for a brief consideration of the factors influencing the relative sizes of the different kinds of rates of return.

Table 14 contains the requisite data. The example has been constructed on the assumption of a moderately rising price level accompanied by more rapidly increasing current costs of particular assets. Under these circumstances accounting operating profit yields the highest operating rate of return. Its measure of profit is swelled by realized cost savings which are evidence that current costs exceed historic costs, and the base is held down to the historic cost level. Current operating profit excludes realized cost

TABLE 14

VARIOUS RATES OF RETURN ON EQUITY, XYZ CORPORATION, 1960

	Profit (before taxes)	Equity base	Rate of return (%)
Operating Profits			
Accounting operating profit	321.00	1389.00	23.1
Real accounting operating profit	273.79	1618.48	16.9
Current operating profit	187.00	2167.00	8.6
Total Money Profits			
Accounting profit	333.00	1389.00	24.0
Realized profit	333.00	2167.00	15.4
Business profit	474.00	2167.00	21.9
Total Real Profits			
Real accounting profit	279.28	1618.48	17.3
Real realized profit	279.28	2167.00	12.9
Real business profit	391.98	2167.00	18.1

savings and, when related to current cost values as the net asset base, yields a substantially smaller operating rate of return. If current costs had been falling and were now generally lower than historic costs, the current operating profit rate would exceed its traditional counterpart. Real accounting operating profit yields a rate between the others because the price level has been rising (this rise, relative to the accounting operating profit rate, reduces profit and increases the base) but not so rapidly as current costs (keeping profit above COP and the base below current cost).

Total accounting profit and realized profit are equal, but in computing the realized profit rate, we recognize the current value of the net assets used to yield that profit. As current costs exceed historic costs, this rate is less than the accounting profit rate. The business profit rate in this instance happens to fall between the others. The base used is the same as for realized profit. The amount of business profit exceeds the amount of realized profit because the rise in this period in the current costs of net assets held in this period exceeds the excess of the current cost over the historic cost of asset services used. If current costs had been stable in this period alone, business profit would just equal current operating profit, but realized profit would not be so drastically affected because current costs of asset services used would still exceed their historic costs by a substantial amount.

The real accounting profit rate is below the accounting profit rate because the price level has been rising, thus reducing profit and increasing the rate base. The real realized profit rate is even lower because the same profit figure is applied against a base of current costs, which have been rising more rapidly than the price level. The real business profit rate utilizes the current cost base also, but the profit figure exceeds that for real realized profit because the excess of current cost changes this period over price level changes this period exceeds the excess of the current cost of services used this period over the historic costs of those services whenever acquired but adjusted for price level changes.

While the relationships among the computed rates will vary depending on relative movements of current costs and the price level (all would be equal if all prices and the price level had been constant over the time span covered by the firm's oldest asset), the most significant rates of return under any conditions are the current operating profit rate, the real business profit rate, and the real realized profit rate. The first indicates the firm's true rate of return from operating net assets having a recognized current value; the second indicates the current rate of return earned on those assets through holding as well as operating activities; the last indicates the rate of return which is related to tax payments.[15]

Real Burden of Taxes

Federal corporate income taxes are presently levied on accounting operating profit and the capital gains tax is levied on realized capital gains (unless used to reduce the tax basis of replacement items, a matter which we shall disregard). Thus taxes for the XYZ Corporation were computed to be $170 (52 per cent of $321 plus 25 per cent of $12), an average rate of 51 per cent on total profit of $333. But of the amount apparently earned, only $279.28 was real, gradual inflation having wiped out the rest. On this amount, the corporation has paid taxes at an average rate of 61 per cent. This real tax rate would be substantially larger given a more rapid rise in the general price level.

Disclosure of the real rate is important information. More significantly, however, a demonstration by business firms that real realized profit can be readily and objectively measured might persuade some congressmen to support a tax amendment designed to place corporate income taxation on a real basis. It should be emphasized, however, that firms would gain in the long run by this decision only to the extent that the price level exhibits an upward trend.

We propose for consideration the following: that a corporation's tax liability be computed on the basis of real business profit but that its current tax payments be related to real realized profit. Further, if it is considered desirable to tax capital gains at lower

[15] When rates of return are used to measure performance and/or monopoly power within and among different industries, as attempted extensively by Bain for example, it would seem to be particularly important to separate holding gains from operating gains. But Bain considers only the adjustment of historic costs for changes in the price level, giving no recognition to the fact that accounting profit throws together two elements of gain, one of which might be a useful index of some types of monopoly power, while the other is surely the key basis on which performance from a social point of view must be judged. See, for example, J. S. Bain, *Industrial Organization,* pp. 363–387.

rates (a matter we will not debate here) there is no reason why cost savings should not be accorded the same treatment. Assuming that all cost savings and capital gains are considered to be long-term gains, that such gains cannot be used to adjust the tax base of replacement items, and that existing tax rates continue in effect, the accompanying illustrative computation can be made for the XYZ Corporation.

	Proposed Tax Liability		Proposed Tax Payment		Existing Liability and Payment	
	Base	Tax	Base	Tax	Base	Tax
Income taxes, 52%	$187	$ 97	$187	$ 97	$321	$167
Capital gains taxes, 25%	205	52	92	23	12	3
Total taxes	$392	$149	$279	$120	$333	$170

The proposed tax payment would result in an average tax rate of 43 per cent on real realized profit of $279, as compared to the existing rate of 61 per cent on that base. Of the total reduction of $50 in taxes in this example, $36 is attributable to the treatment of cost savings ($134 in money terms) as capital gains rather than as operating income, thus reducing the applicable rate by 27 per cent. The subsequent adjustment of these cost savings and of the capital gains to a real basis accounts for only $14 of the tax reduction. Supporters of this proposal should recognize, however, that generally falling prices over a long period of time could lead to higher tax payments than those that would be required under existing law.

IX *Summary and Conclusions:*

IS THE NEEDED CHANGE FEASIBLE?

General agreement is not likely to be achieved overnight on a matter which has aroused so much controversy, over so many years, as the problem of what to do about the effects of changing prices on reported accounting values. Our contribution to the debate is not offered as a definitive solution. Most difficult problems in the social sciences have no definitive solution, and indeed may have no solution at all, as Arnold Toynbee once suggested, but simply an outcome—something is bound to happen. Some things are already happening, of course. But the changes are not necessarily sound ones in our opinion. As one distinguished accountant has put it:

> Inflation, high income taxes, and artificial lowering of interest rates have had an effect on financial accounting not unlike that of prohibition of our drinking habits. Results are now being sought by artificial means which are not permitted to be obtained naturally. . . .[1]

---

[1] G. O. May in *Five Monographs on Business Income,* p. 264.

We urge our proposal in the spirit of furthering discussion, in the belief that it may be a more "natural" means of attacking the problem than those now being tried, and hopefully that it may be the best possible outcome to a situation which has no unique, correct solution.

General Objectives of Accounting Measurement

We have suggested that there are two central objectives toward which accountants should point in formulating measures of a business firm's income over time and position at a moment of time. The principal purpose to be achieved by the collection of accounting data (other than prevention of fraud and theft and the like) is to provide useful information for the evaluation of past business decisions and of the methods used in reaching those decisions. Evaluation, in turn, has two facets: (1) evaluation by management in order to make the best possible decisions for action in an uncertain future; (2) evaluation of management, or more broadly of the performance of the individual firm, by stockholders, creditors (including banks), regulatory agencies of the Government, and other interested outsiders in order that they, too, may make better judgments with respect to the activities of the firm. Evaluation by both insiders and interested outsiders provides the key to the successful functioning of a private, free enterprise economy. If the task is performed effectively, resources will be allocated efficiently.[2] If accountants do not provide the data necessary for measuring performance, resources are misallocated and both business firms and the community at large suffer as a consequence.

A second, and we believe important but subsidiary, objective in developing reports of income and position should be that such information provide a sound and equitable basis for taxation.

---

[2] We are here thinking of the term "efficiency" in the economic sense associated with Paretian optimality. Maximum efficiency is reached in an economy when no individual or firm can be made better off without making another individual or firm worse off. Whether this is a point of maximum welfare depends essentially upon the distribution of income. Maximum efficiency is a recognizable economic ideal, and specific conditions can be set forth for its attainment (the Pareto optimality conditions); maximum welfare depends upon the arbitrary establishment of a social welfare function, given the impossibility of interpersonal comparisons of utilities.

This objective has often been emphasized to such an extent as practically to exclude the first objective; we believe that both are important and that a framework can be evolved to serve both without excluding either.

Profit-Oriented Behavior of the Business Firm

The general theory of profit maximization by the individual firm which is developed in Chapter II provides a simplified picture of the decision-making process under conditions of uncertainty, the process which must be evaluated with the aid of accounting data. Given an initial stock of assets, management forms subjective estimates of future events and compares these estimates with the collective judgment of the market place, planning the present composition of the firm's assets so as to maximize the difference between the subjective value attached to them and their current market value, this difference being termed *subjective goodwill.* Over the life of the plan this subjective goodwill must be converted into market value.

There are two dimensions to any plan and to the activities associated with the carrying out of a plan: a production dimension and a time dimension. Assets owned by the firm are processed through production stages (a vertical flow) and held through time periods (a horizontal flow), as depicted more fully in Chapter III. A business firm can strive to earn profit by combining factors of production having one value into a product which has a greater value, and it can attempt to make gains by holding assets while their prices rise. Both kinds of gains can be anticipated, and the expectations relevant to each can be checked against actual events as they occur.

The ultimate test of the decision-making process employed by the management of a business firm, then, is provided by measuring the extent to which its subjective estimates of future operating and holding gains are realized in terms of market values over the life of a plan, and the degree to which the timing of the conversion into market value was correctly anticipated. The evaluation process involves measuring the total gain in market value in each period, dividing it into operating profit on the one hand and holding gains on the other, and separating each of these gains into that element which was anticipated by management and that element which proved to be a surprise. It is this latter element which reflects errors in the expectations of management. The smaller this error over a long period of time, the more effective is the planning process.

Implications for Accounting

If accounting data are to be useful for the internal evaluation of business decisions, it follows from this approach to the theory of the firm that such data must provide information on changes in the current market value of assets held by the firm, and that these changes must be appropriately subdivided into those resulting from operating activities and those resulting from holding activities. More specifically, accounting data must provide separately, period by period, (1) an accurate measure of profit on operations and (2) an accurate measure of realizable gains which accrue as a result of holding assets which have risen in price. These are the key elements of information needed for evaluation by management of its own activities. To provide such information is the principal function of accounting. But, as we try to show at various points in our work, such data also provide the information necessary for the evaluation of management, that is, for measuring the performance of individual firms by outsiders. Still further, the data, when aggregated, yield the information needed for input-output and national income accounts which serve to measure the performance of the economy as a whole.

Two further pieces of information, while less important for the evaluation process, are of vital significance if accounting is to serve its second principal function, that of providing data which form an equitable basis for taxation: (3) a record of holding gains which are actually realized on assets which have risen in price since time of purchase, either through direct sale of the asset (a realized capital gain) or through use of the asset in production which is sold (a realized cost saving); (4) a division of all gains into two parts, the portion that is real and the portion that is fictional, that is, money gains which simply keep pace with changes in the general price level.

These are the data that are needed for reports on income and position if the purposes of accounting are to be fulfilled. Under present accounting practices, none of the necessary information is provided.

Nature of Required Modifications

In attempting to develop a framework which would serve to provide such data, a dilemma is immediately posed by the ambiguity of the concept of current market value. Current market values can be assigned on either an opportunity cost basis or a current cost basis. The choice involves a fundamental decision, with respect both to the nature of accounting records and to the profit concept which evolves out of those records.

Opportunity Cost versus Current Cost Values

The fundamental difference between the two approaches can best be summarized in terms of their relative departure from the realization principle. We have argued that the activities of a firm have two dimensions, time and production. The realization principle may be thought of as having these same two dimensions. In its time dimension, the realization principle instructs the accountant to assign values to assets on the date of acquisition and not to change them until date of sale. If the realization principle is not recognized, assets will be valued on the basis of prices prevailing at the time of valuation.

The production dimension of the realization principle, on the other hand, is based upon the form of assets upon entry to and exit from the firm. If the principle is followed, entry values must dominate the accounts until final sale; no matter at what stage of production, an asset must be valued at accumulated costs (current or historic) until exit actually occurs. If the principle is not followed, exit values will be used in the valuation of all assets.

When the realization principle is abandoned in both of its dimensions, we have a concept of profit based on opportunity cost, a concept we have termed *realizable profit.* The fundamental basis for asset valuation is current so far as time is concerned, and opportunity cost is by definition an exit value, not an entry value; an asset is not only valued at prices prevailing at time of valuation, but the price chosen is that which could be realized by immediate sale outside the firm. The business profit concept, on the other hand, retains the production dimension of the realization principle. As a result, the values assigned to assets in accordance with this concept are current in nature, but those current values selected are entry values not exit values. These entry values are accumulated in the accounts, although they are kept current as time passes, until actual sale takes place. At that time the accumulated entry values are subtracted from the exit value related to the actual sale in order to determine current operating profit.

We have chosen to concentrate on the business profit concept after developing the distinction between realizable profit and business profit in Chapter III because we believe that the primary function of accounting processes, so far as the production dimension is concerned, is to provide data to aid in the evaluation of the existing mode of production. The decision which is being evaluated on the basis of accounting data is the decision which was actually made with respect to the composition of assets, not the possible alternatives relating to abandonment or replacement of those assets. In effect, we accept the traditional going-concern convention in accounting, which is based upon the assumption that the firm is a continuing, long-run entity with an established set of assets and an established production process. At the same time, we stress that other types of cost data, as they may relate both to the possible sale of existing assets and to the purchase of new (presumably improved) assets, may provide important and useful subsidiary information for the making of new decisions.

This decision in favor of current costs over opportunity costs, which we feel is based upon sound theoretical considerations if a choice must be made, i.e., if both types of data cannot be kept, has the fortunate advantage of allowing us to develop a framework which upsets traditional accounting procedures hardly at all yet at the same time would provide the data which are needed, but are not now provided, for purposes of evaluation and taxation.

Proper Separation of Operating and Holding Gains

The basic distinctions between the modified framework which we propose and that provided by existing practice can be illustrated in one way through recourse again to the realization principle. Business profit adopts the realization principle on a production basis, but not on a time basis. In contrast, accounting profit as presently measured adopts the realization principle in both its production and time dimensions: Assets are valued in entry form at historic costs until time of exit from the firm; at time of sale, then, both holding gains, because prices have risen, and operating gains, because value has been added in the production process, are thrown together as operating profit. The first step to make profit data more useful and more realistic is to separate holding gains from operating gains.

This step can be accomplished with only very slight amendments to present accounting procedures. The current cost of inputs used in producing output which is sold is subtracted from current revenue to yield current operating profit. The difference between this figure and traditional accounting profit comprises realized cost savings, the excess of the current cost of inputs used in production which is sold over and above the original purchase cost of these inputs, and realized capital gains, the excess of proceeds over and above historic costs on the irregular sale or disposal of assets. In other words we simply divide the total profit figure differently, so as to distinguish clearly between the operating and holding components of realized profit.

Recognition of Gains As They Accrue

We have argued extensively in Chapter VII and elsewhere that this confusion of realized cost savings (which are attributable to the firm's holding activities, to wisdom in purchasing assets at prices lower than the prices prevailing at time of use) with operating profit is not only an inaccurate representation of the facts but can have serious consequences with respect to evaluating both particular decisions and general performance, as well as with respect to problems of equity in taxation.[3] While the proper separation of these two types of gains would thus be an important step forward, it is not a sufficient step in and of itself if data on profits are to serve management effectively in evaluating decisions. In order to measure the total change in the

[3] See, for example, the discussion of operating profits of firms which entered an industry at different times, in the section on decision-making and evaluation, Chapter VII.

current value of the firm's assets period by period, that is, the amount of subjective goodwill which has been converted into market value, we must account for holding gains as they arise. Business profit consists of current operating profit plus realizable cost savings, the increase in the current cost of assets while held by the firm during the fiscal period.

Failure to modify existing accounting data so as to record gains or losses as they arise leads to three important types of limitations in the use of accounting data for the evaluation of business decisions. First, it implies that holding activities do not represent a purposeful means by which management can enhance the market position of the firm. Assets which are neither sold directly nor used in producing goods which have been sold during the period, but which nevertheless have changed in value, are carried at the same value at the end of the period as that assigned to them at the beginning of the period. There is thus no report to management, owners, or outsiders of holding gains and losses accruing to the firm unless these gains are realized through sale.

A second, and in many ways more important, consequence of not counting gains when they arise is that when such gains are in fact realized, the gains earned over the full span of time during which the assets were held are attributed entirely to the period in which the gains are realized. This difficulty carries with it two implications. First, as illustrated especially in Chapter V with respect to inventories,[4] it means that when absolutely identical events occur in two periods, accounting data will normally yield a different figure for profits reportedly earned in the two periods, because the data for each period are influenced by data of past periods. Secondly, because when holding gains are realized through sale and thus recorded they are reported simply as net gains, there is no way to determine in what period holding activities were successful and in what periods they were unsuccessful. An illustration of the impact of this second type of limitation on the evaluation of decisions is given in Chapter VII.[5]

Finally, the distortion of balance sheet values which results

---

[4] See the concluding paragraph of the section on profit concept comparison over time.

[5] See the discussion of holding gains on securities, in the section on decision-making and evaluation.

from the failure to report holding gains and losses as they occur makes comparisons among business firms, or among different divisions within a single firm, extremely hazardous. A comparison of the relative net worth of two firms, or of the rates of return on equity, on the basis of historic cost balance sheet values will normally yield very different results from a comparison based on current cost balance sheet values, and indeed the two types of comparison may lead to exactly opposite conclusions as to the relative position of the two firms.

Separation of Real and Fictional Gains

The third type of modification which we propose for the compilation of data on income and position of the individual firm probably has little influence on internal managerial decisions, but would affect considerations relating to the very real burden of taxes, and has some implications for comparison among firms. In accordance with generally accepted accounting principles, changes in the general level of prices are not now accounted for. Even if full account were taken of changes in individual prices, this omission would make it difficult to divide dollar profit into its real and fictional elements. This division is not necessary for most decision-making purposes because the maximization of dollar profit will also maximize real profit. Even the decision as to the amount of dividends to be distributed should not, we feel, be governed by the amount of real profit earned, although it may be useful at least to know that real capital is being dissipated if such is the case.[6] But if the price level is rising and taxes are levied on dollar profits, the real tax rate may be substantially higher than the apparent tax rate. Whether the tax rate on business firms should be levied on real profit while other taxpayers are assessed on their dollar income is a moot question. In any event, the accounts of business firms and their published reports should be designed to reveal the real burden of their tax payments. Finally, we try to show in Chapter VIII that the separation of profit into its real and fictional elements, and the corresponding adjustments which must be made in the equity section of the balance sheet,

[6] See the beginning of the section on the usefulness of real data for decision-making and evaluation, Chapter VIII.

may be useful in the making of certain comparisons on activities as between business firms, and as to the profitability of a single firm over time.[7]

Good managers undoubtedly attempt to compensate for those accounting limitations of which they are aware. It might be argued, therefore, that accounting responsibility ends once historic cost data have been collected and reported and the limitations of the data have been stated. It is doubtful, however, whether management knows, or if informed will understand, all of these limitations. Even in the unlikely event that managements are fully aware of the deficiencies, the success they achieve in compensating for them is probably limited if only because the compensation must be largely subjective in nature. It is not unreasonable to conclude, therefore, that the correction of these deficiencies within a rigorous accounting framework will reduce the area in which subjective judgment is necessary and will increase the efficiency with which business decisions are made.[8]

The Accounting Techniques

The first two accounting deficiencies noted above rest on the neglect of individual price changes; the third stems from neglect in the accounts and in published reports of the effects of changes in the general price level. But as the fundamental purpose to be served by accounting data is the evaluation of business decisions, it is the correction for individual price changes that is most urgently needed. In our judgment, therefore, the emphasis in recent years on the adjustment of historic cost values for price level changes has been misplaced. An adjustment for changes in the general price level is of considerable importance—we have

---

[7] See the section on measurement of real rates of return.

[8] This point of view has been stated succinctly by A. Goudeket of the Philips Company of the Netherlands (whose practical application of individual price adjustments to accounting values is discussed briefly later in this chapter): "The replacement value theory also results in a clear-cut measurement (quantification) of those elements which are otherwise left to guesswork by individuals. . . . The point is sometimes made that informed readers of financial statements understand the principles on which they are based, and the shortcomings of those principles. Hence, they make mental adjustments for such things as replacement values. This adjustment, however, cannot be considered an acceptable compensation." A. Goudeket, "An Application of Replacement Value Theory," p. 46.)

argued for it at some length in earlier chapters—but unless an adjustment is also made for individual price changes, the advantage of the price level adjustment is questionable.

Accounting techniques which may be employed in making adjustments for price changes on individual asset and liability items and thus reporting profit and balance sheet values in the way that we have suggested are presented in Chapters V–VII, while the techniques which could further be used to adjust for changes in the general price level are given in Chapter VIII. We will not try to summarize those methods in any detail here. They are clearly not the only methods which could be employed; practicing accountants who might pursue the objectives we propose would undoubtedly find and devise their own techniques according to the particular type of firm involved and the design of accounts presently used in that firm. But we wish to stress the general principles involved in the techniques which we have developed for purposes of illustration.

First of all, the method involves only end-of-period adjustments to accounts which are presently compiled; there are no elaborate new records to be kept.

Second, the techniques employed do not alter in any fundamental fashion present accounting procedures or destroy any data needed for traditional statements. Records are kept in terms of historic costs, and at the end of a fiscal period adjustments are made, mostly in a limited number of separate ledger accounts, to record current cost values. We need the average-of-period current cost of asset services used in order to measure current operating profit and also the beginning- and end-of-period current cost value of the assets in order to measure realizable cost savings, which together comprise business profit; we need the historic (purchase) cost as well as the average-of-period current cost of asset services used to measure realized cost savings, which together with current operating profit and realized capital gains yield realized profit, a measure which in turn is identical, in the aggregate, to accounting profit as presently measured. Finally, we use the end-of-period current cost values of assets remaining on hand in order to devise a balance sheet based on current values, which can be presented along with a traditional balance sheet based on historic costs.

Third, there is considerable flexibility in the extent to which adjustments must be made. The two principal costs which are "out of line," the items for which current costs may deviate substantially from historic costs because the assets are used at a time different from purchase, relate to inventories and fixed assets. Adjustments for these two types of assets alone would be a long step forward toward realistic accounting, a very important step as we try to indicate at the end of Chapter VII. There we show (table 13) an estimate of the difference such corrections would have made in reported corporate profits, in the aggregate, for the years 1929 to 1949. When we consider the magnitudes involved and then remember that they comprise an average for all firms in the economy so that the deviation of reported accounting operating profit from current operating profit must have been considerably larger for many individual firms, and when we consider that these data still do not account for realizable cost savings which accrued during the period but rather only for cost savings which were actually realized during the period, we do not see how the challenge posed to the accounting profession can be ignored.

Our fourth general principle is that there be provision of maximum information. We compile the information collected through the end-of-period adjustments in a manner which allows the user to choose the data which are important to him in the making of his particular decision. He has at his disposal everything that present accounting data offer, but much more in addition. And yet the integrated statement which shows current operating profit, realized profit, and business profit, and their components, is surely not a difficult statement to compose or to comprehend.[9]

Even if the reader accepts the objectives we have set forth, the general theory espoused, and the possibility of evolving techniques to handle the problem there is, however, still a basis for rejection of our proposal on grounds of practicality, an issue to which we now turn.

The Hurdle of Practicality

Traditional accounting techniques serve highly useful purposes. It is only proper, therefore, that the burden of proof in any

---

[9] See statement 1 in Chapter VII.

discussion of accounting modifications should fall on those who propose the changes. Resistance to change is healthy so long as it prevents hasty and precipitate judgments. Certainly much of the resistance to accounting modifications for price changes has been of this nature, and many of the proposals made have not survived the careful scrutiny of professional accountants.

The origin of some proposed changes, for example, can be traced to the corporate income tax and the fact that, if the proposed change were adopted for tax purposes, the size of the tax paid by corporations would be reduced. The stoutness of the working accountant and his auditor colleague in fighting changes proposed for this reason is commendable. This is especially so when one realizes that it is the corporate employer of these people who would most like to marshall the support of the accounting profession behind these kinds of proposals.

Extensive Codification an Obstacle to Change

Yet the fact that the accountant is usually faced with a barrage of pressures, laws, codes, and conventions, not all of which are without substantial force, is almost bound to influence his judgment and restrict his freedom. There is certainly much evidence, for example, that the income tax law and rulings based upon it have influenced accounting procedures, not always, it must be added, in the direction of progress.

Regulations laid down by such quasi-judicial agencies as the Securities Exchange Commission, the Interstate Commerce Commission, and the Federal Power Commission have also influenced accounting procedures, and state governments have not been inoperative in this area. But governmental rules are only one kind of external influence on the accountant in the performance of his function. He is also influenced by many private organizations, among them trade associations and stock exchanges of which his firm is a member.

Many of these influences have been beneficial by supporting the accountant in the objective performance of his function. Indeed, the accounting profession itself has had substantial influence in the formulation of these laws, rules, and regulations of government. Nevertheless, once rigid codes and procedures have been adopted, they act as a powerful deterrent to change. The modification of these codes and procedures is not a simple process.

A similar retarding influence may often be exercised by those rules and conventions promulgated by the accounting profession itself. Yet this core of rules and conventions is absolutely necessary if accounting is to perform useful services. One of accounting's greatest assets lies in the high degree of uniformity and standardization which has been achieved, and which facilitates comparisons among firms and industries. It is also true, however, that they make change difficult.

In addition to the difficulty of change which usually accompanies extensive codification, there is also the danger that the large body of law, codes, and rules will come to be regarded as a scientific standard against which proposed modifications should be judged. Clearly, however, it is the codes themselves, whether embodied in law or not, which should be judged against objectively determined accounting standards, and changed as the science of measurement progresses.

The Practical Matter of Objectivity

The objectivity principle of accountants is another rock upon which many a proposed change has foundered. Indeed, it has been suggested that the objectivity principle, among others, has often served as a means of rationalizing traditional practices rather than as a tool for scientific examination.[10]

There can be no doubt that the main purpose of objectivity in accounting is to prevent fraud and deceit and to facilitate the independent audit of accounts by avoiding subjective data. But clearly, objectivity is here a relative proposition. The accountant who follows traditional practices makes countless subjective judgments: in deciding on the depreciation pattern of fixed assets, in making an estimate for bad debts allowance, in deciding upon pension liabilities. The degree of objectivity in accounting is never absolute.

Too frequently in our opinion the objectivity principle is used as a means of excluding subjective judgment from accounting

[10] George R. Husband presents an excellent discussion of the role of rationalization in accounting in his "Rationalization in the Accounting Measurement of Income."

decisions without regard for the effect this exclusion may have on the decision-making process of the firm as a whole. If in order to adhere as strictly as possible to the objectivity principle, the accounting department reduces the usefulness or refuses to enhance the usefulness of the accounting data furnished to management, managerial efficiency will be adversely affected. Excessive concern with objectivity may lead the accountant to shirk important responsibilities.

We do not feel, however, that objectivity is a major point at issue in our proposal. Current costs are in most cases as objectively verifiable as are historic costs. And in instances in which current costs must be estimated on the basis of index numbers, it is likely, in the United States at any rate, that government-constructed index numbers could be used or that the Treasury Department or independent auditors could verify and accept the internal construction of an index. If it were required of each firm that once an index was adopted it could not be changed without cause, construction of an index which would favor the firm over any extended period of time would require excellent foresight on the part of the firm's management.

The Search for Accuracy

In those cases where index numbers must be used to estimate current cost, the resulting estimates are bound to be inaccurate even though the index number can be determined and verified objectively. In this sense current costs would be only approximations to the truth. But even if historic costs are known accurately and current costs are but estimates, it does not follow that historic costs are more truthful, that is, that they render reality more accurately.

Reality, we have argued, is composed of the current events of the period being recorded. The historic costs which may be so accurately known are simply not events of the current period. Estimated current costs are certainly superior to historic costs as an approximation to true current costs. In fact, one can argue that the use of historic costs as a statement of reality involves the implicit assumption that prices have not changed since the date of purchase or that, if they have, the best estimate we can make of current costs is to apply an index number of 100 to historic costs.

We suggest that an index number designed to represent current costs is likely to be more accurate.

Difficulties Introduced by Technological Change

Little explicit reference has been made in this volume to technological change although it is an important characteristic of a dynamic economy. One might even argue that technological change is a *sine qua non* of the dynamic economy we profess to treat.

It has been our position, however, that the primary function of accounting processes is to evaluate the existing mode of production in a dynamic setting. To the extent then that past technological change is reflected in the firm's quantity and composition of assets, it is being accounted for. The fact that current or prospective technological changes threaten the existing processes of production should not be construed as placing on the accountant the responsibility for accumulating data in his formal accounts to reflect the operating efficiency of a system of production not yet adopted by the firm. Rather the impact of technological change of this sort should be reflected in the reduced operating profit earned with the existing process of production. It is the accountant's duty to show this reduction when it occurs and to call the attention of management to the impact that technological change is having on the operating efficiency of the firm.

External technological change will affect the firm's existing process of production by altering the relationships among those prices which govern the firm's behavior. As competitors adopt newer techniques, it is to be expected that the prices of the product sold by the firm will fall relative to the prices of its factors of production. The resulting squeeze on profit will reflect the reduced relative efficiency of the firm's process of production. If the firm's current receipts are insufficient to cover the current cost of production including the current cost of the services of fixed assets, a signal has been given for the firm to abandon that process of production.

It follows that if the impact of technological change on the firm's operating efficiency is to be reflected in its accounting data, these data must be reported on the basis of current prices and not on the basis of historic costs. The current operating profit concept meets these requirements while the traditionally reported operating profit may disguise the impact by including gains realized through use as operating profit. Accounting in terms of current costs yields data which will reveal the impact of technological change as soon as it occurs simply because the primary force of technological change acts through prices. The accounting modifications we propose meet the technological change argument at least on theoretical grounds.

Technological change does have a secondary effect which makes the practical application of our proposed modifications more difficult—it destroys markets for some existing assets, thus forcing a reliance on index numbers as a means of estimating current cost. But this practical difficulty carries little weight as an objection to the proposal that accounts be kept on a current cost basis. So long as the existing production process is competitive with others, the assets needed to operate the process will be produced in the economy and current costs will be available. If technological change has proceeded so far that the assets associated with the existing production process are no longer produced, then the existing production process is obsolete and the firm which now uses it will not consider replacement in kind. A principal reason for keeping accounts in terms of current costs has already been achieved.

Secondly, as we have noted above, the use of index numbers is likely to yield better estimates of current costs than is the use of historic costs. Technological change will affect the accuracy of the index number—adjustments for quality changes are notoriously difficult to make—but the resulting bias is not likely to be so great that historic costs themselves would provide better estimates.

Finally there is probably no great harm done if the firm at this stage reverts to an opportunity cost basis for evaluation. Under these circumstances, of course, opportunity costs will be substantially less than current costs. As a result the reported profits of a firm will be larger than they would be on a current cost basis. But as there are no markets in which similar assets can be purchased new, there is no danger that the firm will be misled by these reported profits to replace its assets in kind. Even potential entrants to the industry could not be tempted to adopt the same plan of operation as that used by the existing firm simply because the necessary assets are not being produced. The potential entrant could secure such assets only in the second-hand market, and the prices prevailing there are the opportunity costs which the existing firm would be reporting.

Complexity and the Question of Costs

The modern business corporation is today often a mammoth enterprise involving the use of a great variety of inputs, many complex production and distribution processes, and a multitude of different outputs. We do not deny that the practical task of the accountant if he were to attempt to put our proposal into effect is a difficult one.

Sheer complexity, however, has never really bothered accountants; indeed, they seem to thrive on it and display great ingenuity in developing methods and new machinery for handling problems created by growth, diversification, and technological progress. Accepting the fact that our illustrations of techniques are grossly oversimplified, we still doubt that complexity is really an obstacle to more realistic accounting procedures.

There is, it is true, a question of costs involved. One company, the Philips Company of the Netherlands, a great, complex industrial enterprise, has instituted and used for a number of years a framework for the recognition of current values in its accounts and in its published reports.[11] As we understand it, it is in many ways a different framework from the one we are proposing. But if anything, it would appear to be more complex and involve the *continuous* use of a much more heterogeneous collection of price index numbers than we believe would be necessary in order to make our suggested end-of-period adjustments in the accounts of American corporations. Yet the chief internal auditor of that company has this to say about the costs of the Philips system:

> It is not possible to make a calculation which shows the cost connected with the application of the replacement values. Modern accounting methods and equipment reduce the extra cost to a minimum. Of far

---

[11] For a description of the methods employed, see A. Goudeket, *loc. cit.*

greater importance is the conviction that a more appropriate basis for policy decisions is created, and that is of tremendous value. The extra cost is certainly negligible as compared with this benefit.[12]

The Training Problem

Wilcox and Greer have pointed out that an important reason for making progress slowly on the price change problem is the existence of such a large number of accountants who are trained in existing methods.[13] There is no question but that it takes a long period of time to retrain such a large group and to infuse it with new members. It is also true that much of the detail work in accounting is done by nonprofessional clerks and bookkeepers. Because changes in accounting principles must be capable of broad application often by nonprofessionals, the techniques necessary to put an accounting modification into effect in the formal records must be highly simplified. We feel that the techniques we have suggested are not unduly complicated and could be reduced to a set of rules and procedures which could be followed by appropriately supervised talent. We are also sure, however, that should our arguments in favor of current cost accounting be at all convincing, professional accountants will be able to improve on these techniques.

We hope that this rather cursory review of practical difficulties will not be viewed as a disregard for their importance. After all, the refinement of techniques must await the acceptance of the underlying theory. If this theory demonstrates a useful relationship between economics and accounting, between decision-making and decision evaluation, if we have succeeded in showing that reality is comprised of current events as well as historic events and that the distinction between the two is important, our principal purposes will have been achieved.

But the reader should be fairly warned that the acceptance of the theory implies also a recognition that the responsibility of the accountant in a dynamic economy extends well beyond that

---

[12] *Ibid.*, p. 47.

[13] American Institute of Accountants, Study Group on Business Income, *Changing Concepts of Business Income,* p. 71.

now implicit in the traditional rules and procedures of the profession. The responsibility is a challenging one. We believe that the benefits which could be achieved would far exceed even their current cost.

Selected Bibliography

Selected Bibliography

BOOKS

Abramovitz, M., *An Approach to a Price Theory for a Changing Economy* (New York: Columbia University Press, 1939).

———, *Inventories and Business Cycles* (New York: National Bureau of Economic Research, 1950).

American Institute of Accountants, *Accounting Trends in Corporate Reports* (New York: American Institute of Accountants, 1949).

———, *Changing Concepts of Business Income,* Report of a Study Group on Business Income (New York: Macmillan, 1952).

———, *Restatement and Revision of Accounting Research Bulletins,* Accounting Research Bulletin No. 43, issued by Committee on Accounting Procedure (New York: American Institute of Accountants, 1953).

Andrews, P. W. S., *Manufacturing Business* (London: Macmillan, 1949).

Association of Certified and Corporate Accountants, Taxation and Research Committee, *Accounting for Inflation* (London: Gee, 1952).

Bain, Joe S., *Industrial Organization* (New York: Wiley, 1959).

———, *Price Theory* (New York: Holt, 1952).

Baxter, W. T. (ed.), *Studies in Accounting* (London: Sweet & Maxwell, 1950).

Bergson, Abram, *Soviet National Income and Product in 1937* (New York: Columbia University Press, 1953).

Bergson, Abram, and Hans Heymann, Jr., *Soviet National Income and Product, 1940–1948* (New York: Columbia University Press, 1954).

Berle, A. A., *The 20th Century Capitalist Revolution* (New York: Harcourt, Brace, 1954).

Bonbright, J. C., *The Valuation of Property* (New York: McGraw-Hill, 1937).

Bowen, E. R., *Prices, Pay and Profits—The Solution of the Profit Problem* (New York: Cooperative League, 1957).

Bray, F. S., *The Accounting Mission* (Melbourne: Melbourne University Press, 1951).

———, *Four Essays in Accounting Theory* (London: Oxford University Press, 1953).

———, *The Measurement of Profit* (London: Oxford University Press, 1949).

———, *Social Accounts and the Business Enterprise Sector of the National Economy* (London: Cambridge University Press, 1949).

Brown, E. C., *Effects of Taxation: Depreciation Adjustments for Price Changes* (Boston: Harvard Business School, Division of Research, 1952).

Buchanan, N. S., *The Economics of Corporate Enterprise* (New York: Holt, 1940).

Butters, J. K. (assisted by P. Niland), *Effects of Taxation: Inventory Accounting and Policies* (Boston: Graduate School of Business Administration, Harvard University, 1949).

Canning, J. B., *The Economics of Accounting* (New York: Ronald Press, 1929).

Childs, W. H., *Consolidated Financial Statements* (Ithaca: Cornell University Press, 1949).

Clark, J. M., *Studies in the Economics of Overhead Costs* (Chicago: University of Chicago Press, 1923).

Daniels, M. B., *Financial Statements,* American Accounting Association Monograph No. 2 (Urbana, Illinois: American Accounting Association, 1939).

Dean, A. H., *Business Income under Present Price Levels* (New York: American Institute of Accountants, 1949).

Dean, J., *Capital Budgeting* (New York: Columbia University Press, 1951).

———, *Managerial Economics* (New York: Prentice-Hall, 1951).

———, *The Relation of Cost to Output for a Leather Belt Shop,* Technical Paper No. 2 (New York: National Bureau of Economic Research, 1941).

———, *Statistical Cost Functions of a Hosiery Mill,* Studies in Business Administration of the University of Chicago, v. 11, no. 4, printed in *Journal of Business,* 14 (July, 1941).

———, *Statistical Determination of Costs, with Special Reference to Marginal Costs,* Studies in Business Administration of the University of Chicago, v. 7, no. 1, printed in *Journal of Business,* 9 (October, 1936).

Dean, J., and R. W. James, *The Long-Run Behavior of Costs in a Chain of Shoe Stores: A Statistical Analysis,* Studies in Business Administration of the University of Chicago, v. 12, no. 3, printed in *Journal of Business,* 15 (April, 1942).

Devine, C. T., *Inventory Valuation and Periodic Income* (New York: Ronald Press, 1942).

Dewing, A. S., *Financial Policy of Corporations,* 5th rev. ed. (New York: Ronald Press, 1953).

Drucker, Peter F., *Concept of the Corporation* (New York: John Day, 1946).

Fabricant, S., *Capital Consumption and Adjustment* (New York: National Bureau of Economic Research, 1938).

Finley, J. A., *Handling Higher Replacement Costs,* Studies in Business Policy No. 47 (New York: National Industrial Conference Board, 1950).

Fisher, I., *The Nature of Capital and Income* (New York: Macmillan, 1906).

Foster, W. T., *Practical Financial Statement Analysis,* 3d ed. (New York: McGraw-Hill, 1953).

———, *A Study of the Concept of National Income* (New York: Dun & Bradstreet, 1952).

Foster, W. T., and W. Catchings, *Profits* (Boston: Houghton Mifflin, 1925).

Foulke, R. A., *A Study of the Theory of Corporate Net Profits* (New York: Dun & Bradstreet, 1949).

Fowler, R. F., *The Depreciation of Capital, Analytically Considered* (London: P. S. King & Sons), 1934.

Gaston, J. F., *Effects of Depreciation Policy* (New York: National Industrial Conference Board, 1950).

Gillespie, Cecil C. M., *Accounting System: Procedures and Methods* (New York: Prentice-Hall, 1951).

Gilman, L., *Accounting Concepts of Profit* (New York: Ronald Press, 1939).

Gneib, J. E., *Practical Production Planning and Control* (New York: Funk & Wagnalls, 1948).

Goldsmith, R. W., *A Study of Saving in the United States,* v. I (Princeton: Princeton University Press, 1955).

Graham, B., and D. L. Dodd, *Security Analysis* (New York: McGraw-Hill, 1934).

Grant, E. L., and P. T. Norton, Jr., *Depreciation* (New York: Ronald Press, 1955).

Harrod, R. F., *Economic Essays* (London: Macmillan, 1952).

Hart, A. G., *Anticipations, Uncertainty, and Dynamic Planning* (Chicago: University of Chicago Press, 1940).

Hart, W. L., *Mathematics of Investment* (Boston: D. C. Heath, 1946).

Hatfield, H. R., *Surplus and Dividends* (Cambridge: Harvard University Press, 1943).

Hicks, J. R., *The Social Framework* (Oxford: Clarendon Press, 1st ed., 1943; 2d ed., 1952).

———, *Value and Capital,* 2d ed. (Oxford: Clarendon Press, 1946).

Institute of Cost and Works Accountants, *The Accountancy of Changing Price Levels* (London: Institute of Cost and Works Accountants, 1952).

Jones, R. C., *Effects of Price Level Changes on Business Income, Capital, and Taxes* (Urbana, Illinois: American Accounting Association, 1956).

———, *Price Level Changes and Financial Statements: Case Studies of Four Companies* (Urbana, Illinois: American Accounting Association, 1955).

Keirstead, B. S., *An Essay in the Theory of Profits and Income Distribution* (Oxford: Basil Blackwell, 1953).

Kennedy, R. D., and S. Y. McMullen, *Financial Statements* (Homewood, Illinois: R. D. Irwin, 1952).

Knight, F. H., *Risk, Uncertainty and Profit,* Series of Reprints of Scarce Tracts, No. 16 (London School of Economics and Political Science, 1933).

Kurtz, Edwin B., *Life Expectancy of Physical Property* (New York: Ronald Press, 1930).

Leontief, W., *The Structure of the American Economy, 1919–1939* (New York: Oxford University Press, 1951).

———, *Studies in the Structure of the American Economy* (New York: Oxford University Press, 1953).

Lindahl, Erik, *Studies in the Theory of Money and Capital* (London: Allen & Unwin, 1939).

Littleton, A. C., *Accounting Evolution to 1900* (New York: American Institute Publishing Company, 1933).

———, *Structure of Accounting Theory,* American Accounting Association Monograph No. 5 (Urbana, Illinois: American Accounting Association, 1953).

Littleton, A. C., and B. S. Yamey (eds.), *Studies in the History of Accounting* (Homewood, Illinois: R. D. Irwin, 1956).

Lutz, F. A., *Corporate Cash Balances, 1914–43* (New York: National Bureau of Economic Research, 1945).

Lutz, F. A., and V. Lutz, *The Theory of Investment of the Firm* (Princeton: Princeton University Press, 1951).

McNair, Malcolm P., *The Retail Inventory Method and Lifo* (New York: McGraw-Hill, 1952).

MacNeal, K., *Truth in Accounting* (Philadelphia: University of Pennsylvania Press, 1939).

Marple, R. P., *Capital Surplus and Corporate Net Worth* (New York: Ronald Press, 1936).

Mason, P., *Principles of Public-Utility Depreciation,* American Accounting Association Monograph No. 1 (Urbana, Illinois: American Accounting Association, 1937).

May, G. O., *Business Income and Price Levels: An Accounting Study* (New York: Study Group of Business Income of the American Institute of Accountants, 1949).

———, *Financial Accounting* (New York: Macmillan, 1943).

———, *Twenty-five Years of Accounting Responsibility 1911–1936* (New York: American Institute Publishing Company, 1936).

Mey, J. L. (ed.), *Depreciation and Replacement Policy* (Amsterdam: North Holland Publishing Company, 1961).

Mills, F. C., *The Behavior of Prices* (New York: National Bureau of Economic Research, 1927).

Moonitz, M., *The Entity Theory of Consolidated Statements,* American Accounting Association Monograph No. 4 (Urbana, Illinois: American Accounting Association, 1949).

Morgenstern, O., *On the Accuracy of Economic Observations* (Princeton: Princeton University Press, 1950).

Myer, J. N., *Financial Statement Analysis* (New York: Prentice-Hall, 1939).

Norris, H., *Accounting Theory* (New York: Pitman, 1946).

Oxenfeldt, A. R., *Industrial Pricing and Market Practices* (New York: Prentice-Hall, 1951).

Paton, W. A., *Accounting Theory* (New York: Ronald Press, 1922).

———, *Advanced Accounting* (New York: Macmillan, 1941).

Paton, W. A., and A. C. Littleton, *An Introduction to Corporate Accounting Standards,* American Accounting Association Monograph No. 3 (Urbana, Illinois: American Accounting Association, 1940).

Peragallo, E., *Origin and Evolution of Double Entry Bookkeeping. A Study of Italian Practice from the Fourteenth Century* (New York: American Institute Publishing Company, 1938).

Powelson, J. P., *Economic Accounting* (New York: McGraw-Hill, 1955).

Ruggles, R., and N. D. Ruggles, *National Income Accounts and Income Analysis* (New York: McGraw-Hill, 1956).

Saliers, E. L., *Depreciation; Principles and Applications,* 3d rev. ed. (New York: Ronald Press, 1939).

Sanders, T. H., H. R. Hatfield, and U. Moore, *A Statement of Accounting Principles* (New York: American Institute of Accountants, 1938).

Schlatter, C. F., *Advanced Cost Accounting* (New York: Wiley, 1939).

Schmidt, F., *Die organische Tageswertbilanz,* 3d ed. (Leipzig: Gloeckner, 1929).

Schneider, Erich, *Pricing and Equilibrium* (London: Hodges, 1952).

Shackle, G. L. S., *Expectation in Economics* (Cambridge: Cambridge University Press, 1952).

———, *Expectations, Investments, and Income* (London: Oxford University Press, 1938).

Shoup, C. S., *Principles of National Income Analysis* (Boston: Houghton Mifflin, 1947).

Smith, D. K., and J. K. Butters, *Taxable and Business Income* (New York: National Bureau of Economic Research, 1949).

Solomons, D. (ed.), *Studies in Costing* (London: Sweet & Maxwell, 1952).

Stigler, G. J., and K. E. Boulding (eds.), *Readings in Price Theory* (Homewood, Illinois: R. D. Irwin, 1952).

Sweeney, H. W., *Stabilized Accounting* (New York: Harper, 1936).

Taxation and Research Committee of the Association of Certified and Corporate Accountants, *Accounting for Inflation* (London: Gee, 1952).

Terborgh, G., *Depreciation Policy and the Postwar Price Level* (Chicago: Machinery and Allied Products Institute, 1949).

———, *Dynamic Equipment Policy* (New York: McGraw-Hill, 1949).

———, *Inflation and Postwar Profits* (Chicago: Machinery and Allied Products Institute, 1949).

———, *Realistic Depreciation Policy* (Chicago: Machinery and Allied Products Institute, 1954).

Västhagen, Nils, *De fria avskrivningarna 1938–1951* (Stockholm: Gleerups, 1953).

Vatter, W. J., *The Fund Theory of Accounting and Its Implications for Financial Reports* (Chicago: University of Chicago Press, 1947).

———, *Managerial Accounting* (New York: Prentice-Hall, 1950).

Webb, G. T., *Depreciation of Fixed Assets in Accountancy and Economics* (Sydney: Law Book Company of Australasia, 1954).

Whitin, T. M., *The Theory of Inventory Management* (Princeton: Princeton University Press, 1953).

ARTICLES AND MONOGRAPHS

Alexander, Sidney S., "Income Measurement in a Dynamic Economy," Monograph No. 1, *Five Monographs on Business Income* (New York: American Institute of Accountants, July, 1950), 1–95.

American Accounting Association, Committee on Concepts and Standards, "Accounting Corrections," *Accounting Review* 29 (April, 1954), 186–187.

———, "Inventory Pricing and Changes in Price Levels," *Accounting Review* 29 (April, 1954), 188–193.

———, "Price Level Changes and Financial Statements," *Accounting Review* 26 (October, 1951), 468–474.

———, "Reserves and Retained Income," *Accounting Review* 26 (April, 1951), 152–156.

Anton, H. R., "The Funds Statement as an Internal Report to Management," *Accounting Review* 30 (January, 1955), 71–79.

———, "Funds Statement Practices in the United States and Canada," *Accounting Review* 29 (October, 1954), 620–627.

Aukrust, O., "On the Theory of Social Accounting," *Review of Economic Studies* 16(3) (1949–50), 170–188.

Avery, H. G., "A Study of Net Worth Comparison," *Accounting Review* 29 (January, 1954), 114–120.

Bac, A., "Advantages of 'Break-Even' Income Statement Compared with Conventional Statement," *Journal of Accountancy* 91 (January, 1951), 106–111.

Bain, Joe S., "The Profit Rate as a Measure of Monopoly Power," *Quarterly Journal of Economics* 55 (February, 1941), 271–293.

———, "Relation of Profit Rate to Industry Concentration," *Quarterly Journal of Economics* 65 (August, 1951), 293–324.

Baumol, William J., "Professor Copeland's Study of Moneyflows," *Review of Economics and Statistics* 36 (February, 1954), 102–104.

Baxter, W. T., "Inflation and Accounting Profits," *Westminster Bank Review* (May, 1952), 1–8.

Bedford, N. M., "Accounting Measurements of Economic Concepts," *Journal of Accountancy* 103 (May, 1957), 56–62.

———, "A Critical Analysis of Accounting Concepts of Income," *Accounting Review* 26 (October, 1951), 526–537.

———, "Need for Supplementary Data in Interpretation of Income Reports," *Accounting Review* 27 (April, 1952), 195–201.

———, "Using Supplementary Data to Interpret Reported Income," *Accounting Review* 28 (October, 1953), 517–521.

Bell, A. L., "Fixed Assets and Current Costs," *Accounting Review* 28 (January, 1953), 44–53.

Bhavilai, P., "Concepts of Depreciation and Their Implication in Accounting Theory and Practice," *Accounting Review* 34 (October, 1959), 612–613. [Dissertation abstract.]

Blocker, J. G., "Mismatching of Costs and Revenues," *Accounting Review* 24 (January, 1949), 33–43.

Boni, A. C., "Economic Factors in Selecting Lifo," *New York Certified Public Accountant* 21 (November, 1951), 729–738.

Bordner, H. W., "Financial and Accounting Administration in the Federal Government," *Accounting Review* 24 (October, 1949), 341–353.

Borth, D., "Donated Fixed Assets," *Accounting Review* 23 (April, 1948), 171–178.

Bowers, R., "Business Profit and the Price Level," *Accounting Review* 26 (April, 1951), 167–178.

Bowman, R. T., and R. A. Easterlin, "An Interpretation of the Kuznets and Department of Commerce Income Concepts," *Review of Economics and Statistics* 35 (February, 1953), 41–50.

Bray, F. S., "Accounting Dynamics," *Accounting Research* 5 (April, 1954), 133–153.

———, "Accounting Principles," *Accounting Research* 2 (October, 1951), 353–361.

———, "Design for the Accounts of Society," *Accounting Research* 3 (January, 1952), 15–23.

———, "The Nature of Income and Capital," *Accounting Research* 1 (January, 1949), 27–49.

Bray, F. S., and Thomas Kenny, "National Income Statistics—Inventory Revaluation and Depreciation," *Accounting Research* 1 (July, 1950), 449–450.

Bray, F. S., and R. Stone, "The Presentation of the Central Government Accounts," *Accounting Research* 1 (November, 1948), 1–12.

Break, G. F., "Capital Maintenance and the Concept of Income," *Journal of Political Economy* 62 (February, 1954), 48–62.

Brill, D. H., "Measurement of Savings," *Federal Reserve Bulletin* 35 (November, 1949), 1310–1317.

Broad, S. J., "Cost: Is It a Binding Principle or Just a Means to an End?" *Journal of Accountancy* 97 (May, 1954), pp. 582–586.

———, "The Development of Accounting Standards to Meet Changing Economic Conditions," *Journal of Accountancy* 87 (May, 1949), 378–389.

———, "Valuation of Inventories," *Accounting Review* 25 (July, 1950), 227–234.

Bronfenbrenner, Martin, "Business Income Concepts in the Light of Monetary Theory," Monograph No. 2, *Five Monographs on Business Income* (New York: American Institute of Accountants, July, 1950), 97–142.

Brothers, D. S., "Tax Depreciation Policy and Public Regulation of Business," *Land Economics* 33 (November, 1957), 346–358.

Brown, E. C., "Business-Income Taxation and Investment Incentives," *Income, Employment and Public Policy: Essays in Honor of Alvin H. Hansen* (New York: W. W. Norton, 1948), 300–316.

———, "Tax Allowances for Depreciation Based on Changes in the Price Level," *National Tax Journal* 11 (December, 1948), 311–321.

Brown, H. P., "The Composition of Personal Income," *Economic Record* 25 (June, 1949), 18–36.

Brundage, P., "Conclusions of AIA Study Group on Business Income," *Journal of Accountancy* 93 (February, 1952), 190–198.

Burdett, D. K., "Social Accounting in Relation to Economic Theory," *Economic Journal* 64 (December, 1954), 679–697.

Butters, J. K., "Management Considerations on Lifo," *Harvard Business Review* 27 (May, 1949), 308–329.

Cannon, A. M., "Tax Pressures on Accounting Principles and Accountants' Independence," *Accounting Review* 27 (October, 1952), 419–426.

Carson, A. B., "A Fund-Change-Statement Approach to the Calculation of Inflationary Distortion of Conventional Income Measurements," *Accounting Review* 29 (July, 1954), 373–382.

———, "An Investment-Recovery-First Concept of Taxable Profit," *Accounting Review* 26 (October, 1951), 456–467.

———, "A 'Source and Application of Funds' Philosophy of Financial Accounting," *Accounting Review* 24 (April, 1949), 159–170.

Cerf, A. R., "Price Level Changes, Inventory Valuations, and Tax Considerations," *Accounting Review* 32 (October, 1957), 554–565.

Copeland, M. A., "Accounting Conventions Should Determine Business Income," *Journal of Accountancy* 87 (February, 1949), 107–111.

Corbin, D. A., "A Case Study of Price-Level Adjustments," *Accounting Review* 30 (April, 1955), 268–281.

———, "The Impact of Changing Prices on a Department Store," *Journal of Accountancy* 97 (April, 1954), 430–440.

Coughlin, J. W., "Applicability of the Realization Principle to Money Claims in Common Dollar Accounting," *Accounting Review* 30 (January, 1955), 103–113.

———, "The Guises of Replacement Cost," *Accounting Review* 32 (July, 1957), 434–447.

Davidson, S., "Accelerated Depreciation and the Allocation of Income Taxes," *Accounting Review* 33 (April, 1958), 173–180.

———, "Depreciation and Profit Determination," *Accounting Review* 25 (January, 1950), 45–57.

Day, E. B., "Cash-Balance Approach to Funds Statement," *Journal of Accountancy* 91 (April, 1951), 600–603.

Dean, J., "Measurement of Profits for Executive Decisions," *Accounting Review* 26 (April, 1951), 185–196.

———, "Measurement of Real Economic Earnings of a Machinery Manufacturer," *Accounting Review* 29 (April, 1954), 255–266.

———, "Measuring the Productivity of Capital," *Harvard Business Review* 32 (January–February, 1954), 120–130.

Dein, R. C., "Price-Level Adjustments: Fetish in Accounting," *Accounting Review* 30 (January, 1955), 3–24.

Derksen, J. B. D., "Intertemporal Comparisons of Real National Incomes: An International Survey," *Income and Wealth,* Series I (1951), 245–266.

Devine, C. T., "Cost Accounting and Pricing Policies," *Accounting Review* 25 (October, 1950), 384–389.

———, "Integration of Accounting and Economics in the Elementary Accounting Course," *Accounting Review* 27 (July, 1952), 329–333.

Dobrovolsky, S. P., "Depreciation Policies and Investment Decisions," *American Economic Review* 41 (December, 1951), 906–914.

Dohr, J. L., "The 'Economic Facts of Life' as Shown in the Correlation of Accounting, Economics and Law," *Accounting Research* 3 (January, 1952), 1–14.

———, "An Introduction to the Art of Accounting," *Accounting Review* 22 (April, 1947), 151–161.

———, "Limitations on the Usefulness of Price Level Adjustments," *Accounting Review* 30 (April, 1955), 198–204.

Domar, E. D., "The Case for Accelerated Depreciation," *Quarterly Journal of Economics* 67 (November, 1953), 493–519.

Doyle, L. A., "Uses of Cost Data for Production and Investment Policies," *Accounting Review* 25 (July, 1950), 274–282.

Drake, M. J., "Banker's Problems with Respect to Financial Reports," *Robert Morris Associates Bulletin* 34 (November, 1950), 129–134.

Earley, J. S., "Recent Developments in Cost Accounting and the 'Marginal Analysis,'" *Journal of Political Economy* 63 (June, 1955), 227–242.

Edwards, E. O., "Depreciation Policy under Changing Price Levels," *Accounting Review* 29 (April, 1954), 267–280.

Edwards, J. D., "Contemporary Concepts of Business Net Income—the Shares of Capital and Labour, and the Influence of Public Opinion," *Accounting Research* 5 (April, 1954), 121–132.

Eisner, R., "Accelerated Amortization, Growth and Net Profits," *Quarterly Journal of Economics* 66 (November, 1952), 533-544.

———, "Accelerated Depreciation: Some Further Thoughts," *Quarterly Journal of Economics* 64 (May, 1955), 285–295.

———, "Depreciation Allowances, Replacement Requirements and Growth," *American Economic Review* 42 (December, 1952), 820–831.

———, "Depreciation under the New Tax Law," *Harvard Business Review* 33 (January–February, 1955), 66–74.

Emery, K. G., "Should Goodwill Be Written Off?" *Accounting Review* 26 (October, 1951), 560–567.

Engelmann, K., "In Search of an Accounting Philosophy," *Accounting Review* 29 (July, 1954), 383–390.

———, "The Realization Basis of Determining Income Would Eliminate Distortions Caused by Inflation," *Journal of Accountancy* 90 (October, 1950), 321–323.

Fabricant, Solomon, "Business Costs and Business Income under Changing Price Levels," Monograph No. 3, *Five Monographs of Business Income* (New York: American Institute of Accountants, July, 1950), 143–159.

———, "Revelations of Fixed Assets, 1925–1934," *National Bureau of Economic Research Bulletin* No. 62 (1936).

———, "The Varied Impact of Inflation on the Calculation of Business Income," Monograph No. 4, *Five Monographs on Business Income* (New York: American Institute of Accountants, July, 1950), 155–159.

Fagerberg, D., Jr., "Spotlight on Personal Accounting," *Accounting Review* 29 (July, 1954), 355–364.

Farman, W. L., "Some Basic Assumptions Underlying Social Accounting," *Accounting Review* 26 (January, 1951), 33–39.

Fetter, F. A., "Nature of Capital and Income," *Journal of Political Economy* 15 (March, 1907), 129–148.

———, "Reformulation of the Concepts of Capital and Income in Economics and Accounting," *Accounting Review* 12 (March, 1937), 3–12.

Fill, W. L., "The Break-Even Chart," *Accounting Review* 27 (April, 1952), 202–209.

Finston, H. V., "Managerial Development: Challenge to Accountants," *Journal of Accountancy* 102 (July, 1956), 32–35.

Fisher, Irving, "The Income Concept in the Light of Experience," (English reprint, New Haven, 1927). Originally published in German in Vol. III of the *Wieser Festschrift*, "Die Wirtschaftstheorie der Gegenwart," Vienna, 1927.

Fitzgerald, A. A., "The Classification of Assets," *Accounting Research* 1 (July, 1950), 357–372.

Foss, M. F., and L. E. Holmes, "Trends of Inventories in the Mobilization Period," *Survey of Current Business* 31 (April, 1951), 16–24.

Fox, J. J., "How Emergency Accelerated Amortization Works," *Journal of Accountancy* 91 (June, 1951), 816–821.

Frankel, S. Herbert, "'Psychic' and 'Accounting' Concepts of Income and Welfare," *Oxford Economic Papers*, NS 4 (1952), 1–17.

Freudenthal, D. M., "Lifo: Current Benefits Adopting Last-In-First-Out Inventory Evaluation Method," *Chain Store Age* (March, 1951), 218–219.

———, "Rising Prices Indicate Reconsideration of Lifo: Clarified Lifo's Accounting and Tax Implications," *Commercial and Financial Chronicle* 173 (January, 1951), 441.

Fuerst, E., "The Matrix as a Tool in Macro-Accounting," *Review of Economics and Statistics* 37 (February, 1955), 35–47.

Gilbert, M., G. Jaszi, E. F. Denison, and C. F. Schwartz, "Objectives of National Income Measurement: A Reply to Professor Kuznets," *Review of Economics and Statistics* 30 (August, 1948), 179–195.

Gilbert, M., and R. Stone, "Recent Developments in National Income and Social Accounting," *Accounting Research* 5 (January, 1954), 1–13.

Gilliland, C. E., Jr., "A Simplified Reconciliation of Economic and Accounting Determinants of Depreciation Cost," *Accounting Review* 33 (April, 1958), 277–278. [Dissertation abstract.]

Goldberg, L., "Concepts of Depreciation," *Accounting Review* 30 (July, 1955), 468–484.

———, "A Distinction between 'Profit' and 'Income,'" *Accounting Research* 3 (April, 1952), 133–139.

———, "The Funds Statement Reconsidered," *Accounting Review* 26 (October, 1951), 485–491.

Goode, R., "Accelerated Depreciation Allowances as a Stimulus to Investment," *Quarterly Journal of Economics* 69 (May, 1955), 191–220.

Gordon, M. J., "The Valuation of Accounts at Current Cost," *Accounting Review* 28 (July, 1953), 373–384.

Goudeket, A., "An Application of Replacement Value Theory," *Journal of Accountancy* 110 (July, 1960), 37–47.

Grady, P., "Accounting for Fixed Assets and Their Amortization," *Accounting Review* 25 (January, 1950), 3–19.

———, "Conservation of Productive Capital through Recognition of Current Cost of Depreciation," *Accounting Review* 30 (October, 1955), 617–622.

———, "Economic Depreciation in Income Taxation and in Accounting," *Journal of Accountancy* 107 (April, 1959), 54–60.

———, "The Increasing Emphasis on Accounting as a Social Force," *Accounting Review* 23 (July, 1948), 266–275.

Graham, W. J., "Depreciation and Capital Replacement in an Inflationary Economy," *Accounting Review* 34 (July, 1959), 367–375.

———, "The Effect of Changing Price Levels on the Determination, Reporting, and Interpretation of Income," *Accounting Review* 24 (January, 1949), 15–26.

Green, D., Jr., and G. H. Sorter, "Accounting for Obsolescence—a Proposal," *Accounting Review* 34 (July, 1959), 431–441.

Greer, H. C., "Cost Factors in Price-Making," Parts 1 and 2, *Harvard*

Business Review 30 (July–August, 1952), 33–45, and (September–October, 1952), 127–136.

———, "Managerial Accounting—Twenty Years from Now," *Accounting Review* 29 (April, 1954), 175–185.

Gregory, R. H., and E. L. Wallace, "Solution of Funds Statement Problems—History and Proposed New Method," *Accounting Research* 3 (April, 1952), 99–121.

———, "Work Sheet for Funds Statement Problems," *Accounting Review* 28 (January, 1953), 88–97.

Hammond, J., "Notes on the Calculation of Business Profits during the Present Inflationary Period—France," *Accounting Research* 3 (October, 1952), 346–352.

Hanner, Per V. A., "Accounting and Taxation in Sweden in Relation to the Problem of Inflationary Profits," *Accounting Research* 1 (January, 1950), 257–267.

Henderson, P. D., "Inventory Gains and the National Income," *Bulletin of the Oxford University Institute of Statistics* 13, No. 5 (May, 1951), 164–172.

Hendriksen, E. S., "The Influence of Depreciation Accounting on National Income," *Accounting Review* 26 (October, 1951), 507–515.

Hepworth, S. R., "Smoothing Periodic Income," *Accounting Review* 28 (January, 1953), 32–39.

Hewitt, W. W., "The Concept of Income," *Journal of Political Economy* 33 (April, 1925), 155–178.

Hicks, J. R., "The Valuation of the Social Income," *Economica* 7 (May, 1940), 105–124.

Hirst, R. R., "Inflation—Its Impact on Enterprises," *Economic Record* 25 (December, 1949), 24–30.

Hock, J. R., "Original Cost vs. Market Value as Basis for Depreciation," *Dunsmore Report* (December, 1950), 20–21.

Hodgson, H., "Depreciation and the Future," *Accountant* 125 (July, 1951), 74–78.

Horne, Donald, "The Annual Allowance for Depreciation," *Management Review* 25 (May, 1936), 139–146.

Hosmer, W. A., "Funding Depreciation and Maintenance Reserves under War Conditions," *Harvard Business Review* 21 (Spring, 1943), 369–373.

Husband, G. R., "Professor Dein, Mr. Alexander, and Supplementary Statement Number 2," *Accounting Review* 30 (July, 1955), 383–399.

———, "Rationalization in the Accounting Measurement of Income," *Accounting Review* 29 (January, 1954), 3–14.

Hylton, E. P., "Should Financial Statements Show 'Monetary' or 'Economic' Income?" *Accounting Review* 26 (October, 1951), 503–506.

Jarchow, C. E., "How Do We Stand with Inflation? A Defense of Conventional Accounting," *National Association of Cost Accountants' Bulletin* 31 (February, 1950), 687–698.

Johnson, C. E., "Inventory Valuation—The Accountant's Achilles Heel," *Accounting Review* 29 (January, 1954), 15–26.

Jones, R. C., "The Effect of Inflation on Capital and Profits: The Record of Nine Steel Companies," *Journal of Accountancy* 87 (January, 1949), 9–27.

Kalecki, M., "Further Comments on the Department of Commerce Series," *Review of Economics and Statistics* 30 (August, 1948), 195–197.

Kane, J. E., "Structural Changes and General Changes in the Price Level—Relation to Financial Reporting," *Accounting Review* 26 (October, 1951), 496–502.

Kelley, A. C., "Can Corporate Incomes Be Scientifically Ascertained?" *Accounting Review* 26 (July, 1951), 289–298.

———, "The Presentation of Corporate Income and Earned Surplus," *Accounting Review* 24 (July, 1949), 285–289.

Kempner, J. J., "Revaluation and Depreciation of Plant Assets," *Accounting Review* 27 (October, 1952), 506–513.

Kircher, P., "Accounting Entries and National Accounts," *Accounting Review* 28 (April, 1953), 191–199.

———, "Common Dollar Accounting for Investments," *Journal of Business of the University of Chicago* 22 (October, 1949), 242–248.

Knauth, O. W., "An Executive Looks at Accountancy," *Journal of Accountancy* 103 (January, 1957), 29–32.

Kohler, E. L., "Accounting Concepts and National Income," *Accounting Review* 27 (January, 1952), 50–56.

———, "Recent Developments in the Formulation of Accounting Principles," *Accounting Research* 4 (January, 1953), 30–55.

Kohler, E. L., *et al.*, "Aspects of National Income," *Accounting Review* 27 (April, 1953), 178–238.

Kopta, W. A., "Managerial Utility of Accounting in a Period of Adjustment," *Accounting Review* 29 (July, 1954), 369–372.

Krebs, W. S., "Replacement and Retirement Accounting and Rate Base Valuations," *Accounting Review* 25 (October, 1950), 351–359.

Kuhn, J. W., "The Usefulness of the Factor Cost Concept in National Income Accounting," *Review of Economics and Statistics* 36 (February, 1954), 93–99.

Kuznets, Simon, "Discussion of the New Department of Commerce Series—National Income: A New Version," *Review of Economics and Statistics* 32 (August, 1948), 151–179.

Lacey, K., "Profit Measurement and the Trade Cycle," *Economic Journal* 57 (December, 1947), 456–474.

———, "The Tucker Report and the Technique of Adjusting Taxable Profits for Price Changes," *Economic Journal* 61 (December, 1951), 756–776.

Lawrence, J. S., "Profits and Progress," *Harvard Business Review* 26 (July, 1948), 480–491.

Lindahl, Erik, "The Concept of Income," *Economic Essays in Honour of Gustav Cassel* (London: Allen & Unwin, 1933), 399–407.

Lindholm, R. W., "The Impact of Accelerated Depreciation," *National Tax Journal* 4 (June, 1951), 180–186.

Little, L. T., "Historical Costs or Present Values?" *Economic Journal* 62 (December, 1952), 848–871.

———, "Replacement Costs—An Economist's View," *Accounting Research* 1 (January, 1949), 58–78.

Littleton, A. C., "The Concept of Income Underlying Accounting," *Accounting Review* 12 (March, 1937), 13–22.

———, "Contrasting Theories of Profit," *Accounting Review* 11 (March, 1936), 10–18.

Lotka, A. J., "Industrial Replacement," *Skandinavisk Aktuarietidskrift* 16 (1933), 51–63.

McAnly, H. T., "Lifo Now for All Inventory Pricing," *New York Certified Public Accountant* 21 (July, 1951), 483–492.

———, "The Current Status of Lifo," *Journal of Accountancy* 105 (May, 1958), 55–62.

McBeath, Angus, "Depreciating Assets: Accounting and Taxation," *Accountant* 123 (August 12, 1950), 139–142.

McMullen, S. Y., "Clarifying the Balance Sheet," *Accounting Review* 26 (April, 1951), 157–166.

Machlup, F., "Competition, Pliopoly and Profit," *Economica,* NS 9 (1942), 1–23; 153–173.

Mackenzie, D. H., "Contemporary Theories of Corporate Profits Reporting," *Accounting Review* 24 (October, 1949), 360–368.

McNichols, T. J., and F. V. Boyd, "Adjustment of Fixed Assets to Reflect Price Level Changes," *Accounting Review* 29 (January, 1954), 106–113.

Manning, R. E., "Depreciation in the Tax Laws and Practice of the United States, Australia, Canada, Great Britain, New Zealand, and South Africa," *National Tax Journal* 1 (June, 1948), 154–174.

Margolis, Julius, "The Classification of Sectors in the Social Accounts," *Accounting Review* 28 (April, 1953), 178–186.

Mason, P., "The Price-Level Study of the American Accounting Association," *Accounting Review* 30 (January, 1955), 37–44.

Massel, M. S., "Reappraisal of Depreciation and Obsolescence," *Harvard Business Review* 24 (Autumn, 1945), 85–95.

May, G. O., "The Case Against Change in Present Methods of Accounting for Exhaustion of Business Property," in *Five Monographs on Business Income* (New York: American Institute of Accountants, July, 1950), 261–271.

———, "Concepts of Business Income and Their Measurement," *Quarterly Journal of Economics* 68 (February 1954), 1–18.

———, "Income Accounting and Social Revolution," *Journal of Accountancy* 103 (June, 1957), 36–41.

———, "Periodic Business Income and Changing Price Levels," *Canadian Tax Foundation Tax Bulletin Supplement* (January, 1952), 1014. [This journal was superseded in 1953 by the *Canadian Tax Journal.*]

———, "The Relation of Depreciation Provisions to Replacement," *Journal of Accountancy* 69 (May, 1940), 341–347.

Mayer, J., "Proposals for Improving Income and Product Concepts," *Review of Economics and Statistics* 36 (May, 1954), 191–201.

Maynard, G. P., "Business Income and National Income: A Contrast of Concepts," *Accounting Review* 27 (April, 1952), 189–194.

———, "Modifications of Accounting Data in National Income Estimation," *Accounting Review* 28 (April, 1953), 199–210.

Melvoin, C., "Depreciation in Accountants' Reports," *Journal of Accountancy* 108 (November, 1959), 34–38.

Miller, H. E., W. A. Paton, and H. Taggert, "The 1948 Revision of the American Accounting Association's Statement of Principles," *Accounting Review* 24 (January, 1949), 44–60.

Miller, J. P., "The Pricing Effects of Accelerated Amortization," *Review of Economics and Statistics* 34 (February, 1952), 10–17.

Moonitz, M., "Adaptations to Price-Level Changes," *Accounting Review* 23 (January, 1948), 137–147.

———, "Inventories and the Statement of Funds," *Accounting Review* 18 (July, 1943), 262–266.

———, "The Risk of Obsolescence and the Importance of the Rate of

Interest," *Journal of Political Economy* 51 (August, 1943), 348–355.

Moonitz, M., and C. L. Nelson, "Recent Developments in Accounting Theory," *Accounting Review* 35 (April, 1960), 206–217.

Morgan, J. N., "The Measurement of Gains and Losses," *Quarterly Journal of Economics* 62 (February, 1948), 287–308.

Morrison, L. F., "Some Accounting Limitations of Statement Interpretation," *Accounting Review* 27 (October, 1952), 490–495.

Nad, L. M., "How to Simplify Lifo by Use of Dollar Value Method," *Journal of Accountancy* 91 (February, 1951), 266–271.

Nelson, C. L., "Use of Accounting Data in National-Income Estimation," *Accounting Review* 28 (April, 1953), 186–190.

Nelson, O. S., "Capital Gains from Price Level Increases," *Accounting Review* 26 (January, 1951), 31–32.

Nelson, R. H., "The Momentum Theory of Goodwill," *Accounting Review* 28 (October, 1953), 491–499.

Neuner, E., Jr., "Accelerated Amortization and Regulatory Policy," *Land Economics* 29 (August, 1953), 248–262.

Nicholson, J. L., "National Income at Factor Costs or Market Prices?" *Economic Journal* 65 (June, 1955), 216–224.

Niswonger, C. R., "The Interpretation of Income in a Period of Inflated Prices," *Accounting Review* 24 (January, 1949), 27–32.

Norris, H., "Depreciation Allocations in Relation to Financial Capital, Real Capital, and Productive Capacity," *Accounting Research* 1 (July, 1949), 121–132.

———, "Notes on the Relationship between Economists and Accountants," *Economic Journal* 54, Nos. 215–216 (December, 1944).

Norton, P. T., Jr., "A Sequel to 'An Engineering Viewpoint on Depreciation Accounting,'" *Journal of Accountancy* 105 (June, 1958), 35–40.

Paton, W. A., "Depreciation—Concept and Measurement," *Journal of Accountancy* 108 (October, 1959), 38–43.

———, "The Depreciation Deduction—A Neglected Aspect," *Michigan Business Review* 5 (November, 1953), 23–26.

———, "Measuring Profits under Inflationary Conditions: A Serious Problem for Accountants," *Journal of Accountancy* 89 (January, 1950), 16–27.

Peloubet, M. E., "Choice of Inventory Methods Depends on Specific Needs of Each Business," *Journal of Accountancy* 91 (January, 1951), 70–77.

———, "Has Lifo Fallen?" *Journal of Accountancy* 85 (April, 1948), 298–303.

Pool, A. G., "The Economic and Accounting Concepts of Profit," *Accounting Research* 4 (April, 1953), 144–152.

Preinreich, G. A. D., "Annual Survey of Economic Theory: The Theory of Depreciation," *Econometrica* 6 (July, 1938), 219–241.

———, "The Economic Life of Industrial Equipment," *Econometrica* 8 (January, 1940), 12–44.

———, "Economic Theories of Goodwill," *Journal of Accountancy* 68 (September, 1939), 169–180.

———, "Goodwill in Accountancy," *Journal of Accountancy* 64 (July, 1937), 28–50.

———, "The Law of Goodwill," *Accounting Review* 11 (December, 1936), 317–319.

———, "Note on the Theory of Depreciation," *Econometrica* 9 (January, 1941), 80–88.

———, "The Practice of Depreciation," *Econometrica* 7 (July, 1939), 235–265.

———, "The Theory of Industrial Replacement," *Skandinavisk Aktuarietidskrift* 22 (1939), 1–9.

Prest, A. R., "Replacement Cost Depreciation," *Accounting Research* 1 (July, 1950), 385–402.

Prest, W., "Depreciation and Income," *Economic Record* 15 (June, 1939), 17–23.

Raun, D. L., "Income: A Measurement of Currently Added Purchasing Power through Operations," *Accounting Review* 27 (July, 1952), 352–360.

Reynolds, C. A., "Depreciation of Assets Contributed by Community," *Journal of Accountancy* 91 (May, 1951), 715–717.

Robbins, S. M., "Investor Guideposts in Comparing Income Statements," *Journal of Finance* 7 (March, 1952), 47–65.

Robertson, E. H., "Effect of New Canadian Depreciation Law," *Journal of Accountancy* 91 (March, 1951), 428–433.

Ruggles, R., "The Nature of Price Flexibility and the Determinants of Relative Price Changes in the Economy," *Business Concentration and Price Policy,* a Conference of the Universities—National Bureau Committee for Economic Research, Princeton (1955), 441–505.

Samuelson, Paul A., "Evaluation of Real National Income," *Oxford Economic Papers,* NS 2 (January, 1950), 1–29.

Sanders, T. H., "Depreciation and 1949 Price Levels," *Harvard Business Review* 27 (May, 1949), 293–307.

———, "Inflation and Accounting," *Harvard Business Review* 30 (May–June, 1952), 50–58.

———, "Two Concepts of Accounting," *Harvard Business Review* 27 (July, 1949), 505–520.

Schiff, E., "A Note on Depreciation, Replacement, and Growth," *Review of Economics and Statistics* 36 (February, 1954), 47–56.

Schiff, M., "What Happens to Depreciation," *Journal of Accountancy* 107 (March, 1959), 37–41.

Schlaifer, R., J. K. Butters, and P. Hunt, "Accelerated Amortization," *Harvard Business Review* 29 (May, 1951), 113–126.

Seers, D., and P. F. D. Wallis, "Changes in Real National Income," *Bulletin of the Oxford Institute of Statistics* 11 (June, 1949), 163–176.

Seitelman, N., "The Depletion Problem," *Accounting Review* 28 (January, 1953) 102–109.

Shoup, Carl S., "Development and Use of National Income Data," *A Survey of Contemporary Economics* 1 (Philadelphia: Blakiston, 1948), 288–313.

Silcock, T. H., "Accountants, Economists and Valuation of Fixed Assets," *Economic Journal* 59 (September, 1949), 343–359.

Simon, S. I., "Consolidated Statements and the Law," *Accounting Review* 28 (October, 1953), 505–514.

Singer, F. A., "Depreciation—Better Left Unsaid," *Accounting Review* 32 (July, 1957), 406–412.

Slitor, R. E., "Liberalization of Depreciation," *Proceedings of the National Tax Association* 46 (1953), 466–474.

Smith, C. A., "How Can Accounting Be Integrated with Economics?" *Accounting Review* 27 (January, 1952), 100–103.

Smith, C. W., "Current Useful Concepts of Depreciation for Fixed Assets," *Journal of Accountancy* 92 (August, 1951), 166–174.

Smith, D. T., "Business Profits, during Inflation," *Harvard Business Review* 26 (March, 1948), 216–239.

Soper, H. D., "Inventory Reserves; Why and When," *Accounting Review* 23 (October, 1948), 391–396.

Spear, H. M., "Depreciation Accounting under Changing Price Levels," *Accounting Review* 24 (October, 1949), 369–378.

Stans, M. H., "Modernizing the Income Statement," *Accounting Review* 24 (January, 1949), 3–14.

Staubus, G. J., "Payments for the Use of Capital and the Matching Process," *Accounting Review* 27 (January, 1952), 104–113.

Stead, G. W., "Toward a Synthesis of Accounting Doctrine," *Accounting Review* 23 (October, 1948), 355–359.

Suojanen, W. W., "Accounting Theory and the Large Corporation," *Accounting Review* 29 (July, 1954), 391–398.

———, "Lifo as a Spur to Inflation—the Recent Experience of Copper," *Accounting Review* 32 (January, 1957), 42–50.

Sweezy, Alan R., "A Study of Moneyflows in the United States," *American Economic Review* 53 (September, 1953), 676–680.

Taggart, H. F., "Sacred Cows in Accounting," *Accounting Review* 28 (July, 1953), 313–319.

Tannery, F. F., "Depreciation and the Depreciating Dollar," *National Association of Cost Accountants' Bulletin* 34 (October, 1952), 211–219.

Thirlby, G. F., "The Economist's Description of Business Behaviour," *Economica,* NS 19 (May, 1952), 148–167.

———, "The Subjective Theory of Value and Accounting 'Cost,'" *Economica,* NS 13 (February, 1946), 32–49.

Tilly, V. S., "Depreciation—Does It Relate to Original Cost or to Cost of Replacement?" *Accounting Review* 33 (October, 1958), 622–624.

———, "The Income Statement and Its Significance in Financial Reporting," *Accounting Review* 23 (July, 1948), 296–304.

Tress, R. C., "The Use of Accountancy Terms and Concepts by Economists," *Accounting Research* 3 (October, 1952), 317–331.

Trumbull, W. P., "Price-Level Depreciation and Replacement Cost," *Accounting Review* 33 (January, 1958), 26–34.

Turner, C. L., "Accelerated Depreciation, Amortization, and Obsolescence," *Wartime Accounting* 1942 (papers presented at 55th annual meeting of American Institute of Accountants), 118–127.

Viner, J., "Taxation and Changes in Price Levels," *Journal of Political Economy* 31 (August, 1923), 494–520.

Walden, R. E., "A Course in Accounting Theory," *Accounting Review* 26 (April, 1951), 221–225.

Walter, J. E., "Last-In, First-Out," *Accounting Review* 25 (January, 1950), 63–75.

Warner, G. H., "Depreciation on a Current Basis," *Accounting Review* 29 (October, 1954), 628–633.

Weeden, J. S., "Historical vs. Replacement Cost," *Temple University Economic and Business Bulletin* 3 (December, 1951), 26.

Werntz, W. W., "The Impact of Federal Legislation upon Accounting," *Accounting Review* 28 (April, 1953), 159–169.

———, "The Influences of Administrative Agencies on Accounting in the United States," *Accounting Research* 4 (January, 1953), 77–95.

———, "The Resurgence of the Balance Sheet as a Useful Element in Financial Analysis," *Journal of Accountancy* 96 (November, 1953), 555–569.

Westerfield, R. B., "Building Reserves by Overvaluation of Assets," *Accounting Review* 29 (January, 1954), 45–51.

Weston, J. F., "Consistency and Changing Price Levels," *Accounting Review* 24 (October, 1949), 379–386.

———, "A Generalized Uncertainty Theory of Profit," *American Economic Review* 40 (March, 1950), 40–60.

———, "Revaluations of Fixed Assets," *Accounting Review* 28 (October, 1953), 482–490.

White, W. V., "The Exchequer Accounts," *Accounting Research* 1 (July, 1950), 451–452.

Whitin, T. M., "Some Business Applications of Marginal Analysis—with Particular Reference to Inventory Control," *Accounting Research* 3 (July, 1952), 205–219.

Wilcox, E. B., "The Rise and Fall of Lifo," *Journal of Accountancy* 85 (February, 1948), 98–113.

Wixon, R. "The Measurement and Administration of Income," *Accounting Review* 24 (April, 1949), 184–190.

Woomer, D. B., "Lifo as a Method of Determining Depreciation," *Accounting Review* 24 (July, 1949), 290–295.

Young, W. A., "A Method of Securing a Statement of Application of Funds," *Accounting Review* 10 (September, 1935), 287–293.

Index

Index